The Dramatic Works of John Lilly, (The Euphuist.)

Geo L. Duyckinck
March 12. [illegible]

Library of Old Authors.

a

THE DRAMATIC WORKS

OF JOHN LILLY,

(THE EUPHUIST.)

WITH NOTES AND SOME ACCOUNT OF HIS

LIFE AND WRITINGS

BY F. W. FAIRHOLT, F.S.A.

HONORARY MEMBER OF THE SOCIETY OF ANTIQUARIES OF NORMANDY,
PICARDY, AND POICTIERS, AND CORRESPONDING MEMBER
OF THE SOCIETY OF ANTIQUARIES
OF SCOTLAND.

IN TWO VOLUMES.

VOL. I.

LONDON:

JOHN RUSSELL SMITH,

SOHO SQUARE.

1858.

CONTENTS.

JOHN LILLY AND HIS WORKS.

HATEVER judgment modern critics may pass on the writings of Lilly, it is certain they produced a marked effect on the literature of his own era. His *Euphues* gave the tone to the conversation of the court of Queen Elizabeth; and the gallants and wits who frequented it formed their language upon the model of that once-famed book. "The chief characteristic of his style, besides its smoothness, is the employment of a species of fabulous or unnatural natural philosophy, in which the existence of certain animals, vegetables, and minerals with peculiar properties is presumed, in order to afford similes and illustrations."[1] It was scarcely to be expected that such laborious trifling, founded on the mistakes and inventions of the fabulous writers who flourished in the Middle Ages, would be revived among the learned men of the Elizabethan court, and almost enforced upon such as would wish to pass for polished scholars there. Blount, the editor of his six plays in 1632, says:—"That beautie in court which could not

---

[1] Collier's *History of English Dramatic Poetry*, vol. 3, p. 172.

parley *Euphuisme*, was as little regarded as shee which now there speakes not French." Anthony-à-Wood, in his *Athenæ Oxonienses*, also notes :—" In these bookes of *Euphues* 'tis said that our nation is indebted for a new English in them, which the flower of the youth thereof learned."

Lilly's contemporaries were often loud in his praises. William Webbe, in his *Discourse of English Poetrie*, 1586, speaking of the great improvement the English language had " by the helpe of such rare and singuler wits as from time to time might styll adde some amendment to the same," particularly commends Lilly :—" I thinke there is none that will gainsay, but Master John Lilly hath deserved most high commendations, as he which hath stept one steppe further therein then any either before or since he first began the wyttie discourse of his *Euphues*. Whose workes, surely in respecte of his singuler eloquence and brave composition of apt words and sentences, let the learned examine and make tryall thereof thorough all the partes of rhetoricke, in fitte phrases, in pithy sentences, in gallant tropes, in flowing speeche, in plaine sence; and surely in my judgment, I thinke he wyll yeelde him that verdict which Quintilian giveth of bothe the best orators Demosthenes and Tully, that from one, nothing may be taken away, to the other, nothing may be added." In verses by Henry Upchear, prefixed to *Menaphon or Arcadia*, 1587, occurs the following lines :—

" Of all the flowers a Lillie once I lov'd,
 Whose labouring beautie brancht itself abroade."[1]

---

[1] This obvious pun on our author's name seems to have

In a sonnet by I. Eliote prefixed to *Perimedes*, 1588, he is mentioned in a similar strain :—

> "Marot et de Mornay pour le langage Francois :
> Pour L'Espaignol Guevare, Boccace pour le Toscan :
> Et le gentil Sleidan refait l'Allemand :
> Greene et Lyllè tous deux raffineurs de l'Anglois."

Lodge, in his *Wit's Miserie and the World's Mad-nesse*, 1596, speaking of the demon of envy, and " the divine wits for many things as sufficient as all antiquity," who have to suffer his reproof, gives the first place to Lilly in his enumeration of English authors :—" Lilly, the famous for facility in discourse ; Spencer, best read in ancient poetry ; Daniel, choise in word and invention ; Draiton, diligent and formall ; Th. Nash, true English Aretine."

In verses prefixed to *Alcida*, 1617, occur these Latin lines :—

> "Multis post annis, conjugens carmina prosis,
> Floruit Ascamus, Chekus, Gascoynus, et alter
> Tullius Anglorum nunc vivens Lillius."

But these praises were not universal ; and it is but fair to note that, despite court influence and fashionable sanction, there were some writers who spoke plainly against the affectation which disfigured Lilly's works. Thus Drayton commends Sir Philip Sidney, as the author that

> " did first reduce
> Our tongue from Lilly's writing then in use ;
> Talking of stones, stars, plants, of fishes, flies,

---

been a constant favourite. Harvey, in his *Pierce's Supererogation*, has a whimsical joke upon it in a double sense, where, alluding to the stationers, and the usual water-mark on their paper, he slurs our author by saying they " find more gaine in the lilly-pot blanke, than in the lilly-pot wastepaper *Euphued*."

Playing with words, and idle similies,
As th' English apes, and very zanies be
Of every thing that they do hear and see,
So imitating his ridiculous tricks,
. They speak and write all like meer lunaticks."

Marston, in his comedy entitled *What you Will*, Ac
5, Sc. 1, makes the foolish Simplicius attempt *Eu-*
phuisms in complimenting his mistress; Shakespeare
is thought to have ridiculed the style in the character of
Don Armado in *Love's Labour's Lost;* and it formed one
of the chief objects of satire in Ben Jonson's *Cynthia's*
Revels.[1]

Materials for the biography of Lilly are scanty, but
not more so than for other, and greater, authors of his
era. The earliest consecutive notice of his career is thus
given by Anthony-à-Wood:—"John Lylie, or Lylly,
a Kentish man born, became a student in Magdalen
College in the beginning of 1569, aged sixteen, or there-
abouts, and was afterwards, as I conceive, either one of
the demies or clerks of that house; but always averse to
the crabbed studies of logic and philosophy. For so it
was that his sence being naturally bent to the pleasant
paths of poetry (as if Apollo had given to him a wreath
of his own bays, without snatching or strugling), did in
a manner neglect academical studies, yet not so much
but that he took the degrees in arts, that of master being
compleated 1575.[2] At which time, as he was ésteemed
in the university a noted wit, so afterwards was he in the

---

[1] Sir Walter Scott, in his *Kenilworth*, makes his Sir Piercie
Shafton " parley Euphuism."

[2] In the *Fasti Oxonienses* we find, in the lists of Bachelors of
Arts under April 27, 1573, " John Lilye of Magd. Coll.," and,
under June 1, 1575, an entry, in the same words, as Master of
Arts.

court of Queen Elizabeth, where he was also reputed a rare poet, witty, comical, and facetious."[1] This account would make the year of Lilly's birth 1553. In the Oxford Register he is described as *plebeii filius*, matriculated in 1571, and then said to be seventeen years of age; consequently, 1554 is the correct year of his birth, and perfectly agrees with what he says of himself in his *Euphues and his England*, as being "scarce born" in Queen Mary's reign, that princess commencing her rule in 1553. From the same source we learn that he was rusticated at Oxford [2] for what he calls "glancing at some abuses," but for which he declares he bears no ill-will to his *alma mater*.[3]

There is extant among the Lansdowne manuscripts [4] a Latin letter written by Lilly to Lord Burghley, desiring his patronage and help while a scholar at Oxford,

---

[1] *Athenæ Oxonienses*, edited by Dr. Philip Bliss, 1815, vol. 1, col. 676.

[2] We learn this from his address to the scholars of Oxford, in the second part of *Euphues*, in which he says that it had been objected to the first part that he had "defaced or defamed Oxford" in his description of the education of Euphues; and he then enters on his chief ground of complaint in these words: "Yet may I of all the rest most condemne Oxford of unkindness, of vice I cannot; who seemed to weane me before I could get the teate to suck. Wherein she played the nice mother in sending me into the country to nurse, where I tyred at a dry breast three yeeres, and was at the last enforced to weane myself."

[3] This may have led to Oldys' supposition, that "afterwards, at some disgust, he removed to Cambridge;" but this and other conjectures on Lilly's early career by that writer are shown by Dr. Bliss to be unfounded: "no preferment awaited him there, nor could he want to obtain any academical title, having been previously honoured with a Master's degree at the sister University."

[4] No. xix. art. 16.

which was first pointed out by Collier,[1] who says :——
" The Lord Treasúrer is there addressed in a strain of
extravagant hyperbole ;" but he adds, it is "in a good
style, and a beautiful specimen of penmanship ; it is
indorsed, probably by his lordship's secretary, ' 16 May,
1574, John Lilie, a scholar of Oxford.   An epistle for
yᵉ Queens letters to Magdalen College to admit him
fellow: ' "—

" Viro illustrissimo et insignissimo Heroi Domino Bur-
gleo, totius Angliæ Thesaurario, Regiæ Maiestatis in-
timis a consilijs, et patrono suo colendissimo. J. L.

" Quod in me tuum alumnum benignitas tua munifica
extiterit, (Clarissime Heros) et vltro ne expectanti quidem
studium, operam, et singularem industriam declaraueris,
agnosco pro eo ac decet supplex tuam humanitatem in
literarum studiosos pietatem.   Quare cum incredibilis
mansuetudo tua, non solum merita, sed spem longe su-
perarit, et quod meus pudor nunquam rogasset prolixius
indulserit, habeo tuo honori gratias maximas, et vero
tantas, quantas meæ facultatulæ referre nunquam pote-
runt.   Et licet proiectæ cuiusdam audaciæ et præfrictæ
frontis videri possit, iuuenem rudem et temerarium, virum
amplissimum et prudentem, eum cui nec ætatis accessio
iudicij maturitatem, nec casta disciplina integritatem
morum, nec artium doctrina scientiæ supellectilem est
elargita, insignissimum Heroem, pro regni incolumitate,
salute reip., communium fortunarum defensione excu-
bantem, rursum iniquis precibus interpellare, et impor-

---

[1] *History of English Dramatic Poetry*, vol. 1, p. 240.

tunius obstrepere. Tamen oum optimi cuiusque bonitas commune omnium sit perfugium, subinde percogitans esse animi excelsi cui multum subuenit ei velle plurimum opitulari, ad tuam amplitudinem quam perspectam indies, suspectam nunquam, probatam sæpius habui, supplici prece accedo, passis manibus tuam operam, studium, humanitatem implorans. Hæc summa est, in hoc cardo vertitur, hæc Helena, ut tua celsitudo dignetur serenissimæ regiæ magistatis literas (ut minus latine dicam) mandatorias extorquere, ut ad Magdalenenses deferantur quo in eorum societatem te duce possim obrepere, fortunæ nostræ tanquam fundamento, tibi tanquam firmamento, connituntur. Nisi his subleuer, et sustenter, misere corruo, nihil enim potest quod me consoletur excogitari remedij, nec aliquid esset L. njsi tuus honor tanquam numen quoddam propitium, aut sacra anchora, aut salutare sydus, et Cynosura præluxerit. Adeoque meum corpus tuo honori, et tenues fortunas tuæ voluntati, et animum ad tua mandata conficienda habes expeditissimum. Quare in quem sæpe celsitudo tua benefica, operæ parata, studium semper promptum feruit, eundem hoc tempore supplicem et ad pedes tuos abiectum pro solita tuâ et incredibili humanitate sublevato, ego interim supplices manus ad deum Opt. Max. tendam vt beneficentia Alexandrum, humanitate Traianum, ætate Nestorem, inuicta mentis celsitudine Camillum, Salamonem prudentia, Dauidem sanctimonia, Josiam religionis collapsæ instaurandæ, et incorruptæ conseruandæ cura, possis adæquare. Hoc interim promitto et spondeo meam nec in imbibendis artibus curam, nec in referenda gratia animum, nec in perferendo labore industriam, nec in propaganda tua laude studium, nec religionem in officio, nec fidem in obsequio, vnquam defuturam. Vale.

" Tuæ amplitudinis observantissimus,

" JOANNES LILIUS."

Burghley appears to have befriended Lilly, and afterwards to have taken him into some service of trust in his household. The Lansdowne manuscripts [1] contain another letter from Lilly, when he appears to have been under some imputation of dishonesty. It is written in a hurried manner, very different to the preceding letter, and is endorsed " Julii 1582, John Lilly to my L.," and subscribed " To ye right honorable ye L. Burleigh, L. High Tresorer of England."

" My duetie (right honorable) in most humble manner remembred.

" It hath plesed my Lord upon what colour I cannot tell, certaine I am upon no cause, to be displesed w^t me, ye grief wherof is more then the losse can be. But seeing I am to live in ye world, I must also be judged by the world, for that an honest servaunt must be such as Cæsar wold have his wif, not only free from synne, but from suspicion. And for that I wish nothing more then to commit all my waies to yor wisdome, and the devises of others to yor judgment, I heere yeld both my self and my soule, the one to be tried by yor honnor, the other by the iustic of God, and I doubt not but my dealings being sifted, the world shall find whit meale, wher others thought to shew cours branne. It may be manie

---

[1] No. xxxvi. art. 77.

things wil be objected, but y^t any thing can be proved
I doubt, I know yor L. will soone smell devises from
simplicity, trueth from trecherie, factions from iust servic. And God is my witnes, before whome I speak, and
before whome for my speach I shall aunswer, y^t all my
thoughtes concerning my L. have byne ever reverent,
and almost relligious. How I have dealt God knoweth
and my Lady can coniecture, so faithfullie, as I am as
unspotted for dishonestie as a suckling from theft. This
consciuc of myne maketh me presume to stand to all tri-
alls, ether of accomptes, or counsell, in the one I never
used falshood, nor in the other dissembling. My most
humble suit therefore unto yor L is y^t my accusations be
not smothered and I choaked in ye smoak, but that they
maie be tried in ye fire, and I will stand to the heat.
And my only comfort is, y^t he y^t is wis shall judg
trueth, whos nakednes shall manifest her noblenes. But
I will not troble yor honorable eares w^t meiuie idle
wordes only this upon my knees I ask, y^t yor L will vou-
salf to talk w^t me, and in all things will I shew my self
so honest, y^t my disgrac shall bring to yor L. as great
mervell, as it hath done to me grief, and so thoroughly
will I satisfie everie obiection, y^t yor L shall think me
faithfull, though infortunat. That yor honnor rest
p'suaded of myne honest mynd and my Lady of my true
servic, that all things may be tried to ye uttermost, is my
desire, and the only reward I crave for my just (I iust
I dare tearme it) servic. And thus in all humility sub-
mitting my Caus to yor wisdome and my Consciuc to y^e
triall. I commit yor L to the Almightie.

        " Yo^r L most dutifullie to comma... .
                " Jon...

" for y^t I am for some few daies going into th
countrie, yf yor L be not at leasure to admitt me to yo
speach, at my returne I will give my most dutifull at-
tendaunc at wch time it may be my honesty may ioyne w
yor L. wisdome and both prevent that nether wold allow.
In the meane season what colo^r soever be alledged, ii
I be not honest to my L. and so meane to bee during
his plesure, I desire but yor L. secret opinion, for as [I
know] my L. to be most honorable, so I besech God in
time he be not abused. loth I am to be a prophett, and
to be a wiche I loath

" most dutifull to comand

" JOHN LYLY." [1]

Our author's most celebrated work was entitled: " *Euphues.* The Anatomy of Wit, verie pleasant for all
Gentlemen to read, and most necessary to remember;
wherein are contained the delyghts that Wit followeth
in his youth by the pleasantnesse of Love, and the happinesse he reapeth in age by the perfectnesse of Wise-
dome." 4to. [1580]. And this was followed by " *Euphues and his England,* containing his voyage and
adventures mixed with sundrie pretie discourses of honest

---

[1] The letter covers two sides of a leaf; the postscript is written in a smaller hand on the opposite leaf, with the name at
the extreme edge of the paper in a very minute letter; the two
words in brackets are torn away by the seal.

[2] Collier, in his *Extracts from the Registers of the Stationers
Company*, vol. 2 (published by the Shakespeare Society, 1849),
says that this very popular book " came out originally in 1579
or 1580, with no date on the title-page." He thus prints the
original entry of licence, on the second of December, 1578:
" Gabriel Cawood. Licensed unto him the Anotamie of
Witt, compiled by John Lyllie, under the hande of the bishopp
of London . . . xij^d."

Love, the description of the Countrie, the Court, and the manners of that Isle. Delightful to be read, and nothing hurtfull to be regarded; wherein there is small offence by lightnesse given to the wise, and lesse occasion of loosenesse proffered to the wanton. 4to. 1581."[1]

These works gave a new tone to Court conversation, as has been already noted. Lilly's advent there has been fixed by Oldys[2] in the year 1566, but this is evidently wrong. The same writer says it was in 1576 that he wrote his first letter to the Queen, and in 1597 his second; but this is conjecture also, and evidently not correct. Transcripts[3] are preserved in the Harleian MS. (1877) in the British Museum, and are as follows:

" A Petic'on of John Lilly to the Queenes Ma⁽ᵗⁱᵉ⁾.

' Tempora si numeres quæ nos numeramus
Non venit ante suam nostra querela diem.'

---

[1] Collier, in the work just quoted, also gives an entry of the licensing of the second part of Euphues, July 24, 1579. He says, "there is little doubt that the second part, as it was entered separately, was published separately, but we are not aware that any such edition has come to light: the earliest we have seen is that comprising the two parts, printed by Thomas East in 1581." The entry is as follows:—
" G. Cawood. Lycenced unto him and —— the second part of Euphues. . . . . . vjd."
Lilly himself tells us, in the preface to the second part of his *Euphues*, that the first part was published hurriedly, and that one year had elapsed between that time and the printing of the second part.
[2] MS. notes to Langbaine in Brit. Mus. Lib.
[3] The transcripts are without date; and Oldys' dates do not, in the least degree, tally with the few accurate dates of Lilly's career that we possess, nor with the inferences of the letters themselves: thus, in the first, he tells her Majesty he has been ten years at court in her service; and in the second he says it has reached to thirteen years.

" Most gratious and dread soueraigne, I dare n
pester yor highnes with many words, and want witt 1
wrapp upp much matter in fewe.   This age epitomie
the pater noster thrust into the compasse of a penny
the world into the modell of a tenice ball; all scienc
molted into sentence.   I would I were so compendiou;
as to expresse my hopes, my fortunes, my ouertharts, ir
two sillables, as marchants do riches in fewe ciphers, bu1
I feare to comitt the error I discomend, tediousnes;
like one that vowed to search out what tyme was, spent
all his, and knewe yt not.   I was enterteyned yor Ma{ts}
S'vant by yor owne gratious fauour, strengthened with
condicions, that I should ayme all my courses at the
Reuells (I dare not saye with a promise, but a hopefull
Item to the rev'con) for wch these 10 yeres I have at-
tended with an unwearyed patience, and nowe I knowe
not what Crabb tooke me for an Oyster, that in the
midst of yor sun-shine of your most gratious aspect,
hath thrust a stone betweene the shells to eate me aliue
that onely liue on dead hopes.   If yor sacred Matie thinke
me unworthy, and that, after x yeares tempest, I must
att the Court suffer shipwrack of my tyme, my wittes,
my hopes, vouchsafe in yor neuer-erring judgment,
some planck or refter to wafte me into a country, where
in my sadd and settled devoc'on I may, in euery corner
of a thatcht cottage, write praiers instead of plaies;
prayer for your longe and prosp'rous life, and a repent-
aunce that I haue played the foole so longe, and yett
like

' Quod petimus poena est, nec etiam miser esse recuso,
   Sed precor ut possem mitius esse miser.' "

Collier is of opinion that this application was made for the place of Master of the Revels on the death of Sir Thomas Benger in March, 1577. In the next year, Thomas Blagrave was appointed to the office, *pro tem.*; and in July, 1579, it was granted by letters patent of Edmund Tylney, Esq. " Why the vacancy was not supplied sooner after the death of Benger nowhere appears," says Collier, who inclines to think that Lilly's claim " might possibly have some connection with the delay." Seeing little hope of success, he again addressed her Majesty :—

" John Lillies Second Petic'on to the Queene.

" Most gratious and dread soueraigne, tyme cannot worke my petic'ons, nor my petic'ons the tyme. After many yeares seruice y^t pleased yor Matie to except against tents and toyles : I wish that for tennts I might putt in tenements, so should I be eased of some toyles, some lands, some good fines or forfeitures, that should fall by the just fall of these most false traitors ; that seeing nothing will come by the Revells, I may play upon the Rebells. Thirteene yeres your highnes seruant, but yet nothing. Twenty freinds, that though they saye theye will be sure, I finde them sure to be slowe. A thowsand hopes, but all nothing ; a hundred promises, but yet nothing. Thus casting upp the inventary of my friends, hopes, promises, and tymes, the summa totalis amounteth to just nothing. My last will is shorter than myne invenc'on, but three legacies, patience to my creditors, melancholie without measure to my freinds, and beggerie without shame to my familie.

' Si placet hoc merui quod ô tua fulmina cessent
Virgo parens princeps.'

" In all humilitie I entreate that I may dedicate ꝛ
your sacred Matie Lillie de tristib^s, wherein shal b
seene patience, labours, and misfortunes.

' Quorum si singula nostrum
Frangere non poterant, poterant tamen omnia mentem.'

" The last and the least, that if I bee borne to haue
nothing, I may haue a protecc'on to pay nothinge, w^ch
suite is like his that haveing followed the Court ten m
yeares for recompence of his service, comitted a robbe—
rie, and tooke it out in a p'rdon."

Lilly had produced several dramatic pieces at Court
prior to 1589, when he engaged in the famous *Marprelate* controversy, and published his " *Pap. with a
Hatchet;* alias, a Fig for my Godson: or, crack me this
nut; that is, a sound Box on the Ear for the Idiot Martin, to hold his Peace; written by one that dares call a
Dog a Dog;"[1] which occasioned Harvey to enter into
some gross personalities against himself and his friend
Nash, who was a principal in this discreditable paper-
war.[2] To this Nash replied in his *Have with you to
Saffron Walden*, 1596, in which he thus delineates a

---

[1] In his play of *Mother Bombie*, Act 1, Sc. 3, our author aids
us to understand the meaning of his title (see notes to vol. 2,
p. 271,), and in *Midas*, Act 4, Sc. 3, he uses the last words (see
notes to vol. 2, p. 268).

[2] Sir E. Brydges, in his reprint of Greene's *Groatsworth of
Wit* (4to. 1813), has given an account of the quarrel and its
origin. D'Israeli has also produced it in a more popular form;
but the entire events may be best studied in the *History of the
Martin Marprelate Controversy*, by Rev. W. Maskell (8vo. 1845).

personal trait of our author, who appears to have been a great smoker of tobacco.

"For Master *Lillie* (who is halves with me in this indignitie that is offred), I will not take the tale out of his mouth ; for he is better able to defend himselfe than I am able to say he is able to defend himselfe, and in as much time as hee spendes in taking *Tobacco* one weeke, he can compile that, which would make *Gabriell* repent himselfe all his life after. With a blacke sant he meanes shortly to bee att his chamber window, for calling him *the Fiddlestick of Oxford*."[1]

We are enabled to gather, from such accidental allusions, something like a notion of our author's personal characteristics, and from them we obtain three facts only, that he was a little man, was married, and fond of tobacco.

Lilly's success as a dramatist was considerable. Francis Meres, in his *Palladis Tamia ; Wit's Treasury*, 1598, after naming the best poets for comedy among the ancient Greeks, compares with them the dramatists of his own era, giving our author precedence to Shake-

---

[1] The passage occurs in Harvey's *Pierce's Supererogation, or a new prayse of the old Asse* (1593), and runs thus :—

"Albeit every man cannot compete such graund volumes as *Euphues*, or reare such mighty tomes as *Pap-hatchet ;* yet he might have thought other poore men have tongues and pennes to speake something, when they are provoked unreasonably. But loosers may have their wordes and comedians their actes : such drie bobbers can lustely strike at other, and cunningly rapp themselves. He hath not played the Vicemaster of Poules, and the Foolemaster of the Theater for naughtes : himselfe a mad lad, as ever twangd, never troubled with any substance of witt; or circumstance of honestie, sometime the fiddle-sticke of Oxford, now the very bable of London."

speare. The entire passage is curious, and runs thus :
—" The best for Comedy amongst us bee, Edward Earle
of Oxforde, Doctor Gager of Oxford, Maister Rowley
once a rare scholler of learned Pembrooke Hall in Cambridge, Maister Edwardes, one of her Maiesties Chappell, eloquent and wittie John Lilly, Lodge, Gascoyne,
Greene, Shakespeare, Thomas Nash, Thomas Heywood,
Anthonye Mundye our best plotter, Chapman, Porter,
Wilson, Hathway, and Henry Chettle."

Nash, in his *Have with you*, &c. incidentally notices
the great popularity of his best comedy in these words :
—" If we were wearie with walking, and loth to goe
too farre to seeke sport, into the Arches we might step,
and heare him plead ; which would bee a merrier Comedie than ever was old *Mother Bomby.*"

His antagonist Harvey also notes the general popularity of his dramas ; he says :—" You were best to please
Pap-hatchet, and see Euphues betimes, for fear lest he
be mooved, or some one of his apes hired, to make a
Playe of you ; and then is your credit quite undone for
ever and ever : such is the publique reputation of their
playes." [1]

---

[1] *Pierce's Supererogation*, at the commencement of which he
says :—" Surely Euphues was someway a pretty fellow ; would
God Lilly had alwaies bene Euphues, and never Pap-hatchet."
Nash, in his reply already quoted, declares that Harvey was
first to blame in commencing the attack, " and M. Lilly and
me by name beruffianized and berascalled, and termed us pi-
perly make-playes and make-bates ;" and could not be " made
to hold his peace, till Master Lillie and some others with their
pens drew upon him." This quarrel, which was maintained
for several years " with more vulgar abuse than real wit on
both sides," has been very fully descanted upon by our literary
antiquaries.

Ben Jonson, in his commendatory verses on Shakespeare and his works, has an important reference to Lilly, showing the position he was then considered to occupy, taking precedence of Kyd or Marlowe :—

> " If I thought my judgment were of years,
> I should commit thee surely with thy peers,
> And tell how far thou didst our Lyly outshine,
> Or sporting Kyd, or Marlowe's mighty line."

Modern critics have been favourable to our author. Malone was enthusiastic in his praise ; Bishop Percy has printed his song on Cupid and Campaspe with high commendation ; Hazlitt was a warm admirer of Lilly's *Endimion* ;[1] Lamb quoted him largely ; and the living American author Longfellow has commenced his prose-poem *Hyperion* with a quotation from *Endimion*.

Shakespeare was familiar with his works, and paraphrased some of his best passages.   He was certainly one of those authors Greene accuses him so bitterly of copying.   In the notes to these volumes many such passages are pointed out, and others may readily be added.[2] Such and so many resemblances could not be accidental.

---

[1] " I know few things more perfect in characteristic painting than the exclamation of the Phrygian shepherds, who, afraid of betraying the secret of Midas's ears, fancy that ' the very reeds bow down, as though they listened to their talk ;' nor more affecting in sentiment than the apostrophe addressed by his friend Eumenides to Endimion on waking from his long sleep :—' Behold the twig to which thou laidest down thy head is now become a tree.' "

[2] Collier, in his *History of Dramatic Poetry*, has noted the coincidence between the phrase used by Apelles (*Campaspe*, Act 3, Sc. 5)—" Stars are to be look'd at, not reach'd at ;" and that used by the Duke (*Two Gentlemen of Verona*, Act 3, Sc. 1)—" Wilt thou reach stars, because they shine on thee ?" Shakespeare's lines :—

Despite the popularity of Lilly's works, his success as a court poet, and the honourable position his fellow-authors willingly accorded him, it is to be feared that little else than honour was his lot. His petition to the Queen speaks plainly of necessities borne patiently by him for years; and it detracts still more from the little respect we may feel for that cold-hearted woman, when we find her neglecting the poverty of one who had flattered her assiduously in the works constructed for her amusement, and had assisted the speech of her courtiers by his Euphuism. Blount, in the preface to his reprints, certainly says she "graced and rewarded" him; but this does not appear in other evidence, and may not have been more than payment for his labour at the cheap price of authorship in her era. We find no record of the close of his life, "nor when he died, or where buried, only that he lived till towards the latter end of Queen Elizabeth, if not beyond, for he was in being in 1597, when the *Woman in the Moon* was published." [1]

His plays, with the exception of *Mother Bombie*, are all constructed on classic stories, with many mythological characters. "It may not be unnecessary to state what was probably the intention of the poet, in fixing upon stories apparently so unfit for dramatic represen-

---

"Hark, the lark at heaven's gate sings,
And Phœbus 'gins arise"—

are a close paraphrase of Lilly's song on the lark in *Campaspe*, Act 5 :—

"How at heaven's gate she claps her wings,
The morn not waking till she sings."

[1] Wood—*Athenæ Oxonienses.*

tation as those of *Midas* and *Endimion*. And the true
solution of this seems to be, that these were, what
they were afterwards called, ' *court comedies,*' and intended for the particular amusement and gratification of
Queen Elizabeth. In that of *Midas,* she is compli-
mented as a queen; in that of *Endimion*, her supposed
charms and attractions as a woman are the more parti-
cular·objects which the courtly poet had in view; and it
is surely no mean praise to Lilly if he successfully followed the example of a poet like Spenser. Cynthia,
under which name she is supposed to be depicted, is not
only one of the names of Diana, or the moon, but is that
under which Elizabeth was celebrated by Spenser in his
poem of *Colin Clout's Come Home Again.* That was
the age of allegory in English poetry; and Elizabeth
was not only generally depicted in the poem of that name
as the ' Fairy Queen,' but is unquestionably meant by
Mercilla in Book V. and by Belphœbe in Book II. Who
was the person that sat for the picture of Endymion in
the present drama (or whether any particular person was
intended), is left to the judgment or imagination of the
reader. But as the play in all probability was not re-
presented till any idea of her Majesty's marriage was
out of the question, the sentiments which he avows for
his celestial mistress, in the third scene of the last act,
and the manner in which she receives and acknowledges
them, seem managed with much address, and probably
were in a very high degree acceptable to the Cynthia
who was meant, and before whom the plays were repre-
sented." [1]

---

[1] Introduction to *Endimion* in the *Collection of Old English
Plays,* 6 vols. 8vo. Lond. 1814.

Lilly's dramatic works consist of the following eight plays, here arranged in the order we may believe them to have been written :—

1. *The Woman in the Moone.*—" The Woman in the Moone. As it was presented before her Highnesse; By John Lyllie, Maister of Artes. Imprinted at London for William Jones, and are to be sold at the signe of the Gun, neere Holburne Conduict. 1597." Reprinted for the first time in the ensuing volume. In the concluding lines of the Prologue we are expressly told that this was the first work of the author; this may account for its inferiority to his other productions, which has led Collier to doubt its being his work, although his name is on the title-page.[1]

2. *Campaspe.*—The first edition has the following title :—"A moste excellent Comedie of Alexander, Campaspe, and Diogenes, played beefore the Queene's Maiestie on twelfe day at night, by her Maiesties Children, and the Children of Paules. Imprinted at London, for Thomas Cadman, 1584." This title was altered in the same year to " Campaspe, played beefore the Queene's Maiestie on new yeares day at night, by her Maiesties Children, and the Children of Paules. Imprinted at London for Thomas Cadman, 1584." The third edition has

---

[1] It may be noted here that the reason why it has not been printed first in our volumes, is because Blount's edition of his six plays forms the great basis of the whole; they have consequently been reprinted in the order he adopts, and any variations from the old quartos pointed out in the notes. But the *Woman in the Moone* and *Love's Metamorphosis*, having never been reprinted by him, are given literally, from the old quartos, in our second volume.

the title somewhat varied. " Campaspe. Played beefore the Queene's Maiestie on twelfe day at night, by
her Maiesties Children, and the Children of Paules.
Imprinted at London by Thomas Orwin, for William
Broome. 1591." It has been reprinted by Blount, in
1632, in his duodecimo volume entitled *Sixe Court Co-*
medies (a full notice of which will follow this list); and
also in all the editions of Dodsley, where it has the title
of *Alexander and Campaspe.* (See notes to the present volume, p. 284.)

3. *Sapho and Phao.*—The first edition has the following title :—" Sapho and Phao, played beefore the
Queene's Maiestie on Shrovetewsday, by her Maiesties
Children, and the Boyes of Paules. Imprinted at London by Thomas Cadman. 1584." There is a second
edition with the same title, " Imprinted at London by
Thomas Orwin for William Broome. 1591." It also is
reprinted by Blount.[1]

4. *Endimion.*—The first edition has the following
title :—" Endimion, the Man in the Moone, play'd before the Queene's Majestie at Greenewich on Candlemas
day at night, by the Chyldren of Paules. At London by

---

[1] In an entry of the Stationers Company, April 6, 1584, it
is thus noted :—

" Tho. Cadman. Yt is graunted unto him that if he can gett
the commedie of *Sappho* lawfully alowed unto him, Then none
of this companie shall Interrupt him to enjoye yt.   .   vj d.

Mr. Collier remarks that the first edition was printed without
the author's name; and Lilly's claim to it, he says, has been
disputed, notwithstanding it is in Blount's *Six Plays;* but his
name has been written opposite the above entry in a different
but contemporary hand.

I. Charlewood, for the widdow Broome, 1591." It is reprinted by Blount, and also in Dilke's *Old Plays*, Lond. 1814, vol. 2.

5. *Gallathea.*—The first edition has the following title :—" Gallathea. As it was playde before the Queene's Maiestie at Greene-wiche, on Newyeeres day at Night. By the Chyldren of Paules. At London, printed by John Charlwood for the Widdow Broome. 1592." It is reprinted by Blount.[1]

6. *Midas.*—The first edition has the following title : —" Midas. Plaied before the Queene's Maiestie upon twelfe day at night by the children of Paules. London, printed by Thomas Scarlet for I. B. and are to be sold in Paules churchyard at the signe of the Bible. 1592." It is reprinted by Blount, and also in Dilke's *Old Plays*, 1814, vol. 1.

7. *Mother Bombie.*—The first edition has the following title :—" Mother Bombie. As it was sundrie times plaied by the Children of Powles. London, Imprinted by Thomas Scarlet for Cuthbert Burby, 1594." It is reprinted by Blount, and also in Dilke's *Old Plays*, 1814, vol. 1.

---

[1] Collier extracts from the Stationers Company the following entry under April 1, 1585 :—

" Gal Cawood. Rd of him, for printing a Commoedie of Titirus and Galathea . . . . *[no sum.]*"

To which he appends this note :—" Warton (H.E.P., iv, 232, edit. 1824) speaks of this ' comedy ' as if it had been printed in 1584, but it was not entered until April, 1585; and we may doubt if it were published at that date, seeing that no sum was paid for the license, and that no copy of it is known until it was printed in 1592. It was no doubt Lilly's comedy of *Galathea.*"

8. *Love's Metamorphosis.*—"Love's Metamorphosis. A wittie and courtly Pastorall, written by Mr. John Lyllie. First playd by the children of Paules, and now by the children of the Chappell. London: Printed by William Wood, dwelling at the West end of Paules, at the signe of Time, 1601." Collier inclines to think this "was probably the work of Lyly at an advanced period of life, and it has not the recommendation of the ordinary, though affected graces of his style."[1] It is reprinted, for the first time, in our second volume.

Two other plays have been ascribed to our author:—
1. *A Warning for Faire Women,* 1599, on the authority of Winstanley and Wood; but, very erroneously, as it was written by an anonymous author, and bears no traces of Lilly's style. 2. *The Maid's Metamorphosis,* 1600, also published anonymously, and of which Mr. Collier thinks "there is no sufficient reason to deprive him, unless that it is better in some respects than his other plays." Unlike all other undoubted plays by Lilly it is written in rhyme, except some short comic scenes; and it is so totally unlike his style of thought and phraseology, that it is evidently the production of another mind, and has not been included in this edition of Lilly's dramas; a judgment we venture to think will be confirmed by any one who reads the plays in these two volumes, and who will then read a single page of this old drama.[2]

---

[1] *History of Dramatic Poetry,* vol. 3, p. 189. On the following page, however, he says:—"Although the name of John Lyly is upon the title-page, it may be doubted whether he had any hand in it, as it is so decidedly inferior to his other productions."

[2] It is totally free from Lilly's Euphuism, and contains no

In 1632, Edward Blount, the bookseller and publisher of many plays (having, among the rest, an interest in some of Shakespeare's), brought out an edition in 12mo. of six plays by Lilly. He appears to have had access to the original manuscripts; for in no earlier printed editions do we find the Songs included, some few of which are very beautiful. But there are instances of slovenly printing in the volume, extending so far as the misplacing of many pages. The title runs thus:—"*Sixe Court Comedies.* Often presented and acted before Queene Elizabeth, by the Children of her Maiesties Chappell, and the Children of Paules. Written by the onely rare poet of that time, the wittie, comicall, facetiously-quicke and vnparalleld John Lilly, Master of Arts. *Decies repetita placebunt.* London: Printed by William Stansby for Edward Blount. 1632."

" *The Epistle Dedicatorie*" is addressed "to the Right Honourable Richard Lumley, Viscount Lumley of Waterford," in the following words :—

" My noble Lord,

" It can be no dishonor, to listen to this Poets Musike, whose tunes alighted in the Eares of a great and ever-famous Queene: his Invention was so curiously strung, that *Elizaes* court held his notes in Admiration. Light Ayres are now in fashion ; and these being not sad, fit the season, though perchance not sute so well with your more serious Contemplations.

---

allusions to the fabulous tales of beasts, birds, trees, &c., he is so fond of referring to, and with which his style is completely identified.

" The spring is at hand, and therefore I present you a Lilly, growing in a Grove of Lawrells. For this Poet, sat at the *Sunnes* table : *Apollo* gave him a wreath of his owne *Bayes*, without snatching. The Lyre he played on had no borrowed strings.

" I am (My Lord) no executor, yet I presume to distribute the Goods of the Dead : their value being no way answerable to those Debts of dutie and affection in which I stand obliged to your Lordship. The greatest treasure our Poet left behind him, are these six ingots of refined invention : richer than Gold. Were they Diamonds they are now yours. Accept them (Noble Lord) in part ; and Mee،

" Your Lordships ever obliged and devoted

" ED. BLOUNT."

Then follows this Address :—

" *To the Reader.*—Reader, I haue (for the loue I beare to Posteritie) dig'd vp the Graue of a Rare and Excellent Poet, whom Queene Elizabeth then heard, Graced, and Rewarded. These Papers of his, lay like dead Lawrels in a Churchyard ; But I haue gathered the scattered branches vp, and by a Charme (gotten from Apollo) made them greene againe, and set them vp as Epitaphes to his Memory.

" A sinne it were to suffer these Rare Monuments of wit, to lye couered in Dust, and a shame, such conceipted Comedies, should be Acted by none but wormes. Obliuion shall not so trample on a sonne of the Muses ; And such a sonne, as they called their Darling. Our

Nation are in his debt for a new English whi⸤
taught them. *Ephues* and his *England* bega⸤
that language: All our Ladies were then his Scho⸤
And that Beautie in Court, which could **not** P⸤
Euphueisme, was as litle regarded; as shee **which**⸤
there, speakes not French.

   " These his playes Crown'd him with app**lause**,⸤
the Spectators with pleasure. Thou canst **not** re⸤
the reading of them over; when old John Lilly, is m⸤
with thee in thy chamber, Thou shalt say, few (or n⸤
of our Poets now are such witty companions; **and that**⸤
mee, that brings him to thy acquaintance.

" Thine.   ED. BLOVNT."

[Antograph of Lilly.
Lansdowne MS. No. 36.]

ENDIMION,

THE MAN IN THE MOONE.

PLAYED BEFORE THE QUEENES MAJESTIE AT GREENE-
WICH ON NEW YEERES DAY AT NIGHT BY
THE CHILDREN OF PAVLES.

DRAMATIS PERSONÆ.

ENDIMION, *in love with Cynthia.*
EUMENIDES, *his friend; in love with Semele.*
CORSITES,
PANTALION, }*Lords of Cynthia's Court.*
ZONTES,
PYTHAGORAS, } *Philosophers.*
GYPTES,
GERON, *an old man, husband to Dipsas.*
SIR TOPHAS, *a bragging Soldier.*
SAMIAS, *Page to Endimion.*
DARES, *Page to Eumenides.*
EPITON, *Page to Sir Tophas.*
Master Constable.
Watchmen.
Fairies.
Characters in Dumb Show.

CYNTHIA.
TELLUS, *enamoured of Endimion.*
FLOSCULA, *her confidant.*
SEMELE,
SCINTILLA, }*Ladies of Cynthia's Court.*
FAVILLA,
DIPSAS, *an Enchantress.*
BAGOA, *her Servant.*

THE PROLOGUE.

MOST high and happy Princesse, we must te you a tale of the Man in the Moone, which i it seeme ridiculous for the method, or superfluous fo the matter, or for the meanes incredible, for three fault we can make but one excuse. It is a tale of the Mai in the Moone.

It was forbidden in olde time to dispute of *Chymera* because it was a fiction, wee hope in our times none will apply pastimes, because they are fancies; for there liveth none under the sunne, that knowes what to make of the Man in the Moone. Wee present neither comedie, nor tragedie, nor storie, nor any thing, but that whosoever heareth may say this, Why here is a tale of the Man in the Moone.

ENDIMION.

ACTUS PRIMUS. SCÆNA PRIMA.

ENDIMION. EUMENIDES.

Endimion.

 FIND *Eumenides* in all things both va-
rietie to content, and satietie to glut,
saving onely in my affections; which are
so stayed, and withall so stately; that I
can neither satisfie my heart with love, nor mine eyes with
wonder. My thoughts *Eumenides* are stitched to the
starres, which being as high as I can see, thou maist
imagine how much higher they are then I can reach.

Eum. If you bee enamored of any thing above the
Moone, your thoughts are ridiculous, for that things
immortall are not subject to affections; if allured or en-
chaunted with these transitorie things under the Moone,
you shew your selfe sencelesse, to attribute such loftie
titles, to such love trifles.

End. My love is placed neither under the Moone nor
above.

Eum. I hope you be not sotted upon the Man in the
Moone.

End. No but setled, either to die, or possesse ̄t
Moone herselfe.

Eum. Is *Endimion* mad, or doe I mistake? doe y ̄c
love the Moone *Endimion?*

End. Eumenides, the Moone.

Eum. There was never any so peevish to imagin
the Moone either capable of affection, or shape of ̄ ̄
Mistris : for as impossible it is to make love sit to he ̄
humour which no man knoweth, as a coate to her forme ̄.
which continueth not in one bignesse whilst she is mea—
suring. Cease of *Endimion* to feed so much upon
fancies. That melancholy bloud must be purged, which
draweth you to a dotage no lesse miserable then mon—
strous.

End. My thoughts have no veines, and yet unles they
be let blood, I shall perish.

Eum. But they have vanities, which being reformed,
you may be restored.

End. O faire *Cynthia,* why doe others terme thee
unconstant, whom I have ever found unmoveable?
Injurious time, corrupt manners, unkind men, who
finding a constancie not to be matched in my sweet
Mistris, have christned her with the name of wavering,
waxing, and waning. Is shee inconstant that keepeth
a setled course, which since her first creation altereth
not one minute in her moving? There is nothing
thought more admirable, or commendable in the sea,
then the ebbing and flowing; and shall the Moone,
from whom the sea taketh this vertue, be accounted
fickle for encreasing and decreasing? Flowers in their
buds, are nothing worth till they be blowne; nor blos-

somes accounted till they bee ripe fruite; and shal we
then say they be changeable, for that they grow from
seeds to leaves, from leaves to buds, from buds to their
perfection? then, why be not twigs that become trees,
children that become men, and mornings that grow to
evenings, termed wavering, for that they continue not
at one stay? I, but *Cynthia* being in her fulnesse de-
cayeth, as not delighting in her greatest beauty, or
withering when she should be most honored.   When
malice cannot object any thing, folly will; making that
a vice, which is the greatest vertue.   What thing (my
mistris excepted) being in the pride of her beautie, and
latter minute of her age, that waxeth young againe?
Tell mee *Eumenides*, what is hee that having a mistris
of ripe yeeres, and infinite vertues, great honors, and
unspeakable beautie, but would wish that she might
grow tender againe? getting youth by yeeres, and
never decaying beautie by time; whose faire face, neither
the summers blaze can scorch, nor winters blast chap,
nor the numbring of yeeres breed altering of colours.
Such is my sweet *Cynthia*, whom time cannot touch,
because she is divine, nor will offend because shee is
delicate.   O *Cynthia*, if thou shouldest alwayes continue at thy fulnesse, both Gods and men would con-
spire to ravish thee.   But thou to abate the pride of
our affections, dost detract from thy perfections; thinking it sufficient, if once in a moneth wee enjoy a
glimpse of thy majestie; and then, to increase our griefes,
thou doest decrease thy glemes; comming out of thy
royall robes, wherewith thou dazelest our eyes, downe
into thy swathe clowts, beguiling our eyes; and then—

Eum. Stay there *Endimion*, thou that committest idolatry, wilt straight blaspheme, if thou be suffered. Sleepe would doe thee more good then speech: the Moone heareth thee not, or if she doe, regardeth thee not.

End. Vaine *Eumenides*, whose thoughts never grow higher then the crowne of thy head. Why troublest thou me, having neither head to conceive the cause of my love, or a heart to receive the impressions? follow thou thine owne fortunes, which creepe on the earth, and suffer mee to flie to mine, whose fall though it be desperate, yet shall it come by daring. Farewell.

Eum. Without doubt *Endimion* is bewitched, otherwise in a man of such rare vertues, there could not harbour a minde of such extreme madnesse. I will follow him, least in this fancie of the moone he deprive himselfe of the sight of the sunne. [*Exit.*

ACTUS PRIMUS. SCÆNA SECUNDA.

TELLUS. FLOSCULA.

Tellus. Trecherous and most perjur'd *Endimion*, is *Cynthia* the sweetnesse of thy life, and the bitternesse of my death? What revenge may be devised so full of shame, as my thoughts are replenished with malice? Tell me *Floscula* if falsenesse in love can possibly be punished with extremity of hate. As long as sword, fire, or poyson may be hired, no traytor to my love shall live unrevenged. Were thy oathes without number, thy kisses without measure, thy sighes without end, forged to deceive a poore credulous virgin whose simplicitie had beene worth thy favour and better fortune? If the Gods sit unequall beholders of injuries, or laughers at lovers deceits; then let mischiefe be as well forgiven in women, as perjurie winked at in men.

Flosc. Madame, if you would compare the state of *Cynthia* with your own; and the height of *Endimion* his thoughts, with the meannesse of your fortune; you would rather yeeld then contend, being betweene you and her no comparison; and rather wonder then rage at the greatnesse of his minde, being affected with a thing more then mortall.

Tellus. No comparison *Floscula?* and why so? is not my beautie divine, whose bodie is decked with faire flowers; and veines are vines, yeelding sweet liquour to the dullest spirits; whose eares are corne, to bring strength; and whose haires are grasse to bring abundance? Doth not frankincense, and myrrhe breath out of my nostrils, and all the sacrifice of the Gods, breed in my bowels? Infinite are my creatures, without which, neither thou nor *Endimion,* nor any could love, or live.

Flosc. But know you not faire ladie, that *Cynthia* governeth all things? Your grapes would be but drie huskes, your corne but chaffe, and all your vertues vaine; were it not *Cynthia* that preserveth the one in the bud, and nourisheth the other in the blade, and by her influence both comforteth al things, and by her authority commandeth all creatures; suffer then *Endimion* to follow his affections, though to obtaine her be impossible, and let him flatter himselfe in his owne imaginations, because they are immortall.

Tellus. Loth I am *Endimion* thou shouldest die, because I love thee well; and that shouldest live it grieveth me, because thou lovest *Cynthia* too well. In these extremities what shall I doe? *Floscula* no more words, I am resolved. He shall neither live, nor die.

Flosc. A strange practice, if it be possible.

Tellus. Yes, I will entangle him in such a sweet net, that he shall neither find the meanes to come out, nor desire it. All allurements of pleasure will I cast before his eyes, insomuch that he shall slake that love which hee now voweth to *Cynthia;* and burne in mine, of which hee seemeth carelesse. In this languishing, betweene my amorous devises, and his owne loose desires, there shal such dissolute thoghts take root in his head, and over his heart grow so thicke a skin; that neither hope of preferment, nor feare of punishment, nor counsell of the wisest, nor company of the worthiest; shall alter his humour, nor make him once to thinke of his honour.

Flosc. A revenge incredible, and if it may be, unnaturall.

Tellus. He shall know the malice of a woman, to have neither meane, nor end; and of a woman deluded in love, to have neither rule, nor reason. I can doe it, I must; I will! All his vertues will I shadow with vices; his person (ah sweet person) shall he decke with such rich robes, as hee shall forget it is his owne person; his sharpe wit (ah wit too sharpe, that hath cut off all my joyes) shall hee use, in flattering of my face, and devising sonnets in my favour. The prime of his youth and pride of his time, shall be spent in melancholy passions, carelesse behaviour, untamed thoughts, and unbridled affections.

Flosc. When this is done what then, shall it continue till his death, or shall he dote for ever in this delight?

Tellus. Ah *Floscula*, thou rendest my heart in sunder in putting me in remembrance of the end.

Flosc. Why if this be not the end, all the rest is to no end.

Tellus. Yet suffer me to imitate *Juno*, who would turne *Jupiters* lovers to beasts on the earth though she knew afterwards they should be stars in heaven.

Flosc. Affection that is bred by enchantment, is like a flower that is wrought in silke, in colour and forme most like, but nothing at all in substance or savour.

Tellus. It shall suffice me if the world talke that I am favoured of *Endimion.*

Flosc. Well, use your owne will; but you shall find that love gotten with witchcraft, is as unpleasant, as fish taken with medicines unwholesome.

Tellus. Floscula, they that be so poore that they have neither net nor hooke, will rather poyson dowe then pine with hunger: and she that is so opprest with love, that she is neither able with beautie, nor wit to obtaine her friend, will rather use unlawfull meanes, then try untolerable paines.   I will doe it.   [*Exit.*

Flosc. Then about it.   Poore *Endimion*, what traps are laid for thee, because thou honourest one that all the world wondreth at.   And what plots are cast to make thee unfortunate, that studiest of all men to be the faithfullest.   [*Exit.*

ACTUS PRIMUS. SCÆNA TERTIA.

DARES, SAMIAS, SIR TOPHAS, EPITON.

Dares. Now our masters are in love up to the eares, what have we to doe but to be in knaverie up to the crownes.

Samias. O that we had Sir *Tophas* that brave squire in the midst of our mirth, *et ecce autem*, will you see the devill?

Enter Sir TOPHAS.

Top. Epi.

Epi. Heere sir.

Top. I brook not this idle humour of love, it tickleth not my liver, from whence the love-mongers in former age seemed to inferre they should proceed.

Epi. Love, sir, may lie in your lungs, and I thinke it doth; and that is the cause you blow and are so pursie.

Top. Tush boy! I thinke it but some device of the poet to get money.

Epi. A poet? what's that?

Top. Doest thou not know what a poet is?

Epi. No.

Top. Why foole, a poet is as much as one should say, a poet. But soft, yonder be two wrens, shall I shoot at them?

Epi. They are two lads.

Top. Larkes or wrens, I will kill them.

Epi. Larkes? are you blinde? they are two little boyes.

Top. Birds, or boyes, they are both but a pittance for my breakfast; therefore have at them, for their braines must as it were imbroder my bolts.

Sam. Stay your courage valiant knight, for your wisdome is so wearie that it stayeth it selfe.

Dar. Why Sir *Tophas* have you forgotten your old friends?

Top. Friends? *Nego argumentum.*

Sam. And why not friends?

Top. Because *Amicitia* (as in old annals we find) is *inter pares,* now my prettie companions you shall see how unequall you be to me; but I will not cut you quite off, you shall be my halfe friends; for reaching to my middle, so farre as from the ground to the waste I will be your friend.

Dar. Learnedly. But what shall become of the rest of your bodie, from the waste to the crowne?

Top. My children *quod supra vos nihil ad vos,* you must thinke the rest immortall, because you cannot reach it.

Epi. Nay, I tell yee my master is more then a man.

Dar. And thou lesse then a mouse.

Top. But what be you two?

Sam. I am *Samias,* page to *Endimion.*

Dar. And I *Dares,* page to *Eumenides.*

Top. Of what occupation are your masters?

Dar. Occupation, you clowne, why they are honourable, and warriers.

Top. Then are they my prentises.

Dar. Thine, and why so?

Top. I was the first that ever devised warre, and

therefore by *Mars* himselfe had given me for my armes a whole armorie; and thus I goe as you see, clothed with artillerie; it is not silkes (*milkesops*) nor tyssues, nor the fine wooll of *Ceres;* but yron, steele, swords, flame, shot, terrour, clamour, bloud, and ruine, that rocks asleepe my thoughts, which never had any other cradle but crueltie. Let me see, doe you not bleed?

Dar. Why so?

Top. Commonly my wordes wound.

Sam. What then doe your blowes?

Top. Not onely wound, but also confound.

Sam. How darest thou come so neere thy master *Epi?* Sir *Tophas* spare us.

Top. You shall live. You *Samias* because you are little; you *Dares*, because you are no bigger; and both of you, because you are but two; for commonly I kill by the doozen, and have for every particular adversarie, a peculiar weapon.

Sam. May we know the use for our better skill in warre?

Top. You shall. Heere is a bird-bolt for the ugly beast the black-bird.

Dar. A cruell sight.

Top. Heere is the musket, for the untamed, (or as the vulgar sort terme it) the wilde mallard.

Sam. O desperate attempt!

Epi. Nay, my master will match them.

Dar. I, if he catch them.

Top. Heere is a speare and shield, and both necessary; the one to conquer, the other to subdue or overcome the terrible trowt, which although he be under

the water, yet tying a string to the top of my speare and
an engine of iron to the end of my line, I overthrow
him; and then herein I put him.

Sam. O wonderfull warre! *Dares*, didst thou ever
heare such a dolt?

Dar. All the better, we shall have good sport hereafter, if wee can get leisure.

Sam. Leisure? I will rather loose my masters service
then his company! looke how he *strowtes;* but what is
this, call you it your sword?

Top. No, it is my *simiter;* which I by construction
often studying to bee compendious, call my smiter.

Dar. What, are you also learned, sir?

Top. Learned? I am all *Mars* and *Ars*.

Sam. Nay, you are all masse and asse.

Top. Mocke you mee? You shall both suffer, yet
with such weapons, as you shall make choice of the
weapon wherewith you shall perish. Am I all a masse
or lumpe, is there no proportion in me? Am I all asse?
is there no wit in me. *Epi*, prepare them to the
slaughter.

Sam. I pray sir heare us speake! wee call you masse,
which your learning doth well understand is all man,
for *Mas maris* is a man. Then *As* (as you know) is a
weight, and we for your vertues account you a weight.

Top. The Latine hath saved your lives, the which a
world of silver could not have ransomed. I understand
you, and pardon you.

Dar. Well Sir *Tophas* wee bid you farewell, and at
our next meeting wee will be readie to doe you service.

Top. *Samias* I thanke you ;—*Dares* I thanke you ;
but especially I thanke you both.

Sam. Wisely. Come, next time weele have some
prettie gentlewomen with us to walk, for without doubt
with them he will be very daintie.

Dar. Come let us see what our masters doe, it is high
time.   [*Exeunt.*

Top. Now will I march into the field, where if I
cannot encounter with my foule enemies, I will withdraw
myselfe to the river, and there fortifie for fish : for
there resteth no minute free from fight.   [*Exit.*

ACTUS PRIMUS. SCÆNA QUARTA.

TELLUS, FLOSCULA, DIPSAS.

Tellus. Behold *Floscula*, wee have met with the
woman by chance that wee sought for by travell ; I will
breake my minde to her without ceremonie or circumstance, least we loose that time in advice that should be
spent in execution.

Flosc. Use your discretion, I will in this case neither
give counsell nor consent, for there cannot be a thing
more monstrous then to force affection by sorcerie,
neither do I imagine any thing more impossible.

Tellus. Tush *Floscula!* in obtaining of love, what
impossibilities will I not try? and for the winning of
Endimion, what impieties will I not practise ? *Dipsas,*
whom as many honor for age, as wonder at for cunning ;
listen in few words to my tale, and answer in one word
to the purpose ; for that neither my burning desire can
afford long speech, nor the short time I have to stay

many delayes. Is it possible by herbs, stones, spels, incantation, enchantment, exorcismes, fire, metalls, planets, or any practice; to plant affection where it is not, and to supplant it where it is?

Dipsas. Faire ladie, you may imagine that these horie haires are not void of experience, nor the great name that goeth of my cunning to be without cause. I can darken the sunne by my skill, and remove the moone out of her course; I can restore youth to the aged, and make hils without bottoms; there is nothing that I cannot doe, but that onely which you would have mee doe; and therein I differ from the Gods, that I am not able to rule hearts; for were it in my power to place affection by appointment, I would make such evill appetites, such inordinate lusts, such cursed desires, as all the world should be filled both with superstitious heats, and extreme love.

Tellus. Unhappie *Tellus*, whose desires are so desperate that they are neither to be conceived of any creature, nor to be cured by any art.

Dipsas. This I can, breed slacknesse in love, though never root it out. What is he whom you love, and what shee that he honoureth?

Tellus. Endimion, sweet *Endimion* is hee that hath my heart; and *Cynthia,* too too faire *Cynthia,* the miracle of nature, of time, of fortune, is the ladie that he delights in; and dotes on every day, and dies for ten thousand times a day.

Dipsas. Would you have his love, either by absence or sicknes aslaked? Would you that Cynt... mistrust him, or be jealous of him without c...

Tellus. It is the onely thing I crave, that seeing my love to *Endimion* unspotted, cannot be accepted, his truth to *Cynthia* (though it be unspeakable) may bee suspected.

Dipsas. I will undertake it, and overtake him, that all his love shall be doubted of, and therefore become desperate: but this will weare out with time, that treadeth all things downe but truth.

Tellus. Let us goe.

Dipsas. I follow.   [*Exeunt.*

ACTUS SECUNDUS. SCÆNA PRIMA.

ENDIMION. TELLUS.

Endimion.

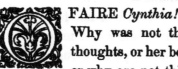 FAIRE *Cynthia!* O unfortunate *Endimion!* Why was not thy birth as high as thy thoughts, or her beauty lesse then heavenly? or why are not thine honours as rare as her beautie? or thy fortunes as great as thy deserts? Sweet *Cynthia,* how wouldst thou be pleased, how possessed? will labours (patient of all extremities) obtaine thy love? There is no mountaine so steepe that I will not climbe, no monster so cruell that I will not tame, no action so desperate that I will not attempt. Desirest thou the passions of love, the sad and melancholy moods of perplexed minds, the not to be expressed torments of racked thoughts? Behold my sad teares, my deepe sighes, my hollow eyes, my broken sleepes, my heavie countenance. Wouldst thou have me vow'd onely to thy beautie, and consume every minute of time in thy ser-

vice? remember my solitarie life, almost these seven
yeares, whom have I entertained but mine owne thoughts,
and thy vertues? What company have I used but contemplation? Whom have I wondred at but thee? Nay,
whom have I not contemned, for thee? Have I not
crept to those on whom I might have trodden, onely
because thou didst shine upon them? Have not injuries
beene sweet to mee, if thou vouchsafest I should beare
them? Have I not spent my golden yeeres in hopes,
waxing old with wishing, yet wishing nothing but thy
love.   With *Tellus*, faire *Tellus*, have I dissembled,
using her but as a cloake for mine affections, that others
seeing my mangled and disordered mind, might thinke
it were for one that loveth me, not for *Cynthia*, whose
perfection alloweth no companion, nor comparison.   In
the midst of these distempered thoughts of mine thou
art not only jealous of my truth, but carelesse, suspicious, and secure: which strange humour maketh my
minde as desperate as thy conceits are doubtfull.   I am
none of those wolves that barke most, when thou shinest
brightest.   But that fish (thy fish *Cynthia* in the floud
Aranis) which at thy waxing is as white as the driven
snow, and at thy wayning, as blacke as deepest dark-
nesse.   I am that *Endimion* (sweete *Cynthia*) that
have carried my thoughts in equall ballance with my
actions, being alwayes as free from imagining ill, as en-
terprizing; that *Endimion*, whose eyes never esteemed
any thing faire, but thy face, whose tongue termed
nothing rare but thy vertues, and whose heart imagined
nothing miraculous, but thy government.   Yea, that
Endimion, who divorcing himselfe from the amiable-

nesse of all ladies, the braverie of all courts, the company
of all men, hath chosen in a solitarie cell to live, onely
by feeding on thy favour, accounting in the world (but
thyselfe) nothing excellent, nothing immortall; thus
maist thou see every vaine, sinew, muscle, and artery
of my love, in which there is no flatterie, nor deceit,
error, nor art.   But soft, here commeth *Tellus*, I must
turne my other face to her like *Janus*, least she be as
suspicious as *Juno*.

Enter TELLUS.

Tellus. Yonder I espie *Endimion*, I will seeme to
suspect nothing, but sooth him, that seeing I cannot
obtain the depth of his love, I may learne the height of
his dissembling; *Floscula* and *Dipsas*, withdraw yourselves out of our sight, yet be within the hearing of our
saluting.   How now *Endimion*, alwaies solitarie? no
company but your owne thoughts? no friend but melancholy fancies?

End. You know (faire *Tellus*) that the sweet remembrance of your love, is the onely companion of my life,
and thy presence, my paradise; so that I am not alone
when nobodie is with mee, and in heaven itselfe when
thou art with me.

Tellus. Then you love me *Endimion.*

End. Or else I live not *Tellus.*

Tellus. Is it not possible for you *Endimion* to dissemble?

End. Not *Tellus*, unlesse I could make me a woman.

Tellus. Why, is dissembling joyned to their sex in-
separable? as heate to fire, heavinesse to earth, moysture
to water, thinnesse to aire?

End. No, but found in their sex, as common as spots upon doves, moles upon faces, caterpillers upon sweet apples, cobwebs upon faire windowes.

Tellus. Doe they all dissemble?

End. All but one.

Tellus. Who is that?

End. I dare not tell. For if I should say you, then would you imagine my flatterie to be extreme; if another, then would you thinke my love to be but indifferent.

Tellus. You will be sure I shall take no vantage of your words. But in sooth *Endimion*, without more ceremonies, is it not *Cynthia?*

End. You know *Tellus*, that of the gods we are forbidden to dispute, because their deities come not within the compasse of our reasons; and of *Cynthia* wee are allowed not to talke but to wonder, because her vertues are not within the reach of our capacities.

Tellus. Why, she is but a woman.

End. No more was *Venus.*

Tellus. Shee is but a virgin.

End. No more was *Vesta.*

Tellus. Shee shall have an end.

End. So shall the world.

Tellus. Is not her beautie subject to time?

End. No more then time is to standing still.

Tellus. Wilt thou make her immortall?

End. No, but incomparable.

Tellus. Take heed *Endimion,* lest like the wrastler in *Olympia,* that striving to lift an impossible weight catcht an incurable straine, thou by fixing thy thoughts above thy reach, fall into a disease without all recure? But I see thou art now in love with *Cynthia.*

End. No *Tellus;* thou knowest that the stately cedar, whose top reacheth unto the cloudes, never boweth his head to the shrubs that grow in the valley; nor ivie that climeth up by the elme, can ever get hold of the beames of the sunne; *Cynthia* I honour in all humilitie, whom none ought, or dare adventure to love; whose affections are immortall, and vertues infinite. Suffer me therefore to gaze on the Moone, at whom, were it not for thyselfe, I would die with wondering. [*Exeunt.*

ACTUS SECUNDUS. SCÆNA SECUNDA.

DARES, SAMIAS, SCINTILLA, FAVILLA.

Dar. Come, *Samias,* diddest thou ever heare such a sighing, the one for *Cynthia,* the other for *Semele,* and both for mooneshine in the water?

Sam. Let them sigh, and let us sing; how say you gentlewomen, are not our masters too farre in love?

Scint. Their tongues happily are dipt to the root in amorous words and sweet discourses, but I thinke their hearts are scarce tipt on the side with constant desires.

Dar. How say you *Favilla,* is not love a lurcher, that taketh mens stomacks away that they cannot eate; their spleene that they cannot laugh; their hearts that they cannot fight; their eyes that they cannot sleepe; and leaveth nothing but livers to make nothing but lovers?

Favil. Away peevish boy, a rod were better under thy girdle, than love in thy mouth: it will be a forward cocke that croweth in the shell.

Dar. Alas! good old gentlewoman, how it becommeth you to be grave.

Scint. *Favilla* though shee be but a sparke, yet is she fire.

Favil. And you *Scintilla* be not much more then a sparke, though you would be esteemed a flame.

Sam. It were good sport to see the fight betweene two sparkes.

Dar. Let them to it, and wee will warme us by their words.

Scint. You are not angry *Favilla?*

Favil. That is *Scintilla*, as you list to take it.

Sam. That, that.

Scint. This it is to be matched with girles, who comming but yesterday from making of babies, would before to morrow be accounted matrons.

Favil. I cry your matronship mercie; because your pantables be higher with corke, therefore your feet must needs be higher in the insteps: you will be mine elder, because you stand upon a stoole, and I on the floore.

Sam. Good, good.

Dar. Let them love, and see with what countenance they will become friends.

Scint. Nay, you thinke to be the wiser, because you meane to have the last word.

Sam. Step betweene them least they scratch. In faith gentlewomen, seeing wee came out to be merry, let not your jarring marre our jests: be friends, how say you?

Scint. I am not angry, but it spited me to see how short she was.

Favil. I meant nothing, till she would me.

Dar. Then so let it rest.

Scint. I am agreed.

Favil. And I, yet I never tooke any thing so unkindly in my life.

Scint. 'Tis I have the cause, that never offered the occasion.

Dar. Excellent and right like a woman.

Sam. A strange sight to see water come out of fire.

Dar. It is their propertie, to carrie in their eyes, fire and water, teares and torches, and in their mouthes, hony and gall.

Scint. You will be a good one if you live; but what is yonder formall fellow?

Enter Sir TOPHAS.

Dar. Sir *Tophas*, Sir *Tophas*, of whom we told you: if you be good wenches make as though you love him, and wonder at him.

Favil. We will doe our parts.

Dar. But first let us stand aside, and let him use his garbe, for all consisteth in his gracing.

Top. Epi.

Epi. At hand sir.

Top. How likest thou this martiall life, where nothing but bloud besprinkleth our bosomes? Let me see, be our enemies fat?

Epi. Passing fat: and I would not change this life to be a lord; and yourselfe passeth all comparison, for other captaines kill and beate, and there is nothing you kill, but you also eate.

Top. I will draw out their guts out of their bellies,

and teare the flesh with my teeth, so mortall is my hate, and so eager my unstanched stomacke.

Epi. My master thinkes himselfe the valiantest man in the world if hee kill a wren: so warlike a thing he accompteth to take away life, though it bee from a larke.

Top. Epi, I finde my thoughts to swell, and my spirit to take wings, in so much that I cannot continue within the compasse of so slender combates.

Favil. This passeth!

Scint. Why, is he not mad?

Sam. No, but a little vaine glorious.

Top. Epi.

Epi. Sir.

Top. I will encounter that blacke and cruell enemie that beareth rough and untewed locks upon his bodie, whose sire throweth downe the strongest walls, whose legs are as many as both ours, on whose head are placed most horrible hornes by nature, as a defence from all harmes.

Epi. What meane you master to be so desperate?

Top. Honour inciteth me, and very hunger compelleth me.

Epi. What is that monster?

Top. The monster *Ovis.* I have said,—let thy wits worke.

Epi. I cannot imagine it; yet let mee see,—a blacke enemie with rough lockes? it may be a sheepe, and *Ovis* is a sheepe: his sire so strong, a ram is a sheepes sire, that being also an engine of war; hornes hee hath, and foure legs,—so hath a sheepe: without doubt this monster is a blacke sheepe. Is it not a sheepe that you meane?

Top. Thou hast hit it, that monster will I kill and sup with.

Sam. Come let us take him off. Sir *Tophas* all haile.

Top. Welcome children, I seldome cast mine eyes so low as to the crownes of your heads, and therefore pardon me that I spake not all this while.

Dar. No harme done; here be faire ladies come to wonder at your person, your valour, your wit, the report whereof hath made them carelesse of their owne honours, to glut their eyes and hearts upon yours.

Top. Report cannot but injure me, for that not knowing fully what I am, I feare she hath beene a niggard in her praises.

Scint. No, gentle knight, Report hath beene prodigall; for shee hath left you no equall, nor herselfe credit, so much hath she told, yet no more than we now see.

Dar. A good wench.

Favil. If there remaine as much pittie toward women, as there is in you courage against your enemies, then shall wee be happy, who hearing of your person, came to see it, and seeing it, are now in love with it.

Top. Love mee ladies? I easily beleeve it, but my tough heart receiveth no impression with sweet words. *Mars* may pierce it, *Venus* shall not paint on it.

Favil. A cruell saying.

Sam. There's a girle.

Dar. Will you cast these ladies away, and all for a little love? do but speake kindly.

Top. There commeth no soft syllable within my lips,
custome hath made my words bloudy, and my heart
barbarous: that pelting word love, how watrish it is in
my mouth, it carrieth no sound; hate, horror, death,
are speeches that nourish my spirits. I like hony but
I care not for the bees, I delight in musique but I love
not to play on the bagpipes, I can vouchsafe to heare
the voice of women, but to touch their bodies I disdaine
it, as a thing childish, and fit for such men as can disgest
nothing but milke.

Scint. A hard heart! shall wee die for your love, and
find no remedie.

Top. I have alreadie taken a surfet.

Epi. Good master pitie them.

Top. Pitie them, *Epi?* no I doe not thinke that this
breast shall bee pestered with such a foolish passion.
What is that the gentlewoman carrieth in a chaine?

Epi. Why, it is a squirrill.

Top. A squirrill? O Gods what things are made for
money.

Dar. Is not this gentleman overwise?

Favil. I could stay all day with him, if I feared not
to be shent.

Scint. Is it not possible to meete againe?

Dar. Yes at any time.

Favil. Then let us hasten home.

Scint. Sir *Tophas,* the God of warre deale better
with you, then you doe with the God of love.

Favil. Our love wee may dissemble, disgest we cannot; but I doubt not but time will hamper you, and
helpe us.

Top. I defie time, who hath no interest in my heart:
come *Epi*, let me to the battaile with that hideous beast,
love is pap and hath no rellish in my taste, because it is
not terrible.

Dar. Indeed a blacke sheepe is a perilous beast, but
let us in till another time.

Favil. I shall long for that time.　　　[*Exeunt.*

ACTUS SECUNDUS. SCÆNA TERTIA.

Endimion, Dipsas, Bagoa.

End. No rest *Endimion?* still uncertain how to
settle thy steps by day, or thy thoughts by night? thy
truth is measured by thy fortune, and thou art judged
unfaithfull because thou art unhappy. I will see if I
can beguile myselfe with sleepe, and if no slumber will
take hold in my eyes, yet will I imbrace the golden
thoughts in my head, and wish to melt by musing:
that as ebone, which no fire can scorch, is yet consumed with sweet savours; so my heart which cannot
be bent by the hardnesse of fortune, may be bruised by
amorous desires. On yonder banke never grew any
thing but lunary, and hereafter I will never have any
bed but that banke. O *Endimion, Tellus* was faire,
but what avayleth beauty without wisdome? Nay, *Endimion*, she was wise, but what avayleth wisdome
without honour? Shee was honorable *Endimion*, belie
her not, I but how obscure is honour without fortune?
Was she not fortunate whom so many followed? Yes,
yes, but base is fortune without majestie: thy majestie
Cynthia all the world knoweth and wondereth at, but

not one in the world that can imitate it, or comprehend
it.   No more *Endimion*, sleepe or die; nay die, for to
sleepe, it is impossible, and yet I know not how it
commeth to passe, I feele such a heavinesse both in
mine eyes and heart, that I am sodainly benummed,
yea in every joint: it may be wearinesse, for when did
I rest? it may be deepe melancholy, for when did I
not sigh? *Cynthia*, I so, I say *Cynthia*.

[*He fals asleepe.*

Dipsas. Little doest thou know *Endimion* when thou
shalt wake, for hadst thou placed thy heart as lowe in
love, as thy head lieth now in sleepe, thou mightest
have commanded *Tellus* whom now instead of a mistris,
thou shalt finde a tombe.   These eies must I seale up
by art, not nature, which are to be opened neither by
art nor nature.   Thou that laist downe with golden
lockes, shalt not awake untill they bee turned to silver
haires: and that chin, on which scarcely appeareth soft
downe, shall be filled with brissels as hard as broome:
thou shalt sleepe out thy youth and flewring time, and
become dry hay before thou knewest thyselfe greene
grasse; and readie by age to step into the grave when
thou wakest, that was youthfull in the court when thou
laidst thee downe to sleepe.   The malice of *Tellus* hath
brought this to passe, which if shee could not have intreated of mee by faire meanes, shee would have commanded by menacing, for from her gather we all our
simples to maintaine our sorceries.   Fanne with this
hemlocke over his face, and sing the inchantment for
sleepe, whilst I goe in and finish those ceremonies that
are required in our art: take heed yee touch not his

face, for the fanne is so seasoned that who so it toucheth
with a leafe shall presently die, and over whom the winde
of it breatheth, hee shall sleepe for ever.   [*Exit.*

Bagoa. Let me alone, I will be carefull. What hap
hadst thou *Endimion* to come under the hands of
Dipsas. O faire *Endimion !* how it grieveth mee that
that faire face must be turned to a withered skin, and
taste the paines of death before it feele the reward of
love. I feare *Tellus* will repent that which the heavens
themselves seemed to rewe; but I heare *Dipsas* comming,
I dare not repine, least shee make me pine, and rocke
mee into such a deepe sleepe, that I shall not awake to
my marriage.

Enter DIPSAS.

Dipsas. How now, have you finished ?
Bagoa. Yea.
Dipsas. Well then let us in, and see that you doe
not so much as whisper that I did this, for if you doe,
I will turne thy haires to adders, and all thy teeth in
thy head to tongues; come away, come away. [*Exeunt.*

A DUMB SHEW.

Musique sounds.

Three ladies enter; one with a knife and a looking
glasse, who by the procurement of one of the other two,
offers to stab *Endimion* as hee sleepes, but the third
wrings her hands, lamenteth, offering still to prevent it,
but dares not.

At last, the first lady looking in the glasse, casts
downe the knife.   [*Exeunt.*

Enters an ancient Man *with bookes with three leaves, offers the same twice.*

Endimion refuseth, hee readeth two and offers the third, where hee stands awhile, and then *Endimion* offers to take it. 　　　　　　　　　　　[*Exit.*

ACTUS TERTIUS. SCÆNA PRIMA.

CYNTHIA, three Lords, TELLUS.

Cynthia.

S the report true, that *Endimion* is stricken into such a dead sleepe, that nothing can either wake him or move him?

Eum. Too true madame, and as much to be pitied as wondred at.

Tellus. As good sleepe and doe no harme, as wake and doe no good.

Cynth. What maketh you *Tellus* to be so short? the time was *Endimion* onely was.

Eum. It is an old saying madame, that a waking dogge doth afarre off barke at a sleeping lion.

Sem. It were good *Eumenides* that you tooke a nap with your friend, for your speech beginneth to be heavie.

Eum. Contrarie to your nature, *Semele*, which hath beene alwayes accounted light.

Cynth. What have wee here before my face, these unseemely and malepart overthwarts? I will tame your tongues, and your thoughts, and make your speeches answerable to your duties, and your conceits fit for my dignitie, else will I banish you both my person and the world.

Eum. Pardon I humbly aske; but such is my un-spotted faith to *Endimion*, that whatsoever seemeth a needle to prick his finger, is a dagger to wound my heart.

Cynth. If you be so deere to him, how happeneth it you neither goe to see him, nor search for remedie for him?

Eum. I have seene him to my griefe, and sought re-cure with despaire, for that I cannot imagine who should restore him that is the wonder to all men: your high-nesse, on whose hands the compasse of the earth is at command, (though not in possession) may shew your-selfe both worthy your sex, your nature, and your favour, if you redeeme that honourable *Endimion*, whose ripe yeares foretell rare vertues, and whose un-mellowed conceits promise ripe counsell.

Cynth. I have had triall of *Endimion*, and conceive greater assurance of his age, then I could hope of his youth.

Tellus. But timely madame crookes that tree that will be a camocke; and yong it prickes that will be a thorne; and therefore hee that began without care to settle his life, it is a signe without amendement he will end it.

Cynth. Presumptuous girle, I will make thy tongue an example of unrecoverable displeasure, *Corsites* carrie her to the castle in the desert, there to remaine and weave.

Cors. Shall shee worke stories or poetries?

Cynth. It skilleth not which, goe to, in both, for shee shall find examples infinite in either what punishment long tongues have. *Eumenides*, if either the sooth-sayers in Egypt, or the enchanters in Thessaly, or the philosophers in Greece, or all the sages of the world, can find remedie, I will procure it; therefore dispatch with all speed: you *Eumenides* into Thessalie: You *Zontes* into Greece, (because you are acquainted in Athens.) You *Pantalion* to Egypt, saying that *Cynthia* sendeth, and if you will, commandeth.

Eum. On bowed knee I give thankes, and with wings on my legs, I flie for remedie.

Zon. We are readie at your highnesse command, and hope to returne to your full content.

Cynth. It shall never be said that *Cynthia*, whose mercie and goodnesse filleth the heavens with joyes, and the world with marvaile, will suffer either *Endimion* or any to perish, if he may be protected.

Eum. Your majesties words have been alwayes deeds, and your deeds vertues.   [*Exeunt.*

ACTUS TERTIUS. SCÆNA SECUNDA.

Corsites, Tellus.

Cors. Heere is the castle (faire *Tellus*) in which you must weave, till either time end your dayes, or *Cynthia* her displeasure. I am sorrie so faire a face should be subject to so hard a fortune, and that the flower of beautie, which is honoured in courts, should heere wither in prison.

Tellus. Corsites, Cynthia may restraine the libertie of my bodie, of my thoughts shee cannot, and therefore doe I esteeme myselfe most free, though I am in greatest bondage.

Cors. Can you then feed on fancie, and subdue the malice of envie by the sweetnesse of imagination.

Tellus. Corsites, there is no sweeter musique to the miserable then despaire; and therefore the more bitternesse I feele, the more sweetnesse I find; for so vaine were libertie, and so unwelcome the following of higher fortune, that I chuse rather to pine in this castle, then to be a prince in any other court.

Cors. A humour contrary to your yeeres, and nothing agreeable to your sex: the one commonly allured with delights, the other alwayes with soveraigntie.

Tellus. I marvaile *Corsites* that you being a captaine, who should sound nothing but terrour, and sucke nothing but bloud, can find in your heart to talke such smooth wordes, for that it agreeth not with your calling to use words so soft, as that of love.

Cors. Ladie, it were unfit of warres to discourse with women, into whose minds nothing can sinke but smoothnes; besides, you must not thinke that souldiers be so rough hewne, or of such knottie mettle, that beautie cannot allure, and you being beyond perfection enchant.

Tellus. Good *Corsites* talke not of love, but let mee to my labour: the little beautie I have, shall be bestowed on my loome, which I now meane to make my lover.

Cors. Let us in, and what favour *Corsites* can shew, *Tellus* shall command.

Tellus. The onely favour I desire, is now and then to walke.   [*Exeunt.*

ACTUS TERTIUS. SCÆNA TERTIA.

Sir TOPHAS, *and* EPI.

Tophas. Epi.

Epi. Heere sir.

Tophas. Unrigge me.   Hey ho!

Epi. What's that?

Tophas. An interjection, whereof some are of mourning : as *eho, vah.*

Epi. I understand you not.

Tophas. Thou seest me.

Epi. I.

Tophas. Thou hearest me.

Epi. I.

Tophas. Thou feelest me.

Epi. I.

Tophas. And not understand'st me?

Epi. No.

Tophas. Then am I but three quarters of a nowne substantive.   But alas *Epi*, to tell thee the troth, I am a nowne adjective.

Epi. Why?

Tophas. Because I cannot stand without another.

Epi. Who is that?

Tophas. Dipsas.

Epi. Are you in love?

Tophas. No : but love hath as it were milkt my thoughts, and drained from my heart the very substance

of my accustomed courage; it worketh in my head like
new wine, so as I must hoope my skonce with iron, least
my head breake, and so I bewray my braines: but I
pray thee first discover mee in all parts, that I may be
like a lover, and then will I sigh and die. Take my
gun, and give me a gowne: *Cædant arma togæ.*

Epi. Heere.

Tophas. Take my sword and shield, and give mee
beard, brush, and cyssers: *bella gerant alii, tu pari
semper ama.*

Epi. Will you be trim'd sir?

Tophas. Not yet: for I feele a contention within me,
whether I shall frame the bodkin beard or the bush.
But take my pike and give me pen: *dicere quæ puduit,
scribere jussit amor.*

Epi. I will furnish you, sir.

Tophas. Now for my bowe and bolts, give me inke
and paper; for my scmiter a pen-knife: for *Scalpel-
lum, calami, atramentum, charta, libelli, sint semper
studiis arma parata meis.*

Epi. Sir, will you give over warres, and play with
that bable called love?

Tophas. Give over warres? no Epi, *Militat omnis
amans, et habet sua castra Cupido.*

Epi. Love hath made you very eloquent, but your
face is nothing faire.

Tophas. *Non formosus erat, sederat facundus Ulisses.*

Epi. Nay, I must seeke a new master if you can
speake nothing but verses.

Tophas. *Quicquid conabar dicere versus erat.* Epi.
I feele all *Ovid de arte amandi* lie as heavie at my
heart as a load of logges. O what a fine thin haire

hath *Dipsas!* What a pretie low forehead! What a
tall and stately nose! What little hollow eyes! What
great and goodly lips! How harmlesse she is being
toothlesse! her fingers fat and short, adorned with long
nailes like a byttern! In how sweet a proportion her
cheekes hang downe to her brests like dugges, and her
paps to her waste like bags! What a low stature shee
is, and yet what a great foot she carrieth! How thriftie
must shee be in whom there is no waste! How vertuous
is she like to be, over whom no man can be jealous!

Epi. Stay master, you forget yourselfe.

Tophas. O *Epi.* even as a dish melteth by the fire,
so doth my wit increase by love.

Epi. Pithily, and to the purpose, but what? begin
you to nod?

Tophas. Good *Epi* let mee take a nap: for as some
man may better steale a horse, then another looke over
the hedge: so divers shall be sleepie when they would
fainest take rest.　　　　　　　　　　*[He sleeps.*

Epi. Who ever saw such a woodcock, love *Dipsas!*
without doubt all the world will now account him valiant,
that ventureth on her, whom none durst undertake.
But heere commeth two wagges.

Enter DARES *and* SAMIAS.

Sam. Thy master hath slept his share.

Dar. I thinke he doth it because he would not pay
me my boord wages.

Sam. It is a thing most strange, and I thinke mine
will never returne, so that we must both seeke new
masters, for wee shall never live by our manners.

Epi. If you want masters, joyne with me, and serve

Sir *Tophas,* who must needs keepe more men, because
hee is toward mariage.

Sam. What *Epi,* where's thy master?

Epi. Yonder sleeping in love.

Dar. Is it possible?

Epi. He hath taken his thoughts a hole lower, and
saith, seeing it is the fashion of the world, he will vaile
bonet to beautie.

Sam. How is he attired?

Epi. Lovely.

Dar. Whom loveth this amorous knight?

Epi. *Dipsas.*

Sam. That ugly creature? Why she is a foole, a
scold, fat, without fashion, and quite without favour.

Epi. Tush you be simple, my master hath a good
mariage.

Dar. Good? as how?

Epi. Why in marrying *Dipsas,* hee shall have every
day twelve dishes of meate to his dinner, though there
be none but *Dipsas* with him.   Foure of flesh, foure of
fish, foure of fruit.

Sam. As how *Epi?*

Epi. For flesh these; woodcocke, goose, byttern, and
rayle.

Dar. Indeed hee shall not misse, if *Dipsas* be there.

Epi. For fish these; crab, carpe, lumpe, and powting.

Sam. Excellent, for of my word, she is both crabbish,
lumpish, and carping.

Epi. For fruit these; fritters, medlers, hartichokes,
and lady longings.   Thus you see hee shall fare like a
king, though he be but a begger.

Dar. Well, *Epi*, dine thou with him, for I had rather fast then see her face. But see thy master is asleepe, let us have a song to wake this amorous knight.

Epi. Agreed.

Sam. Content.

Tʜᴇ ꜰɪʀsᴛ Sᴏɴɢ.

Epi. Here snores *Tophas*,
That amorous asse,
Who loves *Dipsas*,
With face so sweet,
Nose and chinne meet.

All three. { At sight of her each fury skips
　　　　　 { And flings into her lap their whips.

Dar. Holla, holla in his eare.

Sam. The witch sure thrust her fingers there.

Epi. Crampe him, or wring the foole by th' nose.

Dar. Or clap some burning flax, to his toes.

Sam. What musique's best to wake him?

Epi. Baw wow, let bandogs shake him.

Dar. Let adders hisse in's eare.

Sam. Else eare-wigs, wriggle there.

Epi. No, let him batten, when his tongue
Once goes, a cat is not worse strung.

All three. { But if he ope nor mouth, nor eies,
　　　　　 { He may in time sleepe himselfe wise.

Top. Sleepe is a binding of the sences, love a loosing.

Epi. Let us heare him awhile.

Top. There appeared in my sleepe a goodly owle, who sitting upon my shoulder, cried twit, twit, and before mine eyes presented herselfe the expresse image of *Dipsas*. I marvailed what the owle said, till at the last, I perceived twit, twit, to it, to it: onely by contraction admonished by this vision, to make account of my sweet *Venus*.

Sam. Sir *Tophas*, you have over-slept yourselfe.

Top. No youth, I have but slept over my love.

Dar. Loue? Why it is impossible, that into so noble and unconquered a courage, love should creepe; having first a head as hard to pierce as steele, then to passe to a hart arm'd with a shirt of male.

Epi. I but my master yawning one day in the sun, Love crept into his mouth before hee could close it, and there kept such a tumbling in his bodie that he was glad to untrusse the points of his heart, and entertaine Love as a stranger.

Top. If there remaine any pitie in you, plead for me to *Dipsas*.

Dar. Plead? Nay, wee will presse her to it. Let us goe with him to *Dipsas*, and there shall wee have good sport. But Sir *Tophas* when shall wee goe? for I find my tongue voluble, and my heart venturous, and all myselfe like myselfe.

Sam. Come *Dares*, let us not loose him till wee find our masters, for as long as he liveth, wee shall lacke neither mirth nor meate.

Epi. We will travice. Will you go sir?

Top. *I prœ, sequar.* [*Exeunt.*

ACTUS TERTIUS. SCÆNA QUARTA.

Eumenides, Geron.

Eum. Father, your sad musique being tuned on the same key that my hard fortune is, hath so melted my minde, that I wish to hang at your mouthes end till life end.

Ger. These tunes gentleman have I beene accustomed with these fiftie winters, having no other house to shrowde myselfe but the broad heavens, and so familiar with mee hath use made miserie, that I esteeme sorrow my chiefest solace. And welcommest is that guest to me, that can rehearse the saddest tale, or the bloudiest tragedie.

Eum. A strange humour, might I enquire the cause?

Ger. You must pardon me if I denie to tell it, for knowing that the revealing of griefes is as it were a renewing of sorrow, I have vowed therefore to conceale them, that I might not onely feele the depth of everlasting discontentment, but despaire of remedie. But whence are you? What fortune hath thrust you to this distresse?

Eum. I am going to Thessalie, to seeke remedie for *Endimion* my dearest friend, who hath beene cast into a dead sleepe, almost these twentie yeeres, waxing olde, and readie for the grave, being almost but newly come forth of the cradle.

Ger. You need not for recure travell farre, for who so can cleerly see the bottome of this fountaine shall have remedie for any thing.

Eum. That me thinketh is unpossible, why what vertue can there be in water?

Ger. Yes, whosoever can shed the teares of a faithfull lover shall obtaine any thing hee would; reade these words engraven about the brim.

Eum. Have you knowne this by experience, or is it placed here of purpose to delude men?

Ger. I onely would have experience of it, and then

should there be an end of my miserie. And then would I tell the strangest discourse that ever yet was heard.

Eum. Ah *Eumenides!*

Ger. What lacke you gentleman, are you not well?

Eum. Yes father, but a qualme that often commeth over my heart doth now take hold of me; but did never any lovers come hither?

Ger. Lusters, but not lovers; for often have I seene them weepe, but never could I heare they saw the bottome.

Eum. Came there women also?

Ger. Some.

Eum. What did they see?

Ger. They all wept that the fountaine overflowed with teares, but so thick became the water with their teares, that I could scarce discerne the brimme, much lesse behold the bottome.

Eum. Be faithfull lovers so skant?

Ger. It seemeth so, for yet heard I never of any.

Eum. Ah *Eumenides,* how art thou perplexed? call to minde the beautie of thy sweet mistris, and the depth of thy never dying affections: how oft hast thou honoured her, not onely without spot, but suspition of falshood? And how hardly hath she rewarded thee, without cause or colour of despight. How secret hast thou beene these seven yeeres, that hast not, nor once darest not to name her, for discontenting her. How faithfull! that hath offered to die for her, to please her. Unhappie *Eumenides!*

Ger. Why gentleman did you once love?

Eum. Once? I father, and ever shall.

Ger. Was she unkind, and you faithfull?

Eum. Shee of all women the most froward, and I of all creatures the most fond.

Ger. You doted then, not loved: for affection is grounded on vertue, and vertue is never peevish: or on beautie, and beautie loveth to be praised.

Eum. I but if all vertuous ladies should yeeld to all that be loving, or all amiable gentlewomen entertaine all that be amorous, their vertues would be accounted vices, and beauties deformities; for that love can be but between two, and that not proceeding of him that is most faithfull, but most fortunate.

Ger. I would you were so faithfull, that your teares might make you fortunate.

Eum. Yea father, if that my teares cleare not this fountaine, then may you sweare it is but a meere mockerie.

Ger. So saith every one yet, that wept.

Eum. Ah, I faint, I die! Ah sweete *Semele* let me alone, and dissolve by weeping into water.

Ger. This affection seemeth strange, if hee see nothing, without doubt this dissembling passeth, for nothing shall draw me from the beliefe.

Eum. Father, I plainly see the bottome, and there in white marble engraven these words, *Aske one for all, and but one thing at all.*

Ger. O fortunate *Eumenides,* (for so have I heard thee call thyselfe) let me see. I cannot discerne any such thing. I thinke thou dreamest.

Eum. Ah father thou art not a faithfull lover, and therefore canst not behold it.

Ger. Then aske, that I may be satisfied by the event, and thyselfe blessed.

Eum. Aske? so I will: and what shall I doe but aske, and whom should I aske but *Semele,* the possessing of whose person is a pleasure that cannot come within the compasse of comparison; whose golden lockes seeme most curious, when they seeme most carelesse; whose sweet lookes seeme most alluring, when they are most chaste; and whose wordes the more vertuous they are, the more amorous they be accounted. I pray thee fortune when I shall first meete with faire *Semele,* dash my delight with some light disgrace, least imbracing sweetnesse beyond measure, I take a surfet without recure: let her practise her accustomed coynesse, that I may diet myselfe upon my desires: otherwise the fulnesse of my joyes will diminish the sweetnesse, and I shall perish by them before I possesse them. Why doe I trifle the time in words? The least minute being spent in the getting of *Semele,* is more worth then the whole world: therefore let mee aske, What now *Eumenides?* Whither art thou drawne? Hast thou forgotten both friendship and dutie? Care of *Endimion,* and the commandement of *Cynthia?* Shall he die in a leaden sleep, because thou sleepest in a golden dreame? I, let him sleepe ever, so I slumber but one minute with *Semele.* Love knoweth neither friendship nor kindred. Shall I not hazard the losse of a friend, for the obtayning of her for whom I would often loose myselfe? Fond *Eumenides,* shall the inticing beautie of a most disdainfull ladie, be of more force then the rare fidelitie of a tried friend? The love of men to women is a thing

common, and of course: the friendship of man to man
infinite and immortall. Tush, *Semele* doth possesse my
love. I but *Endimion* hath deserved it. I will helpe
Endimion. I found *Endimion* unspotted in his truth.
I but I shall find *Semele* constant in her love. I will
have *Semele.* What shall I do? Father thy gray
haires are embassadors of experience. Which shall I
aske?

Ger. Eumenides release *Endimion*, for all things
(friendship excepted) are subject to fortune: love is but
an eye-worme, which onely tickleth the head with hopes,
and wishes: friendship the image of eternitie, in which
there is nothing moveable, nothing mischievous. As
much difference as there is between beautie and vertue,
bodies and shadowes, colours and life—so great oddes
is there betweene love and friendship. Love is a came-
lion, which draweth nothing into the mouth but aire,
and nourisheth nothing in the body but lungs: believe
me *Eumenides*, desire dies in the same moment that
beautie sickens, and beautie fadeth in the same instant
that it flourisheth. When adversities flow, then love
ebbes: but friendship standeth stifly in stormes. Time
draweth wrinckles in a faire face, but addeth fresh
colours to a fast friend, which neither heate, nor cold,
nor miserie, nor place, nor destinie, can alter or diminish.
O friendship! of all things the most rare, and therefore
most rare because most excellent, whose comforts in
miserie is alwayes sweete, and whose counsels in pros-
peritie are ever fortunate. Vaine love, that onely comming neere to friendship in name, would seeme to be
the same, or better, in nature.

Eum. Father I allow your reasons, and will therefore conquer mine owne. Vertue shall subdue affections, wisdome lust, friendship beautie. Mistresses are in every place, and as common as hares in *Atho*, bees in *Hybla*, foules in the ayre: but friends to be found, are like the Phænix in *Arabia*, but one, or the *Philadelphi* in *Arays*, never above two. I will have *Endimion:* sacred fountaine, in whose bowels are hidden divine secrets, I have increased your waters with the teares of unspotted thoughts and therefore let mee receive the reward you promise: *Endimion*, the truest friend to me, and faithfullest lover to *Cynthia*, is in such a dead sleepe, that nothing can wake or move him.

Ger. Doest thou see any thing?

Eum. I see in the same piller, these words: *When she whose figure of all is the perfectest, and never to be measured: alwayes one, yet never the same: still inconstant, yet never wavering: shall come and kisse* Endimion *in his sleepe, he shall then rise, else never.* This is strange.

Ger. What see you else?

Eum. There commeth over mine eyes either a darke mist, or upon the fountaine a deepe thicknesse: for I can perceive nothing. But how am I deluded? or what difficult (nay impossible) thing is this?

Ger. Me thinketh it easie.

Eum. Good father and how?

Ger. Is not a circle of all figures the perfectest?

Eum. Yes.

Ger. And is not *Cynthia* of all circles the most absolute?

Eum. Yes.

Ger. Is it not impossible to measure her, who still worketh by her influence, never standing at one stay?

Eum. Yes.

Ger. Is shee not alwayes *Cynthia,* yet seldome in the same bignesse; alwayes wavering in her waxing or wayning, that our bodies might the better be governed, our seasons the daylier give their increase; yet never to be removed from her course as long as the heavens. continue theirs?

Eum. Yes.

Ger. Then who can it be but *Cynthia,* whose vertues being all divine, must needs bring things to passe that be miraculous? Goe, humble thyselfe to *Cynthia,* tell her the successe of which myselfe shall be a witnesse. And this assure thyselfe, that shee that sent to find meanes for his safetie will now worke her cunning.

Eum. How fortunate am I if *Cynthia* be she that may doe it.

Ger. How fond art thou if thou do not beleeve it?

Eum. I will hasten thither that I may intreat on my knees for succour, and imbrace in mine armes my friend.

Ger. I will goe with thee, for unto *Cynthia* must I discover all my sorrowes, who also must worke in mee a contentment.

Eum. May I now know the cause?

Ger. That shall be as we walke, and I doubt not but the strangenesse of my tale will take away the tediousnesse of our journey.

Eum. Let us goe.

Ger. I follow.   [*Exeunt.*

ACTUS QUARTUS.   SCÆNA PRIMA.

Tellus, Corsites.

Tellus.

MARVELL *Corsites* giveth me so much libertie: all the world knowing his charge to be so high, and his nature to be most strange; who hath so ill intreated ladies of great honour, that he hath not suffered them to looke out of windowes, much lesse to walke abroad: it may be he is in love with me, for (*Endimion*, hard-hearted *Endimion*, excepted) what is hee that is not enamoured of my beautie? But what respectest thou the love of all the world? *Endimion* hates thee. Alas poore *Endimion*, my malice hath exceeded my love: and thy faith to *Cynthia*, quenched my affections. Quenched *Tellus*? nay kindled them afresh; insomuch that I find scorching flames for dead embers, and cruell encounters of warre in my thoughts, in steed of sweet parlees. Ah that I might once againe see *Endimion*: accursed girle, what hope hast thou to see *Endimion*: on whose head already are growne gray haires, and whose life must yeeld to nature, before *Cynthia* end her displeasure. Wicked *Dipsas*, and more devillish *Tellus*, the one for cunning too exquisite, the other for hate too intolerable. Thou wast commanded to weave the stories and poetries wherein were shewed both examples and punishments of tatling tongues, and thou hast only imbrodered the sweet face of *Endimion*, devices of love, melancholy imaginations, and what not, out of thy worke, that thou shouldest studie to picke out of thy minde. But here commeth *Corsites*, I must seeme yeelding and stout, full of mildnesse, yet tempered with a majestie: for if I be too flexible, I shall give him more hope then I meane; if too froward, enjoy lesse libertie then I would; love him I cannot, and therefore will practise that which is most contrary to our sex to dissemble.

Enter Corsites.

Cor. Faire *Tellus*, I perceive you rise with the larke, and to your selfe sing with the nightingale.

Tellus. My lord I have no playfellow but fancy, being barred of all company I must question with myselfe, and make my thoughts my friends.

Cor. I would you would account my thoughts also your friends, for they be such as are only busied in wondering at your beautie and wisdome; and some such as have esteemed your fortune too hard; and divers of that kinde that offer to set you free, if you will set them free.

Tellus. There are no colours so contrarie as white and blacke, nor elements so disagreeing as fire and water, nor any thing so opposite as mens thoughts and their words.

Cor. He that gave *Cassandra* the gift of prophecying, with the curse that spake she never so true she should never be beleeved, hath I thinke poysoned the fortune of men, that uttering the extremities of their inward passions are always suspected of outward perjuries.

Tellus. Well *Corsites* I will flatter myselfe and beleeve you. What would you doe to enjoy my love?

Cor. Set all the ladies of the castle free, and make
you the pleasure of my life: more I cannot doe, lesse
I will not.

Tellus. These be great words, and fit for your calling: for captaines must promise things impossible. But
will you doe one thing for all.

Cor. Anything sweet *Tellus*, that am readie for all.

Tellus. You know that on the lunarie banke sleepeth
Endimion.

Cor. I know it.

Tellus. If you will remoove him from that place by
force, and convey him into some obscure cave by policie:
I give you here the faith of an unspotted virgin, that
you onely shall possesse me as a lover, and in spight of
malice, have me for a wife.

Cor. Remove him *Tellus?* Yes *Tellus*, hee shall be
removed, and that so soone, as thou shalt as much commend my diligence as my force. I goe.

Tellus. Stay, will yourselfe attempt it?

Cor. I *Tellus:* as I would have none partaker of my
sweet love, so shall none be partners of my labours:
but I pray thee goe at your best leisure, for *Cynthia*
beginneth to rise, and if shee discover our love we both
perish, for nothing pleaseth her but the fairenesse of
virginitie. All things must be not onely without lust,
but without suspicion of lightnesse.

Tellus. I will depart, and goe you to *Endimion.*

Cor. I flie *Tellus*, being of all men the most fortunate.   [*Exit.*

Tellus. Simple *Corsites*, I have set thee about a taske being but a man, the gods themselves cannot performe : for little doest thou know how heavy his head lies, how hard his fortune : but such shifts must women have to deceive men, and under colour of things easie, intreat that which is impossible : otherwise we should be cumbred with importunities, oathes, sighes, letters, and all implements of love, which to one resolved to the contrary, are most lothsome. I will in, and laugh with the other ladies at *Corsites* sweating. [*Exit.*

ACTUS QUARTUS. SCÆNA SECUNDA.

SAMIAS, DARES *and* EPITON.

Sam. Will thy master never awake?

Dar. No, I thinke hee sleepes for a wager : but how shall we spend the time? Sir *Tophas* is so farre in love that hee pineth in his bed, and commeth not abroad?

Sam. But here commeth *Epi*, in a pelting chafe.

Epi. A poxe of all false proverbs, and were a proverbe a page, I would have him by the eares.

Sam. Why art thou angry?

Epi. Why? you know it is said, the tyde tarrieth no man.

Sam. True.

Epi. A monstrous lie ; for I was tide two houres, and tarried for one to unlose mee.

Dar. Alas poore *Epi*.

Epi. Poore? No, no, you base conceited slaves, I am

a most compleate gentleman, although I be in (
with Sir *Tophas*.

Dar. Art thou out with him.

Epi. I, because I cannot get him a lodgi1
Endimion, he would faine take a nap for fortie
yeeres.

Dar. A short sleepe, considering our long li1

Sam. Is he still in love?

Epi. In love? why he doth nothing but make

Sam. Canst thou remember any one of his p

Epi. I, this is one.

> The beggar Love that knowes not where to lodg
> At last within my heart when I slept,
> He crept,
> I wakt, and so my fancies began to fodge.

Sam. That's a very long verse.

Epi. Why the other was short, the first is
from the thumbe to the little finger, the secon
the little finger to the elbow, and some hee n
reach to the crowne of his head, and downe ag
the sole of his foot: it is set to the tune of the
Saunce, *ratio est*, because *Dipsas* is a blacke sai

Dar. Very wisely, but pray thee *Epi* how a
compleate, and being from thy master what occ:
wilt thou take?

Epi. No my harts, I am an absolute *Microco*
pettie world of my selfe, my library is my head
have no other bookes but my braines: my ward1
my backe, for I have no more apparell then is
bodie; my armorie at my finger ends, for I
other artillarie then my nailes; my treasure
purse. *Sic omnia mea mecum porto.*

Dar. Good!

Epi. Now sirs, my palace is paved with grasse, and tiled with stars: for *cœlo tegitur qui non habet urnam*, he that hath no house, must lie in the yard.

Sam. A brave resolution. But how wilt thou spend thy time?

Epi. Not in any melancholy sort, for mine exercise I will walke horses, *Dares.*

Dar. Too bad.

Epi. Why is it not said: It is good walking when one hath his horse in his hand?

Sam. Worse, and worse, but how wilt thou live?

Epi. By angling; O tis a stately occupation to stand foure houres in a colde morning, and to have his nose bitten with frost before his baite be mumbled with a fish.

Dar. A rare attempt, but wilt thou never travell?

Epi. Yes in a westerne barge, when with a good winde and lustie pugges one may goe ten miles in two dayes.

Sam. Thou art excellent at thy choice, but what pastime wilt thou use, none?

Epi. Yes the quickest of all.

Sam. What! dice?

Epi. No, when I am in haste, one and twentie games at chesse to passe a few minutes.

Dar. A life for a little lord, and full of quicknesse.

Epi. Tush, let mee alone! but I must needs see if I can find where *Endimion* lieth; and then goe to a certaine fountaine hard by, where they say faithfull lovers shall have all things they will aske. If I can find out any of these, *ego et magister meus erimus in tuto*, I and my master shal be friends. He is resolved to weepe some three or foure palefuls to avoide the rheume of loue that wambleth in his stomacke.

Enter the Watch.

Sam. Shall wee never see thy master *Dares?*

Dar. Yes, let us goe now, for to-morrow *Cynthia* will be there.

Epi. I will goe with you. But how shall we see for the Watch?

Sam. Tush, let me alone! I'le begin to them. Masters God speed you.

1 Watch. Sir boy, we are all sped alreadie.

Epi. So me thinkes, for they smell all of drinke like a beggars beard.

Dar. But I pray sirs, may wee see *Endimion?*

2 Watch. No, wee are commanded in *Cynthias* name that no man shall see him.

Sam. No man? Why wee are but boyes.

1 Watch. Masse neighbours he sayes true, for if I sweare I will never drinke my liquor by the quart, and yet call for two pints, I thinke with a safe conscience I may carouse both.

Dar. Pithily, and to the purpose.

2 Watch. Tush, tush, neighbours, take me with you.

Sam. This will grow hote.

Dar. Let them alone.

2 Watch. If I say to my wife, wife I will have no raisons in my pudding, shee puts in corance, small raisons are raisons, and boyes are men. Even as my wife should have put no raisons in my pudding, so shall there no boyes see *Endimion.*

Dar. Learnedly.

Epi. Let Master Constable speake: I thinke he is the wisest among you.

Master Constable. You know neighbours 'tis an old said saw, *Children and fooles speake true.*

All say. True.

Mast. Const. Well, there you see the men be the fooles, because it is provided from the children.

Dar. Good.

Mast. Const. Then say I neighbours, that children must not see *Endimion,* because children and fooles speake true.

Epi. O wicked application!

Sam. Scurvily brought about!

1 *Watch.* Nay hee sayes true, and therefore till *Cynthia* have beene here he shall not be uncovered. Therefore away!

Dar. A watch quoth you? a man may watch seven yeeres for a wise word, and yet goe without it. Their wits are all as rustie as their bils. But come on Master Constable shall wee have a song before we goe?

Const. With all my heart.   [*Exeunt.*

THE SECOND SONG.

Watch. Stand: Who goes there?
We charge you appeare
Fore our Constable here.
(In the name of the Man in the Moone)
To us Bilmen relate,
Why you stagger so late,
And how you come drunke so soone.

Pages. What are yee (scabs ?)

Watch. The Watch :

This the Constable.

Pages. A patch.

Const. Knock'em downe unlesse they all stand.

If any run away,

Tis the old watchmans play,

To reach him a bill of his hand.

Pages. O gentlemen hold,

Your gownes freeze with cold,

And your rotten teeth dance in your head;

Epi. Wine, nothing shall cost yee.

Sam. Nor huge fires to roast yee.

Dares. Then soberly let us be led.

Const. Come my browne bils wee'l roare,

Bownce loud at taverne dore,

Omnes. And i'th' morning steale all to bed.

ACTUS QUARTUS. SCÆNA TERTIA.

CORSITES *solus.*

Corsites. I am come in sight of the Lunarie banke;
without doubt *Tellus* doteth upon me, and cunningly
that I might not perceive her love, she hath set me to
a taske that is done before it is begun. *Endimion,* you
must change your pillow, and if you be not wearie of
sleepe I will carrie you where at ease you shall sleepe
your fill. It were good that without more ceremonies
I tooke him, least being espied I be intrapt, and so incurre the displeasure of *Cynthia,* who commonly setteth
watch that *Endimion* have no wrong. [*He tries to lift*
Endimion.] What now, is your mastership so heavie?
or are you nail'd to the ground? Not stirre one whit?
then use all thy force though he feele it and wake.

What stone still? turn'd I thinke to earth, with lying
so long on the earth.   Didst thou not *Corsites* before
Cynthia pull up a tree, that fortie yeeres was fastned
with roots and wreathed in knots to the ground? Didst
not thou with maine force pull open the iron gates,
which no ramme or engine could move? Have my
weake thoughts made braun-fallen my strong armes?
or is it the nature of love or the quintessence of the
minde to breede numnesse, or lythernesse, or I know
not what languishing in my joynts and sinewes, being
but the base strings of my bodie? Or doth the remembrance of *Tellus* so refine my spirits into a matter so
subtill and divine, that the other fleshie parts cannot
worke whilst they muse? Rest thyselfe, rest thyselfe;
nay, rent thyselfe in pieces *Corsites*, and strive in spight
of love, fortune, and nature, to lift up this dulled bodie,
heavier then dead, and more sencelesse then death.

Enter Fairies.

But what are these so faire fiends that cause my haires
to stand upright, and spirits to fall downe? Hags; out
alas, Nymphs I crave pardon. Aye me, but what doe
I heere.

> [*The* Fairies *daunce, and with a Song pinch
> him, and hee falleth asleepe, they kisse* En-
> dimion, *and depart.*

THE THIRD SONG BY *Fairies.*

Omnes. Pinch him, pinch him, blacke and blue,
Sawcie mortalls must not view
What the Queene of Stars is doing,
Nor pry into our fairy woing.

1 *Fairy.* Pinch him blue.

2 *Fairy.* And pinch him blacke.

3 *Fairy.* Let him not lacke

Sharpe nailes to pinch him blue and red,

Till sleepe has rock'd his addle head.

4 *Fairy.* For the trespasse hee hath done,

Spots ore all his flesh shall runne.

Kisse *Endimion*, kisse his eyes,

Then to our midnight heidegyes.

CYNTHIA, FLOSCULA, SEMELE, PANELION,
PYTHAGORAS, GYPTES, CORSITES.

Cynth. You see *Pythagoras* what ridiculo
you hold, and I doubt not but you are now (
minde.

Pythag. Madame, I plainly perceive that
fection of your brightnesse hath pierced thi
thicknesse that covered my mind ; in so much
no lesse glad to be reformed, then ashamed to 1
my grossenesse.

Gyptes. They are thrice fortunate that live
palace, where truth is not in colours, but life
not in imagination, but execution.

Cynth. I have alwayes studied to have rath
vertues then painted Gods ; the bodie of truth,
tombe. But let us walke to *Endimion*, it m
lieth in your arts to deliver him ; as for *Eume*
feare he is dead.

Pythag. I have alledged all the naturall r
can for such a long sleepe.

Gyptes. I can doe nothing till I see him.

Cynth. Come *Floscula*, I am sure you are g
you shall behold *Endimion*.

Flosc. I were blessed if I might have him recovered.

Cynth. Are you in love with his person?

Flosc. No, but with his vertue.

Cynth. What say you *Semele?*

Sem. Madame, I dare say nothing for feare I offend.

Cynth. Belike you cannot speake except you be spightfull. But as good be silent as saucie. *Panelion,* what punishment were fit for *Semele,* in whose speech and thoughts is onely contempt and sowernesse?

Panel. I love not madame to give any judgment. Yet sith your highnesse commandeth, I thinke, to commit her tongue close prisoner to her mouth.

Cynth. Agreed; *Semele,* if thou speake this twelve moneth thou shalt forfet thy tongue. Behold *Endimion,* alas poore gentleman, hast thou spent thy youth in sleepe that once vowed all to my service. Hollow eyes? gray haires? wrinckled cheekes? and decayed limbes? Is it destinie, or deceit that hath brought this to passe? If the first, who could prevent thy wretched starres? If the latter, I would I might know thy cruell enemy. I favoured thee *Endimion* for thy honour, thy vertues, thy affections: but to bring thy thoughts within the compasse of thy fortunes I have seemed strange, that I might have thee stayed, and now are thy dayes ended before my favour begin. But whom have we here, is it not *Corsites?*

Zon. It is, but more like a leopard then a man.

Cynth. Awake him. How now *Corsites,* what make you here? How came you deformed? Looke on thy hands, and then thou seest the picture of thy face.

Cors. Miserable wretch, and accursed. How am I

deluded? Madame, I aske pardon for my offence, and you see my fortune deserveth pitie.

Cynth. Speake on, thy offence cannot deserve greater punishment: but see thou rehearse the truth, else shalt thou not find me as thou wishest me.

Cors. Madame, as it is no offence to be in love being a man mortall, so I hope can it be no shame to tell with whom, my ladie being heavenly. Your majestie committed to my charge the faire *Tellus*, whose beautie in the same moment tooke my heart captive that I undertooke to carrie her bodie prisoner. Since that time have I found such combats in my thoughts betweene love and dutie, reverence and affection, that I could neither endure the conflict, nor hope for the conquest.

Cynth. In love? A thing farre unfitting the name of a captaine, and (as I thought) the tough and unsmoothed nature of *Corsites.* But forth.

Cors. Feeling this continuall warre, I thought rather by parley to yeeld, then by certaine danger to perish. I unfolded to *Tellus* the depth of my affections, and framed my tongue to utter a sweet tale of love, that was wont to sound nothing but threats of warre. She too faire to be true, and too false for one so faire, after a nice deniall, practised a notable deceit; commanding mee to remove *Endimion* from this caban, and carrie him to some darke cave; which I seeking to accomplish, found impossible; and so by fairies or fiends have beene thus handled.

Cynth. How say you my lords, is not *Tellus* alwayes practising of some deceits? In sooth *Corsites*, thy face is now too foule for a lover, and thine heart too fond

for a souldier. You may see when warriors become
wantons how their manners alter with their faces. Is
it not a shame *Corsites*, that having lived so long in
Mars his campe thou shouldst now be rockt in *Venus*
cradle. Doest thou weare *Cupids* quiver at thy girdle,
and make launces of lookes? Well *Corsites*, rouse thy
selfe, and be as thou hast beene, and let *Tellus* who
is made all of love, melt her selfe in her owne loosenesse.

Cors. Madame, I doubt not but to recover my former
state; for *Tellus* beautie never wrought such love in my
mind, as now her deceit hath despight; and yet to be
revenged of a woman, were a thing then love it selfe
more womanish.

Gyptes. These spots gentlemen are to be worne out,
if you rub them over with this lunarie; so that in place
where you received this maime, you shall find a medicine.

Cors. I thanke you for that. The gods blesse mee
from love, and these pretie ladies that haunt this greene.

Flosc. *Corsites*, I would *Tellus* saw your amiable
face.

Zont. How spightfully *Semele* laugheth, that dare not
speake.

Cynthia. Could you not stirre *Endimion* with that
doubled strength of yours?

Cors. Not so much as his finger with all my force.

Cynth. *Pythagoras* and *Gyptes*, what thinke you of
Endimion? what reason is to be given, what remedie?

Pyth. Madam, it is impossible to yeild reason for
things that happen not in compasse of nat

most certaine, that some strange enchantment hath bound all his sences.

Cynth. What say you *Gyptes.*

Gyptes. With *Pythagoras,* that it is enchantment, and that so strange that no art can undoe it, for that heavinesse argueth a malice unremoveable in the enchantresse, and that no power can end it, till she die that did it, or the heavens shew some means more miraculous.

Flosc. O *Endimion,* could spight it selfe devise a mischiefe so monstrous as to make thee dead with life, and living being altogether dead? Where others number their yeares, their houres, their minutes, and step to age by staires, thou onely hast thy yeares and times in a cluster, being olde before thou remembrest thou wast young.

Cynth. No more *Floscula,* pittie doth him no good, I would any thing else might, and I vow by the unspotted honour of a ladie he should not misse it: but is this all *Gyptes,* that is to be done?

Gyptes. All as yet. It may be that either the enchantresse shall die, or else be discovered; if either happen I will then practise the utmost of my art. In the meane season, about this grove would I have a watch, and the first living thing that toucheth *Endimion* to be taken.

Cynth. *Corsites* what say you, will you undertake this?

Cors. Good madame pardon mee! I was overtaken too late, I should rather breake into the midst of a maine battaile, then againe fall into the hands of those faire babies.

Cynth. Well, I will provide others. *Pythagoras* and
Gyptes, you shall yet remayne in my court, till I heare
what may be done in this matter.

Pyth. We attend.

Cynth. Let us goe in.   [*Exeunt.*

ACTUS QUINTUS. SCÆNA PRIMA.

SAMIAS, DARES.

Samias.

UMENIDES hath told such strange tales
as I may well wonder at them, but never
beleeve them.

 Dar. The other old man what a sad
speech used he, that caused us almost all to weepe.
Cynthia is so desirous to know the experiment of her
owne vertue, and so willing to ease *Endimions* hard
fortune, that shee no sooner heard the discourse, but
shee made her selfe in a readinesse to try the event.

 Sam. We will also see the event; but whist! here
commeth *Cynthia* with all her traine: let us sneake
in amongst them.

Enter CYNTHIA, FLOSCULA, SEMELE, PANELION, &c.

 Cynth. Eumenides, it cannot sinke into my head that
I should be signified by that sacred fountaine, for many
things are there in the world to which those words may
be applyed.

 Eum. Good madame vouchsafe but to trie, else shall
I thinke my selfe most unhappy that I asked not my
sweet mistris.

Cynth. Will you not yet tell me her name?

Eum. Pardon me good madame, for if *Endimion* awake, hee shall: my selfe have sworne never to reveale it.

Cynth. Well, let us to *Endimion.* I will not be so stately (good *Endimion*) not to stoope to doe thee good: and if thy libertie consist in a kisse from mee, thou shalt have it. And although my mouth hath beene heretofore as untouched as my thoughts, yet now to recover thy life, (though to restore thy youth it be impossible) I will doe that to *Endimion* which yet never mortall man could boast of heretofore, nor shall ever hope for hereafter.   [*Shee kisseth him.*

Eum. Madam he beginneth to stirre.

Cynth. Soft *Eumenides*, stand still.

Eum. Ah, I see his eyes almost open.

Cynth. I command thee once againe stirre not: I will stand behind him.

Pan. What doe I see, *Endimion* almost awake?

Eum. *Endimion, Endimion*, art thou deafe or dumbe? or hath this long sleepe taken away thy memorie? Ah my sweete *Endimion*, seest thou not *Eumenides?* thy faithfull friend, thy faithfull *Eumenides*, who for thy safetie hath beene carelesse of his owne content. Speake *Endimion, Endimion, Endimion.*

End. Endimion? I call to minde such a name.

Eum. Hast thou forgotten thyselfe *Endimion?* then doe I not marvaile thou remembrest not thy friend. I tel thee thou art *Endimion*, and I *Eumenides:* behold also *Cynthia*, by whose favour thou art awaked, and by whose vertue thou shalt continue thy naturall course.

Cynth. *Endimion,* speake sweet *Endimion,* knowest thou not *Cynthia?*

End. O heavens, whom doe I-behold, faire *Cynthia,* divine *Cynthia?*

Cynth. I am *Cynthia,* and thou *Endimion.*

End. *Endimion,* What doe I heere? What, a gray beard? hollow eyes? withered body? decayed limbes? and all in one night?

Eum. One night? thou hast heere slept fortie yeeres, by what enchaunteresse as yet it is not knowne: and behold the twig to which thou layedst thy head is now become a tree; callest thou not *Eumenides* to remembrance?

End. Thy name I doe remember by the sound, but thy favour I doe not yet call to minde; onely divine *Cynthia,* to whom time, fortune, destinie, and death, are subject, I see and remember; and in all humilitie, I regard and reverence.

Cynth. You have good cause to remember *Eumenides,* who hath for thy safety forsaken his owne solace.

End. Am I that *Endimion* who was wont in court to lead my life; and in justs, turneyes, and armes, to exercise my youth? am I that *Endimion?*

Eum. Thou art that *Endimion,* and I *Eumenides,* wilt thou not yet call mee to remembrance?

End. Ah sweete *Eumenides,* I now perceive thou art hee, and that my selfe have the name of *Endimion;* but that this should be my bodie I doubt, for how could my curled lockes be turned to gray hairs, and my strong bodie to a dying weaknesse, having waxed olde and not knowing it.

Cynth. Well *Endimion* arise, a while sit downe, for
that thy limbes are stiffe, and not able to stay thee, and
tell what hast thou seene in thy sleepe all this while?
What dreames, visions, thoughts, and fortunes? For
it is impossible, but in so long time, thou shouldest see
things strange.

End. Faire *Cynthia* I will rehearse what I have
seene, humbly desiring that when I exceed in length
you give mee warning, that I may end: for to utter all
I have to speake would bee troublesome, although happily the strangenesse may somewhat abate the tediousnesse.

Cynth. Well *Endimion* begin.

End. Mee thought I saw a ladie passing faire, but
very mischievous; who in the one hand carried a knife
with which she offered to cut my throate, and in the
other a looking-glasse, wherein seeing how ill anger
became ladies, shee refrained from intended violence.
Shee was accompanied with other damsels, one of which
with a sterne countenance, and as it were with a setled
malice engraven in her eyes, provoked her to execute
mischiefe: another with visage sad and constant onely
in sorrow, with her armes crossed, and watery eyes,
seemed to lament my fortune, but durst not offer to
prevent the force. I started in my sleepe, feeling my
very veines to swell, and my sinewes to stretch with
feare, and such a cold sweate bedewed all my bodie,
that death it selfe could not be so terrible as the vision.

Cynth. A strange sight. *Gyptes* at our better leisure shall expound it.

End. After long debating with her selfe, mercie

overcame anger; and there appeared in her heavenly face such a divine majestie, mingled with a sweet mildnesse, that I was ravished with the sight above measure; and wished that I might have enjoyed the sight without end; and so she departed with the other ladies, of which the one retained still an unmoveable crueltie, the other a constant pittie.

Cynthia. Poore *Endimion*, how wast thou affrighted? What else?

End. After her immediately appeared an aged man with a beard as white as snow, carrying in his hand a booke with three leaves, and speaking as I remember these words. *Endimion, receive this booke with three leaves, in which are contained counsels, policies, and pictures:* and with that hee offered mee the booke, which I rejected: wherewith moved with a disdainfull pitie, he rent the first leafe in a thousand shivers; the second time hee offered it, which I refused also; at which bending his browes, and pitching his eyes fast to the ground, as though they were fixed to the earth, and not againe to be removed—then sodainly casting them up to the heavens, hee tore in a rage the second leafe, and offered the booke only with one leafe. I know not whether feare to offend, or desire to know some strange thing, moved me,—I tooke the booke, and so the old man vanished.

Cynth. What diddest thou imagine was in the last leafe?

End. There portraid to life, with a cold quaking in every joynt, I beheld many wolves barking at thee *Cynthia*, who having ground their teeth to bite, did with striving bleed themselves to death. There might I see ingratitude with an hundred eyes, gazing for benefits; and with a thousand teeth, gnawing on the bowels wherein she was bred. Trecherie stood all clothed in white, with a smiling countenance, but both her hands bathed in bloud. Enuie with a pale and megar face (whose bodie was so leane, that one might tell all her bones, and whose garment was so totterd, that it was easie to number every thread) stood shooting at starres, whose darts fell downe againe on her owne face. There might I behold drones or beetles, I know not how to term them, creeping under the wings of a princely eagle, who being carried into her nest, sought there to suck that vein, that would have killed the eagle. I mused that things so base, should attempt a fact so barbarous, or durst imagine a thing so bloudie. And many other things madame, the repetition whereof, may at your better leisure seeme more pleasing: for bees surfet sometimes with honey, and the gods are glutted with harmony, and your highnesse may be dulled with delight.

Cynth. I am content to bee dieted, therefore let us in. *Eumenides,* see that *Endimion* be well tended, least either eating immoderatly, or sleeping againe too long, he fall into a deadly surfet, or into his former sleepe. See this also be proclaimed, that whosoever will discover this practice, shall have of *Cynthia* infinite thankes, and no small rewards. [*Exit.*

Flosc. Ah *Endimion,* none so joyfull as *Floscula,* of thy restoring.

Eum. Yes, *Floscula,* let *Eumenides* be somewhat

gladder, and do not that wrong to the setled friendship of a man, as to compare it with the light affection of a woman. Ah my deare friend *Endimion,* suffer me to die, with gazing at thee.

End. *Eumenides,* thy friendship is immortall, and not to be conceived ; and thy good will *Floscula,* better then I have deserved. But let us all waite on *Cynthia :* I marvell *Semele* speaketh not a word.

Eum. Because if shee doe, shee loseth her tongue.

End. But how prospereth your love ?

Eum. I never yet spake word since your sleepe.

End. I doubt not but your affection is old, and your appetite cold.

Eum. No *Endimion,* thine hath made it stronger, and now are my sparkes growne to flames, and my fancies almost to frenzies : but let us follow, and within we will debate all this matter at large.   [*Exeunt.*

ACTUS QUINTUS. SCÆNA SECUNDA.

Sir Tophas, Epiton.

Top. Epi, love hath justled my libertie from the wall, and taken the upper hand of my reason.

Epi. Let mee then trip up the heeles of your affection, and thrust your good will into the gutter.

Top. No *Epi,* love is a lord of misrule, and keepeth Christmas in my corps.

Epi. No doubt there is good cheere : what dishes of delight doth his lordship feast you with withall ?

Top. First, with a great platter of plum-porridge of pleasure, wherein is stued the mutton of mistrust.

Epi. Excellent love lap.

Top. Then commeth a pye of patience, a hen of honey, a goose of gall, a capon of care, and many other viands; some sweet, and some sowre; which proveth love to bee as it was said of, in olde yeeres, *Dulce venenum.*

Epi. A brave banquet.

Top. But *Epi.* I pray thee feele on my chinne, some thing pricketh me. What doest thou feele or see.

Epi. There are three or foure little haires.

Top. I pray thee call it my beard, how shall I be troubled when this yong spring shall grow to a great wood!

Epi. O, sir, your chinne is but a quyller yet, you will be most majesticall when it is full fledge. But I marvell that you love *Dipsas,* that old crone.

Top. *Agnosco veteris vestigia flammæ,* I love the smoke of an old fire.

Epi. Why she is so cold, that no fire can thawe her thoughts.

Top. It is an olde goose, *Epi,* that will eate no oates; old kine will kicke, old rats gnaw cheese, and olde sackes will have much patching: I preferre an olde cony before a rabbet sucker, and an ancient henne before a young chicken peeper.

Epi. *Argumentum ab antiquitate,* My master loveth anticke worke.

Top. Give mee a pippin that is withered like an old wife.

Epi. Good sir.

Top. Then, *à contrario sequitur argumentum.* Give me a wife that lookes like an old pippin.

Epi. Nothing hath made my master a foole, but flat schollership.

Top. Knowest thou not that olde wine is best?

Epi. Yes.

Top. And thou knowest that like will to like?

Epi. I.

Top. And thou knowest that *Venus* loved the best wine.

Epi. So.

Top. Then I conclude, that *Venus* was an old woman in an old cup of wine. For, *est* Venus *in vinis, ignis in igne fuit.*

Epi. O lepidum caput, O mad cap master! You were worthy to winne *Dipsas,* were shee as olde againe, for in your love you have worne the nap of your wit quite off, and made it thred-bare. But soft, who comes heere?

Top. My solicitors.

Sam. All haile Sir *Tophas,* how feele you your selfe?

Top. Stately in every joynt, which the common people terme stiffnesse. Doth *Dipsas* stoope? will shee yield? will she bend?

Dar. O sir as much as you would wish, for her chin almost toucheth her knees.

Epi. Master, shee is bent I warrant you.

Top. What conditions doth shee aske?

Sam. Shee hath vowed she will never love any that hath not a tooth in his head lesse than she.

Top. How many hath she?

Dar. One.

Epi. That goeth hard master, for then you must have none.

Top. A small request, and agreeable to the gravitie of her yeeres. What should a wiseman doe with his mouth full of bones like a charnell house. The turtle true hath nere a tooth.

Sam. Thy master is in a notable vaine, that will loose his teeth to be like a turtle.

Epi. Let him loose his tongue too, I care not.

Dar. Nay, you must also have no nailes, for she long since hath cast hers.

Top. That I yeeld to, what a quiet life shall *Dipsas* and I leade when we can neither bite nor scratch? You may see youthes how age provides for peace.

Sam. How shall wee doe to make him leave his love, for wee never spake to her?

Dar. Let me alone. Shee is a notable witch, and hath turned her maide *Bagoa* to an aspen tree for bewraying her secrets.

Top. I honour her for her cunning, for now when I am wearie of walking on two legs, what a pleasure may she doe me to turn mee to some goodly asse, and helpe me to foure.

Dar. Nay, then I must tell you the troth; her husband *Geron* is come home, who this fiftie yeeres hath had her to wife.

Top. What doe I heare? Hath shee an husband? Goe to the sexton, and tell him desire is dead, and will him to digge his grave. O heavens, an husband? What death is agreeable to my fortune?

Sam. Be not desperate, and we will helpe you to find a young ladie.

Top. I love no grissels they are so brittle they will cracke like glasse, or so daintie, that if they be touched they are straight of the fashion of waxe: *animus majoribus instat.* I desire old matrons. What a sight would it be to embrace one whose haire were as orient as the pearle! whose teeth shall be so pure a watchet, that they shall staine the truest turkis! whose nose shal throw more beames from it then the fiery carbuncle! whose eies shal be environed about with rednesse exceeding the deepest corall! And whose lips might compare with silver for the palenesse! Such a one if you can helpe mee to, I will by peece-meale curtall my affections towards *Dipsas,* and walke my swelling thoughts till they be cold.

Epi. Wisely provided. How say you my friends, will you angle for my master's cause?

Sam. Most willingly.

Dar. If wee speed him not shortly I will burne my cap, wee will serve him of the spades, and digge an old wife out of the grave that shall be answerable to his gravitie.

Top. Youthes adiew; hee that bringeth me first newes, shall possesse mine inheritance.

Dar. What, is thy master landed?

Epi. Know you not that my master is *liber tenens?*

Sam. What's that?

Epi. A free-holder. But I will after him.

Sam. And we to heare what newes of *Endimion* for the conclusion.   [*Exeunt.*

ACTUS QUINTUS. SCÆNA TERTIA.

PANELION, ZONTES.

Pan. Who would have thought that *Tellus* being so faire by nature, so honorable by birth, so wise by education, would have entred into a mischiefe to the gods so odious, to men so detestable, and to her friend so malicious.

Zon. If *Bagoa* had not bewrayed it, how then should it have come to light? But wee see that gold and faire words, are of force to corrupt the strongest men; And therefore able to worke silly women like waxe.

Pan. I marvell what *Cynthia* will determine in this cause.

Zon. I feare as in all causes, heare of it in justice, and then judge of it in mercy; for how can it be that shee that is unwilling to punish her deadliest foes with disgrace, will revenge injuries of her traine with death.

Pan. That old witch *Dipsas*, in a rage having understood her practice to be discovered, turned poore *Bagoa* to an aspen tree; but let us make hast and bring *Tellus* before *Cynthia*, for she was comming out after us.

Zon. Let us goe. [*Exeunt.*

CYNTHIA, SEMELE, FLOSCULA, DIPSAS, ENDIMION, EUMENIDES.

Cynth. Dipsas, thy yeeres are not so many as thy vices; yet more in number then commonly nature doth affoord, or justice should permit. Hast thou almost these fifty yeeres practised that detested wickednesse of witchcraft? Wast thou so simple, as for to know the nature of simples, of all creatures to bee most sinfull? Thou hast threatned to turne my course awry, and alter by thy damnable art the government that I now possesse by the eternall gods. But know thou *Dipsas,* and let all the enchanters know, that *Cynthia* being placed for light on earth is also protected by the powers of heaven. Breath out thou mayest words, gather thou mayest hearbs, find out thou mayest stones agreeable to thine art, yet of no force to appall my heart, in which courage is so rooted, and constant perswasion of the mercie of the gods so grounded, that all thy witchcraft I esteeme as weake, as the world doth thy case wretched. This noble gentleman *Geron,* (once thy husband, but now thy mortall hate;) didst thou procure to live in a desert, almost desperate. *Endimion* the flowre of my court and the hope of succeeding time, hast thou bewitched by art, before thou wouldest suffer him to flourish by nature.

Dipsas. Madame, things past may be repented, not recalled: there is nothing so wicked that I have not done, nor any thing so wished for as death. Yet among all the things that I committed, there is nothing so much tormenteth my rented and ransackt thoughts, as that in the prime of my husbands youth I divorced him by my devillish art; for which, if to die might be amends, I would not live till to morrow. If to live and still be more miserable would better content him, I would wish of all creatures to be oldest and ugliest.

Geron. Dipsas, thou hast made this difference be-

tweene mee and *Endimion*, that being both young, thou
hast caused mee to wake in melancholy, losing the joyes
of my youth; and him to sleepe, not remembring youth.

Cynth. Stay, here commeth *Tellus*, we shall now
know all.

Enter Corsites, Tellus, Panelion, &c.

Cors. I would to *Cynthia* thou couldest make as good
an excuse in truth, as to me thou hast done by wit.

Tellus. Truth shall be mine answere, and therefore
I will not studie for an excuse.

Cynth. Is it possible *Tellus*, that so few yeeres should
harbour so many mischiefes? Thy swelling pride have
I borne, because it is a thing that beauty maketh blame-
lesse, which the more it exceedeth fairenesse in measure, the more it stretcheth it selfe in disdaine. Thy
devises against *Corsites* I smile at; for that wits, the
sharper they are, the shrewder they are. But this
unacquainted and most unnaturall practice with a vile
enchauntresse against so noble a gentleman as *Endimion*, I abhorre as a thing most malicious, and will
revenge as a deed most monstrous. And as for you
Dipsas, I will send you into the desert amongst wilde
beasts, and try whether you can cast lions, tygres,
bores, and beares, into as dead a sleepe as you did *Endimion*; or turn them to trees, as you have done *Bagoa*.
But tell me *Tellus*, what was the cause of this cruell
part, farre unfitting thy sexe, in which nothing should
be but simplenesse: and much disagreeing from thy
face, in which nothing seemed to be but softnesse.

Tellus. Divine *Cynthia*, by whom I receive my life,

and am content to end it; I can neither excuse my
fault without lying, nor confesse it without shame; yet
were it possible that in so heavenly thoughts as yours,
there could fall such earthly motions as mine, I would
then hope, if not to be pardoned without extreme punishment, yet to be heard without great marvell.

Cynth. Say on *Tellus*, I cannot imagine any thing
that can colour such a crueltie.

Tellus. *Endimion,* that *Endimion* in the prime of his
youth, so ravisht my heart with love, that to obtaine my
desires, I could not find meanes, nor to recite them
reason. What was she that favoured not *Endimion,*
being young, wise, honourable, and vertuous; besides,
what metall was she made of (be shee mortall) that is
not affected with the spice, nay, infected with the poyson of that (not to be expressed, yet alwayes to be felt)
love? which breaketh the braines, and never bruseth
the brow: consumeth the heart, and never toucheth the
skinne: and maketh a deepe skarre to bee seene, before
any wound at all be felt. My hart too tender to withstand such a divine furie, yeelded to love. Madame I,
not without blushing confesse, yeelded to love.

Cynth. A strange effect of love, to work such an
extreme hate. How say you *Endimion,* all this was for
love?

End. I say Madam then the gods send me a womans
hate.

Cynth. That were as bad, for then by contrarie you
should never sleepe. But on, *Tellus,* let us heare the
end.

Tellus. Feeling a continuall burning in all my bowels, and a bursting almost in every veine, I could not smoother the inward fire, but it must needs be perceived by the outward smoke; and by the flying abroad of divers sparkes, divers judged of my scalding flames. *Endimion* as full of art as wit, marking mine eyes, (in which he might see almost his owne,) my sighes, by which he might ever heare his name sounded; aimed at my heart, in which he was assured his person was imprinted; and by questions wrung out that, which was readie to burst out. When he saw the depth of my affections, hee sware, that mine in respect of his were as fumes to Ætna, valleyes to Alpes, ants to eagles, and nothing could be compared to my beautie but his love, and eternitie. Thus drawing a smooth shoe upon a crooked foot, he made mee beleeve, that (which all of our sexe willingly acknowledge) I was beautifull. And to wonder (which indeed is a thing miraculous) that any of his sexe should be faithfull.

Cynth. *Endimion*, how will you cleere your selfe?

End. Madame, by mine owne accuser.

Cynth. Well *Tellus* proceed, but briefly, least taking delight in uttering thy love thou offend us with the length of it.

Tellus. I will madame quickly make an end of my love and my tale. Finding continuall increase of my tormenting thoughts, and that the enjoying of my love made deeper wounds then the entring into it; I could finde no meanes to ease my griefe but to follow *Endimion*, and continually to have him in the object of mine eyes, who had mee slave and subject to his love. But in the moment that I feared his falshood, and fried my selfe most in mine affections, I found, (ah griefe, even then I lost my selfe!) I found him in most melancholy and desperate tearmes, cursing his starres, his state, the earth, the heavens, the world, and all for the love of—

Cynth. Of whom? *Tellus* speake boldly.

Tellus. Madame, I dare not utter for feare to offend.

Cynth. Speake, I say; who dare take offence, if thou be commanded by *Cynthia?*

Tellus. For the love of *Cynthia.*

Cynth. For my love *Tellus*, that were strange. *Endimion* is it true?

End. In all things madame. *Tellus* doth not speake false.

Cynth. What will this breed to in the end? Well *Endimion*, we shall heare all.

Tellus. I seeing my hopes turned to mishaps, and a setled dissembling towards me, and an unmoveable desire to *Cynthia*, forgetting both my selfe and my sex, fell unto this unnaturall hate; for knowing your vertues *Cynthia* to be immortall, I could not have an imagination to withdraw him. And finding mine owne affections unquenchable, I could not carrie the minde that any else should possesse what I had pursued. For though in majestie, beautie, vertue, and dignitie, I alwayes humbled and yeelded my selfe to *Cynthia*; yet in affections, I esteemed my selfe equall with the goddesses; and all other creatures according to their states with my selfe. For starres to their bignesse have their lights, and the sunne hath no more. And little pitchers when they can hold no more, are as full as great vessels that run over. Thus madame in all truth, have I

uttered the unhappinesse of my love, and the cause of
my hate; yeelding wholy to that divine judgement
which never erred for want of wisdome, or envied for
too much partialitie.

Cynth. How say you my lords to this matter? But
what say you *Endimion*, hath *Tellus* told troth?

End. Madame in all things, but in that she said I
loved her, and swore to honour her.

Cynth. Was there such a time when as for my love
thou didst vow thy selfe to death, and in respect of it
loth'd thy life? speake *Endimion*, I will not revenge it
with hate.

End. The time was madame, and is, and ever shall
be, that I honoured your highnesse above all the world;
but to stretch it so farre as to call it love, I never durst.
There hath none pleased mine eye but *Cynthia*, none
delighted mine eares but *Cynthia*, none possessed my
heart but *Cynthia*. I have forsaken all other fortunes
to follow *Cynthia*, and heere I stand readie to die if it
please *Cynthia*. Such a difference hath the gods set
betweene our states, that all must be dutie, loyaltie, and
reverence, nothing (without it vouchsafe your highnesse)
be termed love. My unspotted thoughts, my languishing bodie, my discontented life, let them obtaine by
princely favour, that which to challenge they must not
presume, onely wishing of impossibilities: with imagination of which, I will spend my spirits, and to my selfe
that no creature may heare, softly call it love. And if
any urge to utter what I whisper, then will I name it
honour. From this sweet contemplation if I be not
driven, I shall live of all men the most content, taking

more pleasure in mine aged thoughts, then ever I did in my youthfull actions.

Cynth. *Endimion*, this honorable respect of thine, shall be christned love in thee, and my reward for it, favour.   Persever *Endimion* in loving mee, and I account more strength in a true heart, then in a walled citie.   I have laboured to win all, and studie to keep such as I have wonne; but those that neither my favour can move to continue constant, nor my offered benefits get to be faithfull, the gods shall either reduce to truth, or revenge their trecheries with justice.   *Endimion* continue as thou hast begun, and thou shalt find that *Cynthia* shineth not on thee in vaine.

End. Your highnesse hath blessed me, and your words have againe restored my youth: me thinks I feele my joynts strong, and these mouldy haires to molt, and all by your vertue *Cynthia*, into whose hands the ballance that weigheth time and fortune are committed.

Cynth. What young againe? then it is pitie to punish *Tellus*.

Tellus. Ah *Endimion*, now I know thee and aske pardon of thee: suffer mee still to wish thee well.

End. *Tellus*, *Cynthia* must command what she will.

Flosc. *Endimion*, I rejoyce te see thee in thy former estate.

End. Good *Floscula*, to thee also am I in my former affections.

Eum. *Endimion*, the comfort of my life, how am I ravished with a joy matchlesse, saving onely the enjoying of my mistris.

Cynth. *Endimion*, you must now tell who *Euménides* shrineth for his saint.

End. *Semele* madame.

Cynth. *Semele Eumenides?* is it *Semele?* the very waspe of all women, whose tongue stingeth as much as an adders tooth?

Eum. It is *Semele, Cynthia :* the possessing of whose love, must only prolong my life.

Cynth. Nay sith *Endimion* is restored, we will have all parties pleased. *Semele,* are you content after so long trial of his faith, such rare secrecie, such unspotted love, to take *Eumenides?* Why speake you not? Not a word?

End. Silence madame consents : that is most true.

Cynth. It is true *Endimion. Eumenides,* take *Semele.* Take her I say.

Eum. Humble thankes madame, now onely doe I begin to live.

Sem. A hard choice madame, either to be married if I say nothing, or to lose my tongue if I speake a word. Yet doe I rather choose to have my tongue cut out, then my heart distempered : I will not have him.

Cynth. Speakes the parrat? shee shall nod hereafter with signes : cut off her tongue, nay, her head, that having a servant of honourable birth, honest manners, and true love, will not be perswaded.

Sem. He is no faithfull lover madame, for then would hee have asked his mistris.

Ger. Had he not beene faithfull, he had never seene into the fountaine, and so lost his friend and mistris.

Eum. Thine owne thoughts sweet *Semele,* witnesse against thy words, for what hast thou found in my life but love? and as yet what have I found in my love but bitternesse? Madame pardon *Semele,* and let my tongue ransome hers.

Cynth. Thy tongue *Eumenides?* what shouldst thou live wanting a tongue to blaze the beautie of *Semele?* Well *Semele,* I will not command love, for it cannot be enforced: let me entreat it.

Sem. I am content your highnesse shall command, for now only doe I think *Eumenides* faithfull, that is willing to lose his tongue for my sake: yet loth, because it should doe me better service. Madame, I accept of *Eumenides.*

Cynth. I thanke you *Semele.*

Eum. Ah happie *Eumenides,* that hast a friend so faithfull, and a mistris so faire: with what sodaine mischiefe wil the gods daunt this excesse of joy? Sweet *Semele,* I live or die as thou wilt.

Cynth. What shall become of *Tellus? Tellus* you know *Endimion* is vowed to a service, from which death cannot remove him. *Corsites* casteth still a lovely looke towards you, how say you? Will you have your *Corsites,* and so receive pardon for all that is past?

Tellus. Madame most willingly.

Cynth. But I cannot tell whether *Corsites* be agreed.

Cors. I, madame, more happie to enjoy *Tellus* then the monarchie of the world.

Eum. Why she caused you to be pincht with fairies.

Cors. I but her fairenesse hath pinched my heart more deeply.

Cynth. Well enjoy thy love. But what have you wrought in the castle *Tellus?*

Tellus. Onely the picture of *Endimion.*

Cynth. Then so much of *Endimion* as his picture commeth to, possesse and play withall.

Cors. Ah my sweet *Tellus,* my love shall be as thy beautie is, matchlesse.

Cynth. Now it resteth *Dipsas,* that if thou wilt for-sweare that vile art of enchanting, *Geron* hath promised againe to receive thee; otherwise if thou be wedded to that wickednesse, I must and will see it punished to the uttermost.

Dipsas. Madame, I renounce both substance and shadow of that most horrible and hatefull trade; vowing to the gods continuall penance, and to your highnes obedience.

Cynth. How say you *Geron,* will you admit her to your wife?

Ger. I, with more joy then I did the first day: for nothing could happen to make me happy, but onely her forsaking that leude and detestable course. *Dipsas* I imbrace thee.

Dipsas. And I thee *Geron,* to whom I will hereafter recite the cause of these my first follies.

Cynth. Well *Endimion,* nothing resteth now but that wee depart. Thou hast my favour, *Tellus* her friend, *Eumenides* in Paradise with his *Semele, Geron* contented with *Dipsas.*

Top. Nay soft, I cannot handsomely goe to bed without *Bagoa.*

Cynth. Well *Sir Tophas,* it may be there are more vertues in me then my selfe knoweth of; for I awaked *Endimion,* and at my words he waxed young; I will trie whether I can turne this tree againe to thy true love.

Top. Turne her to a true love or false, so shee bee a wench I care not.

Cynth. *Bagoa, Cynthia* putteth an end to thy hard fortunes, for being turned to a tree for revealing a truth, I will recover thee againe, if in my power be the effect of truth.

Top. *Bagoa,* a bots upon thee!

Cynth. Come my lords let us in. You *Gyptes* and *Pythagoras,* if you cannot content your selves in our court, to fall from vaine follies of philosophers to such vertues as are here practised, you shall be entertained according to your deserts; for *Cynthia* is no step-mother to strangers.

Pythag. I had rather in *Cynthia's* court spend ten yeeres, then in Greece one houre.

Gyptes. And I chuse rather to live by the sight of *Cynthia,* then by the possessing of all Egypt.

Cynth. Then follow.

Eum. We all attend.   [*Exeunt.*

THE EPILOGUE.

A MAN walking abroad, the wind and sun strove for soveraignty, the one with his blast, the other with his beames. The wind blew hard, the man wrapped his garment about him harder: it blustred more strongly, he then girt it fast to him: I cannot prevaile, said the wind. The sun casting her christall beames, began to warme the man: hee unlosed his gowne: yet it shined brighter: he then put it off. I yeeld, said the wind, for if thou continue shining, he will also put off his coate.

Dread Soveraigne, the malicious that seeke to overthrow us with threats, doe but stiffen our thoughts, and make them sturdier in stormes: but if your Highnesse vouchsafe with your favourable beames to glance upon us, wee shall not only stoope, but with all humilitie, lay both our hands and hearts, at your Majesties feet.

CAMPASPE.

PLAYED BEFORE THE QUEENES MAJESTIE ON TWELFE

DAY AT NIGHT, BY HER MAJESTIES CHILDREN,

AND THE CHILDREN OF PAULES.

DRAMATIS PERSONÆ.

ALEXANDER, *King of Macedon.*
HEPHESTION, *his General.*
CLYTUS,
PARMENIO, } *Warriors.*
MILECTUS,
PHRYGIUS,
MELIPPUS, *Chamberlain to Alexander.*
ARISTOTLE,
DIOGENES,
CRISIPPUS,
CRATES, } *Philosophers.*
CLEANTHES,
ANAXARCHUS,
CRYSUS,
APELLES, *a Painter.*
SOLINUS, } *Citizens of Athens.*
SYLVIUS,
PERIM,
MILO, } *Sons to Sylvius.*
TRICO,
GRANICUS, *Servant to Plato.*
MANES, *Servant to Diogenes.*
PSYLLUS, *Servant to Apelles.*
Page to *Alexander.*
Citizens of Athens.

CAMPASPE, } *Theban Captives.*
TIMOCLEA,
LAIS, *a Courtezan.*

SCENE—*Athens.*

THE PROLOGUE AT THE
BLACKE FRIERS.

THEY that feare the stinging of waspes make fannes of peacocks tailes, whose spots are like eyes: And *Lepidus*, which could not sleepe for the chattering of birds, set up a beast, whose head was like a dragon: and wee which stand in awe of report, are compelled to set before our owle, *Pallas* shield, thinking by her vertue to cover the others deformity. It was a signe of famine to *Ægypt*, when *Nylus* flowed lesse than twelve cubites, or more than eighteene: and it may threaten despaire unto us, if we be lesse courteous than you looke for, or more cumbersome. But as *Theseus* being promised to be brought to an eagles nest, and travailing all the day, found but a wren in a hedge, yet said, this is a bird: so we hope, if the shower of our swelling mountaine seeme to bring forth some elephant, performe but a mouse, you will gently say, this is a beast! *Basill* softly touched, yieldeth a sweete sent, but chafed in the hand, a ranke savour: we feare, even so, that our labours slily glanced on, will breed some content, but examined to the proofe, small commendation. The haste in performing shall be our excuse. There went two nights to the begetting of *Hercules*. Feathers appeare not on the Phœnix under seven moneths, and the mulberie is twelve in budding : but our travailes are like the hare's, who at one time bringeth forth, nourisheth, and engendreth againe ; or like the brood of *Trochilus*, whose egges in the same moment that they are laid, become birds.   But howsoever we finish our worke, we crave pardon if we offend in matter, and patience if wee transgresse in manners. Wee have mixed mirth with councell, and discipline with delight, thinking it not amisse in the same garden to sow pot-hearbes, that wee set flowers.   But wee hope, as harts that cast their hornes, snakes their skins, eagles their bils, become more fresh for any other labour : so our charge being shaken off, we shall be fit for greater matters.   But least like the *Myndians*, wee make our gates greater than our towne, and that our play runs out at the preface, we here conclude : wishing that although there be in your precise judgements an universall mislike, yet we may enjoy by your wonted courtesies a generall silence.

THE PROLOGUE AT THE COURT.

WE are ashamed that our bird, which fluttereth by twilight seeming a swan; should bee proved a bat set against the sun. But as *Jupiter* placed *Silenus* asse among the starres, and *Alcibiades* covered his pictures being owles and apes, with a curtaine imbroidered with lions and eagles; so are we enforced upon a rough discourse, to draw on a smooth excuse; resembling lapidaries, who thinke to hide the cracke in a stone by setting it deepe in gold. The gods supped once with poore *Baucis*, the Persian kings sometimes shaved stickes: our hope is your Highnesse wil at this time lend an eare to an idle pastime. *Appion* raising *Homer* from hell, demanded only who was his father, and we calling *Alexander* from his grave, seeke only who was his love. Whatsoever wee present, we wish it may be thought the dancing of *Agrippa* his shadowes, who in the moment they were seene, were of any shape one would conceive: or *Lynces*, who having a quicke sight to discerne, have a short memory to forget. With us it is like to fare, as with these torches which giving light to others, consume themselves: and we shewing delight to others shame ourselves.

CAMPASPE.

ACTUS PRIMUS. SCÆNA PRIMA.

CLYTUS, PARMENIO, TIMOCLEA, CAMPASPE,
ALEXANDER, HEPHESTION.

Clytus.

PARMENIO, I cannot tell whether I should more commend in *Alexanders* victories, courage, or courtesie; in the one being a resolution without feare, in the other a liberalitie above custome: *Thebes* is razed, the people not racked, towers throwne downe, bodies not thrust aside, a conquest without conflict, and a cruell warre in a milde peace.

Par. *Clytus*, it becommeth the sonne of *Philip*, to bee none other than *Alexander* is: therefore seeing in the father a full perfection, who could have doubted in the sonne an excellency? For as the moone can borrow nothing else of the sunne but light, so of a sire, in whom nothing but vertue was, what could the child receive but singular? It is for turkies to staine each other, not for diamonds; in the one to bee made a difference in goodnesse, in the other no comparison.

Clytus. You mistake mee *Parmenio*, if whilest I commend *Alexander*, you imagine I call *Philip* into question; unlesse happily you conjecture (which none of judgement will conceive) that because I like the fruit, therefore I heave at the tree; or coveting to kisse the childe, I therefore goe about to poyson the teat.

Par. I, but *Clytus*, I perceive you are borne in the east, and never laugh but at the sunne rising; which argueth though a dutie where you ought, yet no great devotion where you might.

Clytus. We will make no controversie of that which there ought to be no question; onely this shall be the opinion of us both, that none was worthy to be the father of *Alexander* but *Philip*, nor any meete to be the sonne of *Philip* but *Alexander.*

Par. Soft *Clytus*, behold the spoiles and prisoners! a pleasant sight to us, because profit is joyned with honour; not much painfull to them, because their captivitie is eased by mercie.

Timo. Fortune, thou didst never yet deceive vertue, because vertue never yet did trust fortune. Sword and fire will never get spoyle, where wisdome and fortitude beares sway. O *Thebes*, thy wals were raised by the sweetnesse of the harpe, but rased by the shrilnes of the trumpet. *Alexander* had never come so neer the wals, had *Epaminondas* walkt about the wals: and yet might the *Thebanes* have beene merry in their streets, if hee had beene to watch their towers. But destinie is seldome foreseene, never prevented. We are here now captives, whose neckes are yoaked by force, but whose hearts cannot yeeld by death. Come *Campaspe* and the rest, let us not be ashamed to cast our eyes on him, on whom we feared not to cast our darts.

Par. Madame, you need not doubt, it is *Alexander*, that is the Conquerour.

Timo. *Alexander* hath overcome, not conquered.

Par. To bring all under his subjection is to conquer.

Timo. He cannot subdue that which is divine.

Par. *Thebes* was not.

Timo. Vertue is.

Clytus. *Alexander* as hee tendreth vertue, so hee will you; hee drinketh not bloud, but thirsteth after honour, hee is greedie of victorie, but never satisfied with mercie. In fight terrible, as becommeth a captaine; in conquest milde, as beseemeth a king. In all things, than which nothing can be greater, hee is *Alexander*.

Camp. Then if it be such a thing to be *Alexander*, I hope it shall be no miserable thing to be a virgin. For if hee save our honours, it is more than to restore our goods. And rather doe I wish he preserve our fame than our lives; which if he doe, we will confesse there can be no greater thing than to be *Alexander*.

Alex. *Clytus*, are these prisoners? of whence these spoiles?

Clytus. Like your Majestie, they are prisoners, and of *Thebes*.

Alex. Of what calling or reputation?

Clytus. I know not, but they seeme to be ladies of honour.

Alex. I will know: madam, of whence you are I know; but who, I cannot tell.

Timo. *Alexander*, I am the sister of *Theagines*,

who fought a battell with thy father, before the citie of
Chyeronte, where he died, I say which none can gainsay, valiantly.

Alex. Lady, there seeme in your words sparkes of
your brothers deedes, but worser fortune in your life
than his death : but feare not, for you shall live without
violence, enemies, or necessitie : but what are you faire
ladie, another sister to *Theagines?*

Camp. No sister to *Theagines*, but an humble hand-
maid to *Alexander*, born of a meane parentage, but to
extreme fortune.

Alex. Well ladies, for so your vertues shew you,
whatsoever your births be, you shall be honorably entreated. *Athens* shall be your *Thebes*, and you shall
not be as abjects of warre, but as subjects to *Alexander*.
Parmenio, conduct these honourable ladies into the
citie, charge the souldiers not so much as in words to
offer them any offence, and let all wants bee supplied so
farre forth as shall be necessarie for such persons and
my prisoners. [*Exeunt Parmenio et captivi.*] *Hephestion*, it resteth now that wee have as great care to
governe in peace, as conquer in warre : that whilest
armes cease, arts may flourish, and joyning letters with
launces wee endevour to bee as good philosophers as
souldiers, knowing it no lesse prayse to bee wise, than
commendable to be valiant.

Hep. Your Majestie therein sheweth that you have
as great desire to rule as to subdue : and needs must
that commonwealth be fortunate, whose captaine is a
philosopher, and whose philosopher a captaine.

[*Exeunt.*

ACTUS PRIMUS. SCÆNA SECUNDA.

MANES, GRANICHUS, PSYLLUS.

Manes. I serve in stead of a master, a mouse, whose house is a tub, whose dinner is a crust, and whose bed is a boord.

Psyllus. Then art thou in a state of life, which philosophers commend. A crum for thy supper, an hand for thy cup, and thy clothes for thy sheets. For *Natura paucis contenta*.

Gran. Manes, it is pitie so proper a man should be cast away upon a philosopher: but that *Diogenes* that dogge should have *Manes* that dog-bolt, it grieveth nature and spiteth art: the one having found thee so dissolute, absolute I would say, in bodie, the other so single, singular in minde.

Manes. Are you merry? it is a signe by the trip of your tongue, and the toyes of your head, that you have done that to day, which I have not done these three dayes.

Psyllus. What's that?

Manes. Dined.

Gran. I think *Diogenes* keepes but cold cheare.

Manes. I would it were so, but hee keepeth neither hot nor cold.

Gran. What then, lukewarme? That made *Manes* runne from his master the last day.

Psyllus. Manes had reason: for his name foretold as much.

Manes. My name? how so, sir boy?

Psyllus. You know that it is called *Mons à Movendo*, because it stands still.

Manes. Good.

Psyllus. And thou art named *Manes, à Manendo*, because thou runnest away.

Manes. Passing reasons! I did not run away, but retire.

Psyllus. To a prison, because thou wouldst have leisure to contemplate.

Manes. I will prove that my bodie was immortall: because it was in prison.

Gran. As how?

Manes. Did your masters never teach you that the soule is immortall?

Gran. Yes.

Manes. And the bodie is the prison of the soule.

Gran. True.

Manes. Why then, thus to make my body immortall, I put it in prison.

Gran. Oh bad!

Psyllus. Excellent ill!

Manes. You may see how dull a fasting wit is: therefore *Psyllus* let us goe to supper with *Granichus*: *Plato* is the best fellow of all philosophers. Give me him that reades in the morning in the schoole, and at noone in the kitchen.

Psyllus. And me.

Gran. Ah sirs, my master is a king in his parlour for the body: and a god in his studie for the soule. Among all his men he commendeth one that is an excellent musition, then stand I by and clap another on the shoulder and say, this is a passing good cooke.

Manes. It is well done *Granichus ;* for give mee pleasure that goes in at the mouth, not the eare ; I had rather fill my guts, than my braines.

Psyllus. I serve *Apelles,* who feedeth me, as *Diogenes* doth *Manes ;* for at dinner the one preacheth abstinence, the other commendeth counterfaiting : when I would eate meate, he paints a spit, and when I thirst, O saith he, is not this a faire pot ? and pointes to a table which containes the banquet of the gods, where are many dishes to feed the eye, but not to fill the gut.

Gran. What doest thou then ?

Psyllus. This doth hee then, bring in many examples that some have lived by savours, and proveth that much easier it is to fat by colours, and telles of birdes that have been fatted by painted grapes in winter : and how many have so fed their eyes with their mistresse picture, that they never desired to take food, being glutted with the delight in their favours. Then doth he shew me counterfeites, such as have surfeited with their filthy and lothsome vomites, and with the riotous bacchanalls of the god *Bacchus,* and his disorderly crew, which are painted all to the life in his shop. To conclude, I fare hardly, though I goe richly, which maketh me when I should begin to shadow a ladies face, to draw a lambs head, and sometime to set to the body of a maid, a shoulder of mutton : for *semper animus meus est in patinis.*

Manes. Thou art a god to mee : for could I see but a cookes shop painted, I would make mine eyes fatte as butter. For I have nought but sentences to fill my maw, as *plures occidit crapula quam gladius : musa jejunantibus amica :* repletion killeth delicatly : and an old saw of abstinence by *Socrates: The belly is the heads grave.* Thus with sayings, not with meate, he maketh a gallimafray.

Gran. But how doest thou then live?

Manes. With fine jests, sweet ayre, and the dogs almes.

Gran. Well, for this time I will stanch thy gut, and among pots and platters thou shalt see what it is to serve *Plato.*

Psyllus. For joy of it *Granichus* let's sing.

Manes. My voice is as cleare in the evening as in the morning.

Gran. Another commoditie of emptines.

SONG.

Gran. O for a bowle of fatt canary,
Rich Palermo, sparkling sherry,
Some nectar else, from *Juno's* daiery,
O these draughts would make us merry.

Psyllus. O for a wench, (I deale in faces,
And in other dayntier things,)
Tickled am I with her embraces,
Fine dancing in such fairy ringes.

Manes. O for a plump fat leg of mutton,
Veale, lambe, capon, pigge, and conney,
None is happy but a glutton,
None an asse but who wants money.

Chor. Wines (indeed,) and girles are good,
But brave victuals feast the bloud,
For wenches, wine, and lusty cheere,
Jove would leape down to surfet heere.

ACTUS PRIMUS.　SCÆNA TERTIA.

MELIPPUS, PLATO, ARISTOTLE, CRYSIPPUS, CRATES, CLEANTHES, ANAXARCHUS, ALEXANDER, HEPHESTION, PARMENIO, CLYTUS, DIOGENES.

Melip. I had never such adoe to warne schollers to come before a king: First, I came to *Crisippus*, a tall leane old mad man, willing him presently to appeare before *Alexander;* hee stood staring on my face, neither moving his eyes nor his body; I urging him to give some answer, hee tooke up a booke, sate downe and saide nothing: *Melissa* his maide told mee it was his manner, and that oftentimes shee was fain to thrust meat into his mouth: for that he would rather sterve than cease studie: well thought I, seeing bookish men are so blockish, and great clearkes such simple courtiers, I will neither be partaker of their commons, nor their commendations. From thence I came to *Plato* and to *Aristotle,* and to divers other; none refusing to come, saving an olde obscure fellow, who sitting in a tub turned towardes the sunne, read Greeke to a young boy; him when I willed to appeare before *Alexander,* he answered, if *Alexander* would faine see mee, let him come to mee; if learne of me, let him come to mee; whatsoever it be, let him come to me: why, said I, he is a king; he answered, why I am a philosopher; why, but he is *Alexander;* I, but I am *Diogenes.* I was halfe angry to see one so crooked in his shape, to bee so crabbed in his sayings. So going my way, I said, thou shalt repent it, if thou comest not to *Alexander :*

nay, smiling answered hee, *Alexander* may repent it if hee come not to *Diogenes*: vertue must bee sought, not offered: and so turning himselfe to his cell, hee grunted I know not what, like a pig under a tub. But I must bee gone, the philosophers are comming. [*Exit.*

Plato. It is a difficult controversie, *Aristotle*, and rather to be wondered at than beleeved, how naturall causes should worke supernaturall effects.

Aris. I do not so much stand upon the apparition is seene in the moone; neither the *Demonium* of *Socrates*; as that I cannot by naturall reason give any reason of the ebbing and flowing of the sea; which makes me in the depth of my studies to crie out, *O ens entium miserere mei.*

Plato. *Cleanthes*, and you attribute so much to nature by searching for things which are not to be found, that whilest you studie a cause of your owne, you omitt the occasion it selfe. There is no man so savage in whom resteth not this divine particle, that there is an omnipotent, eternall, and divine mover, which may be called God.

Cleant. I am of this minde, that that first mover, which you terme God, is the instrument of all the movings which we attribute to nature. The earth which is masse, swimmeth on the sea, seasons divided in themselves, fruits growing in themselves, the majestie of the skie, the whole firmament of the world, and whatsoever else appeareth miraculous, what man almost of meane capacitie but can prove it natural?

Anax. These causes shall be debated at our philosophers feast, in which controversie I will take part with

Aristotle, that there is *Natura naturans*, and yet not God.

Cra. And I with *Plato*, that there is *Deus optimus maximus*, and not nature.

Aris. Here commeth *Alexander*.

Alex. I see *Hephestion*, that these philosophers are here attending for us.

Hep. They are not philosophers, if they know not their duties.

Alex. But I much mervaile *Diogenes* should bee so dogged.

Hep. I doe not thinke but his excuse will be better than *Melippus* message.

Alex. I will goe see him *Hephestion*, because I long to see him that would command *Alexander* to come, to whom all the world is like to come. *Aristotle* and the rest, sithence my comming from *Thebes* to *Athens*, from a place of conquest to a pallace of quiet, I have resolved with my selfe in my court to have as many philosophers, as I had in my camp souldiers. My court shal be a schoole wherein I wil have used as great doctrine in peace, as I did in warre discipline.

Aris. We are all here ready to be commanded, and glad we are that we are commanded, for that nothing better becommeth kings than literature, which maketh them come as neare to the gods in wisdome, as they doe in dignitie.

Alex. It is so *Aristotle*, but yet there is among you, yea and of your bringing up, that sought to destroy *Alexander; Calistenes, Aristotle*, whose treasons against his prince shall not be borne out with the reasons of his philosophie.

Aris. If ever mischief entred into the heart of *Ca-listenes*, let *Calistenes* suffer for it; but that *Aristotle* ever imagined any such thing of *Calistenes*, *Aristotle* doth denie.

Alex. Well *Aristotle*, kindred may blinde thee, and affection me; but in kings causes I will not stand to schollers arguments. This meeting shal be for a commandement, that you all frequent my court, instruct the young with rules, confirme the olde with reasons: let your lives bee answerable to your learnings, least my proceedings be contrary to my promises.

Hep. You said you would aske every one of them a question, which yesternight none of us could answere.

Alex. I will. *Plato*, of all beasts, which is the subtilest?

Plato. That which man hitherto never knew.

Alex. *Aristotle*, how should a man be thought a god?

Aris. In doing a thing unpossible for a man.

Alex. *Crisippus*, which was first, the day or the night?

Cris. The day, by a day.

Alex. Indeede! strange questions must have strange answers. *Cleanthes*, what say you, is life or death the stronger?

Cle. Life, that suffereth so many troubles.

Alex. *Crates*, how long should a man live?

Crates. Till hee thinke it better to die than to live.

Alex. *Anaxarchus*, whether doth the sea or the earth bring forth most creatures?

Anax. The earth, for the sea is but a part of the earth.

Alex. *Hephestion*, me thinkes they have answered all well, and in such questions I meane often to trie them.

Hep. It is better to have in your court a wise man, than in your ground a golden mine. Therefore would I leave war, to study wisdom, were I *Alexander*.

Alex. So would I, were I *Hephestion*. But come let us goe and give release, as I promised to our *Theban* thrall. [*Exeunt*.

Plato. Thou art fortunate *Aristotle*, that *Alexander* is thy scholler.

Aris. And all you happy that he is your soveraigne.

Crisip. I could like the man well, if he could be contented to bee but a man.

Aris. He seeketh to draw neere to the gods in knowledge, not to be a god.

Plato. Let us question a little with *Diogenes*, why he went not with us to *Alexander*. *Diogenes*, thou didst forget thy duety, that thou wentst not with us to the king.

Diog. And you your profession that went to the king.

Plato. Thou takest as great pride to be peevish, as others do glory to be vertuous.

Diog. And thou as great honour being a philosopher to be thought court-like, as others shame that be courtiers, to be accounted philosophers.

Aris. These austere manners set aside, it is well knowne that thou didst counterfeite money.

Diog. And thou thy manners, in that thou didst not counterfeite money.

Aris. Thou hast reason to contemne the court, being both in bodie and minde too crooked for a courtier.

Diog. As good be crooked, and indevour to make my selfe straight, from the court; as bee straight, and learne to be crooked at the court.

Cris. Thou thinkest it a grace to be opposite against *Alexander*.

Diog. And thou to be jump with *Alexander*.

Anax. Let us goe: for in contemning him, we shal better please him, than in wondering at him.

Aris. Plato, what doest thou thinke of *Diogenes?*

Plato. To be *Socrates,* furious.   Let us go.

[*Exeunt philosophi.*

ACTUS SECUNDUS. SCÆNA PRIMA.

Diogenes, Psyllus, Manes, Granichus.

Psyllus.

EHOLD *Manes* where thy master is; seeking either for bones for his dinner, or pinnes for his sleeves.   I will goe salute him.

Manes. Doe so; but mum, not a word that you saw *Manes.*

Gran. Then stay thou behinde, and I will goe with *Psyllus.*

Psyllus. All hayle, *Diogenes,* to your proper person.

Diog. All hate to thy peevish conditions.

Gran. O dogge!

Psyllus. What doest thou seeke for here?

Diog. For a man and a beast.

Gran. That is easie without thy light to bee found, be not all these men?

Diog. Called men.

Gran. What beast is it thou lookest for?

Diog. The beast my man, *Manes.*

Psyllus. Hee is a beast indeed that will serve thee!

Diog. So is he that begat thee.

Gran. What wouldest thou do, if thou shouldst find *Manes?*

Diog. Give him leave to doe as hee hath done before.

Gran. What's that?

Diog. To run away.

Psyllus. Why, hast thou no neede of *Manes?*

Diog. It were a shame for *Diogenes* to have neede of *Manes,* and for *Manes* to have no neede of *Diogenes.*

Gran. But put the case he were gone, wouldst thou entertaine any of us two?

Diog. Upon condition.

Psyllus. What?

Diog. That you should tell me wherefore any of you both were good.

Gran. Why, I am a scholler, and well seene in philosophy.

Psyllus. And I a prentice, and well seene in painting.

Diog. Well then *Granichus,* be thou a painter to amend thine ill face; and thou *Psyllus* a philosopher to correct thine evill manners. But who is that *Manes?*

Manes. I care not who I were, so I were not *Manes.*

Gran. You are taken tardie.

Psyllus. Let us slip aside *Granichus,* to salutation betweene *Manes* and his master.

Diog. Manes, thou knowest the last day I threw away my dish, to drinke in my hand, because it was superfluous; now I am determined to put away my man, and serve my selfe: *Quia non egeo tui vel te.*

Manes. Master, you know a while agoe I ran away, so doe I meane to doe againe, *quia scio tibi non esse argentum.*

Diog. I know I have no money, neither will have ever a man: for I was resolved long sithence to put away both my slaves: money and *Manes.*

Manes. So was I determined to shake of both my dogges, hunger and *Diogenes.*

Psyllus. O sweet consent betweene a crowde and a Jewes harpe.

Gran. Come let us reconcile them.

Psyllus. It shall not neede: for this is their use, now doe they dine one upon another. [*Exit Diogenes.*

Gran. How now *Manes,* art thou gone from thy master?

Manes. No, I did but now binde my selfe to him.

Psyllus. Why you were at mortall jarres.

Manes. In faith no, we brake a bitter jest one upon another.

Gran. Why thou art as dogged as he.

Psyllus. My father knew them both little whelps.

Manes. Well, I will hie me after my master.

Gran. Why, is it supper time with *Diogenes?*

Manes. I, with him at all time when he hath meate.

Psyllus. Why then every man to his home, and let us steale out againe anone.

Gran. Where shall we meet?

Psyllus. Why at *Ala vendibili suspensa hœdera non est opus.*

Manes. O *Psyllus, habeo te loco parentis,* thou blessest me.   [*Exeunt.*

ACTUS SECUNDUS. SCÆNA SECUNDA.

ALEXANDER, HEPHESTION, PAGE, DIOGENES, APELLES.

Alex. Stand aside sir boy, till you be called. *Hephestion,* how doe you like the sweet face of *Campaspe?*

Hep. I cannot but commende the stout courage of *Timoclea.*

Alex. Without doubt *Campaspe* had some great man to her father.

Hep. You know *Timoclea* had *Theagines* to her brother.

Alex. *Timoclea* still in thy mouth! art thou not in love?

Hep. Not I.

Alex. Not with *Timoclea* you meane; wherein you resemble the lapwing, who crieth most where her nest is not. And so you lead me from espying your love with *Campaspe,* you crie *Timoclea.*

Hep. Could I as well subdue kingdomes, as I can my thoughts; or were I as farre from ambition, as I am from love; all the world would account mee as valiant in armes, as I know my selfe moderate in affection.

Alex. Is love a vice?

Hep. It is no vertue.

Alex. Well, now shalt thou see what small difference

I make betweene *Alexander* and *Hephestion*. And sith
thou hast been alwaies partaker of my triumphes, thou
shalt bee partaker of my torments.   I love *Hephestion*,
I love! I love *Campaspe*, a thing farre unfit for a
Macedonian, for a king, for *Alexander*. Why hangest
thou downe thy head *Hephestion?* Blushing to heare
that which I am not ashamed to tell.

Hep. Might my words crave pardon and my counsell credit, I would both discharge the duetie of a subject, for so I am, and the office of a friend, for so I will.

Alex. Speake *Hephestion;* for whatsoever is spoken,
Hephestion speaketh to *Alexander*.

Hep. I cannot tell *Alexander*, whether the report be
more shamefull to be heard, or the cause sorrowful to
be beleeved? What! is the son of *Philip*, king of
Macedon, become the subject of *Campaspe*, the captive
of *Thebes?* Is that minde, whose greatnes the world
could not containe, drawn within the compasse of an
idle alluring eie? Wil you handle the spindle with
Hercules, when you should shake the speare with *Achil-
les?* Is the warlike sound of drum and trump turned
to the soft noise of lyre and lute? the neighing of
barbed steeds, whose lowdnes filled the aire with terrour,
and whose breathes dimmed the sun with smoake, con-
verted to delicate tunes and amorous glances? O *Alexander*, that soft and yeelding minde should not bee in
him, whose hard and unconquered heart hath made so
many yeeld. But you love,—ah griefe! but whom?
Campaspe? ah shame! a maide forsooth unknowne,
unnoble, and who can tell whether immodest? whose
eyes are framed by art to enamour, and whose heart

was made by nature to enchant. I, but shee is beautiful; yea, but not therefore chaste: I, but she is comely in all parts of the bodie: but shee may bee crooked in some part of the minde: I, but shee is wise, yea, but she is a woman: Beautie is like the blackberry, which seemeth red, when it is not ripe, resembling precious stones that are polished with honie, which the smoother they looke, the sooner they breake. It is thought wonderfull among the sea-men, that *Mugill* of all fishes the swiftest, is found in the belly of the *Bret* of all the slowest: And shall it not seeme monstrous to wise men, that the heart of the greatest conquerour of the world, should be found in the hands of the weakest creature of nature? of a woman? of a captive? *Herrwyns* have faire skins, but foule livers; sepulchres fresh colours, but rotten bones; women faire faces, but false hearts. Remember *Alexander* thou hast a campe to governe, not a chamber; fall not from the armour of *Mars* to the armes of *Venus;* from the fierie assaults of warre, to the maidenly skirmishes of love; from displaying the eagle in thine ensigne, to set downe the sparrow. I sigh *Alexander* that where fortune could not conquer, folly should overcome. But behold all the perfection that may be in *Campaspe;* a haire curling by nature, not art; sweete alluring eyes; a faire face made in despite of *Venus*, and a stately port in disdaine of *Juno;* a wit apt to conceive, and quicke to answere; a skin as soft as silke, and as smooth as jet; a long white hand, a fine little foot; to conclude, all parts answerable to the best part; what of this? Though she have heavenly gifts, vertue and beautie; is shee not of

earthly metall, flesh and bloud? You *Alexander* that
would be a god, shew your selfe in this worse than a
man, so soone to be both overseene and over-taken in
a woman, whose false teares know their true times,
whose smooth words wound deeper than sharpe swords.
There is no surfet so dangerous as that of honie, nor
any poyson so deadly as that of love; in the one physicke cannot prevaile, nor in the other counsell.

Alex. My case were light *Hephestion*, and not worthy
to be called love, if reason were a remedie, or sentences
could salve, that sense cannot conceive. Little do you
know, and therefore sleightly doe you regard, the dead
embers in a private person, or live coales in a great
prince, whose passions and thoughts doe as farre exceed
others in extremitie as their callings doe in majestie.
An eclipse in the sunne is more than the falling of a
starre; none can conceive the torments of a king, unlesse he be a king, whose desires are not inferiour to
their dignities. And then judge *Hephestion* if the agonies of love be dangerous in a subject, whether they be
not more than deadly unto *Alexander*, whose deepe and
not to bee conceived sighes, cleave the heart in shivers;
whose wounded thoughts can neither be expressed nor
endured. Cease then *Hephestion* with arguments to
seeke to refell that, which with their deitie the gods
cannot resist; and let this suffice to answere thee, that it
is a king that loveth, and *Alexander;* whose affections
are not to be measured by reason, being immortall; nor
I feare me to be borne, being intolerable.

Hep. I must needs yeeld; when neither reason nor
counsell can bee heard.

Alex. Yeeld *Hephestion*, for *Alexander* doth love, and therefore must obtaine.

Hep. Suppose shee loves not you ; affection commeth not by appointment or birth ; and then as good hated as enforced.

Alex. I am a king, and will command.

Hep. You may, to yeeld to lust by force ; but to consent to love by feare, you cannot.

Alex. Why, what is that which *Alexander* may not conquer as he list ?

Hep. Why, that which you say the gods cannot resist, love.

Alex. I am a conquerour, shee a captive ; I as fortunate, as shee faire : my greatnesse may answere her wants, and the gifts of my minde, the modestie of hers : Is it not likely then that she should love ? Is it not reasonable ?

Hep. You say that in love there is no reason, and therefore there can be no likelyhood.

Alex. No more *Hephestion :* in this case I will use mine own counsell, and in all other thine advice ; thou mayst be a good souldier, but never good lover. Call my page. Sirrha, goe presently to *Apelles*, and will him to come to me without either delay or excuse.

Page. I goe.

Alex. In the meane season to recreate my spirits, being so neere, wee will goe see *Diogenes*. And see where his tub is. *Diogenes !*

Diog. Who calleth ?

Alex. Alexander : how happened it that you would not come out of your tub to my palace ?

Diog. Because it was as farre from my tub to your palace, as from your palace to my tub.

Alex. Why then doest thou owe no reverence to kings?

Diog. No.

Alex. Why so?

Diog. Because they be no gods.

Alex. They be gods of the earth.

Diog. Yea, gods of earth.

Alex. Plato is not of thy minde.

Diog. I am glad of it.

Alex. Why?

Diog. Because I would have none of *Diogenes* minde, but *Diogenes.*

Alex. If *Alexander* have any thing that may pleasure *Diogenes*, let me know, and take it.

Diog. Then take not from mee, that you cannot give mee, the light of the world.

Alex. What doest thou want?

Diog. Nothing that you have.

Alex. I have the world at command.

Diog. And I in contempt.

Alex. Thou shalt live no longer than I will.

Diog. But I shall die whether you will or no.

Alex. How should one learne to bee content?

Diog. Unlearne to covet.

Alex. Hephestion, were I not *Alexander*, I would wish to bee *Diogenes.*

Hep. He is dogged, but discreet; I cannot tell how sharpe, with a kind of sweetnes; full of wit, yet too too wayward.

Alex. *Diogenes,* when I come this way againe, I will both see thee, and confer with thee.

Diog. Doe.

Alex. But here commeth *Apelles,* how now *Apelles,* is *Venus* face yet finished?

Apel. Not yet: beautie is not so soone shadowed, whose perfection commeth not within the compasse either of cunning or of colour.

Alex. Well, let it rest unperfect; and come you with mee, where I will shew you that finished by nature, that you have beene trifling about by art.

ACTUS TERTIUS. SCÆNA PRIMA.

APELLES, CAMPASPE.

Apelles.

LADIE, I doubt whether there bee any colour so fresh, that may shadow a countenance so faire.

Camp. Sir, I had thought you had bin commanded to paint with your hand, not to glose with your tongue; but as I have heard, it is the hardest thing in painting to set downe a hard favour, which maketh you to despaire of my face; and then shall you have as great thankes to spare your labour, as to discredit your art.

Apel. Mistris, you neither differ from your selfe nor your sexe: for knowing your owne perfection, you seeme to disprayse that which men most commend, drawing them by that meane into an admiration, where feeding themselves they fall into an extasie; your mo-

destie being the cause of the one, and of the other, your
affections.

Camp. I am too young to understand your speech,
though old enough to withstand your devise: you have
bin so long used to colours, you can doe nothing but
colour.

Apel. Indeed the colours I see, I feare will alter the
colour I have: but come madam, will you draw neere:
for *Alexander* will be here anon. *Psyllus*, stay you
here at the window, if any enquire for mee, answere,
Non lubet esse domi.   [*Exeunt.*

ACTUS TERTIUS. SCÆNA SECUNDA.

Psyllus, Manes.

Psyllus. It is alwayes my masters fashion, when any
faire gentlewoman is to be drawne within, to make
me to stay without. But if hee should paint *Jupiter*
like a bull, like a swanne, like an eagle, then must
Psyllus with one hand grind colours, and with the other
hold the candle. But let him alone, the better hee
shadowes her face, the more will he burne his owne
heart. And now if any man could meet with *Manes*,
who I dare say, lookes as leane, as if *Diogenes* dropped
out of his nose—

Manes. And here comes *Manes*, who hath as much
meate in his maw, as thou hast honestie in thy head.

Psyllus. Then I hope thou art very hungry.

Manes. They that know thee, know that.

Psyllus. But doest thou not remember that wee have
certaine liquor to conferre withall.

Manes. I, but I have businesse; I must goe cry a thing.

Psyllus. Why, what hast thou lost?

Manes. That which I never had, my dinner!

Psyllus. Foule lubber, wilt thou crie for thy dinner?

Manes. I meane, I must crie; not as one would say crie; but crie, that is make a noyse.

Psyllus. Why. foole, that is all one; for if thou crie, thou must needs make a noyse..

Manes. Boy, thou art deceived; Crie hath divers significations, and may be alluded to many things; Knave but to one, and can be applyed but to thee.

Psyllus. Profound *Manes!*

Manes. Wee *Cynickes* are mad fellowes, didst thou not finde I did quip thee?

Psyllus. No verily! why, what's a quip?

Manes. Wee great girders call it a short saying of a sharpe wit, with a bitter sense in a sweet word.

Psyllus. How canst thou thus divine, divide, define, dispute, and all on the sodaine?

Manes. Wit will have his swing; I am bewitcht, inspired, inflamed, infected.

Psyllus. Well, then will I not tempt thy gybing spirit.

Manes. Doe not *Psyllus*, for thy dull head will bee but a grindstone for my quicke wit, which if thou whet with overthwarts, *periisti, actum est de te.* I have drawne bloud at one's braines with a bitter bob.

Psyllus. Let me crosse my selfe: for I die, if I crosse thee.

Manes. Let me doe my businesse, I my selfe am

afraid, lest my wit should waxe warme, and then must it needs consume some hard head with fine and prettie jests.   I am sometimes in such a vaine, that for want of some dull pate to worke on, I begin to gird my selfe.

Psyllus. The gods shield me from such a fine fellow, whose words melt wits like waxe.

Manes. Well then, let us to the matter.   In faith my master meaneth to morrow to flie.

Psyllus. It is a jest.

Manes. Is it a jest to flie? shouldest thou flie so soone, thou shouldest repent it in earnest.

Psyllus. Well, I will be the cryer.

Manes and Psyllus one after another. O ys, O ys, O ys, All manner of men, women, or children, that will come to morrow into the market place, betweene the houres of nine and ten, shall see *Diogenes* the Cynicke flie.

Psyllus. I doe not thinke he will flie.

Manes. Tush, say flie.

Psyllus. Flie.

Manes. Now let us goe: for I will not see him againe till midnight, I have a backe way into his tub.

Psyllus. Which way callest thou the backe way, when every way is open?

Manes. I meane to come in at his backe.

Psyllus. Well let us goe away, that we may returne speedily.   [*Exeunt.*

ACTUS TERTIUS.   SCÆNA TERTIA.

APELLES, CAMPASPE.

Apel. I shall never draw your eyes well, because they blinde mine.

Camp. Why then paint mee without eyes, for I am blind.

Apel. Were you ever shadowed before of any?

Camp. No.   And would you could so now shadow me, that I might not be perceived of any.

Apel. It were pitie, but that so absolute a face should furnish *Venus* Temple amongst these pictures.

Camp. What are these pictures?

Apel. This is *Læda,* whom *Jove* deceived in likenesse of a Swan.

Camp. A faire woman, but a foule deceit.

Apel. This is *Alcmena,* unto whom *Jupiter* came in shape of *Amphitrion* her husband, and begate *Hercules.*

Camp. A famous sonne, but an infamous fact.

Apel. Hee might doe it, because hee was a God.

Camp. Nay, therefore it was evill done, because he was a God.

Apel. This is *Danae,* into whose prison *Jupiter* drizled a golden showre, and obtained his desire.

Camp. What gold can make one yeeld to desire?

Apel. This is *Europa,* whom *Jupiter* ravished; this *Antiopa.*

Camp. Were all the Gods like this *Jupiter?*

Apel. There were many Gods, in this, like *Jupiter.*

Camp. I thinke in those dayes love was well ratified among men on earth, when lust was so full authorised by the Gods in Heaven.

Apel. Nay, you may imagine there were women passing amiable, when there were Gods exceeding amorous.

Camp. Were women never so faire, men would be false.

Apel. Were women never so false, men would be fond.

Camp. What counterfeit is this *Apelles*?

Apel. This is *Venus* the Goddesse of love.

Camp. What, bee there also loving Goddesses?

Apel. This is shee that hath power to command the very affections of the heart.

Camp. How is she hired, by prayer, by sacrifice, or bribes?

Apel. By prayer, sacrifice, and bribes.

Camp. What prayer?

Apel. Vowes irrevocable.

Camp. What sacrifice?

Apel. Hearts ever sighing, never dissembling.

Camp. What bribes?

Apel. Roses and kisses: but were you never in love?

Camp. No, nor love in me.

Apel. Then have you injuried many!

Camp. How so?

Apel. Because you have been loved of many.

Camp. Flattered perchance of some.

Apel. It is not possible that a face so faire, and a wit so sharpe, both without comparison, should not be apt to love.

Camp. If you begin to tip your tongue with cunning, I pray dip your pensill in colours; and fall to that you must doe, not that you would doe.

ACTUS TERTIUS. SCÆNA QUARTA.

CLYTUS, PARMENIO, ALEXANDER, HEPHESTION, CRYSUS, DIOGENES, APELLES, CAMPASPE.

Clytus. *Parmenio* I cannot tell how it commeth to passe, that in *Alexander* now a dayes there groweth an unpatient kind of life: in the morning he is melancholy, at noone solemne; at all times either more sowre or severe, than hee was accustomed.

Par. In King's causes I rather love to doubt than conjecture, and thinke it better to bee ignorant than inquisitive: they have long eares and stretched armes, in whose heads suspition is a proofe, and to be accused is to be condemned.

Clytus. Yet betweene us there can bee no danger to find out the cause: for that there is no malice to withstand it. It may be an unquenchable thirst of conquering maketh him unquiet: it is not unlikely his long ease hath altered his humour: that he should be in love, it is impossible.

Par. In love *Clytus?* no, no, it is as farre from his thought, as treason in ours: he, whose ever waking eye, whose never tired heart, whose body patient of labour, whose mind unsatiable of victorie hath alwayes beene noted, cannot so soone be melted into the weake conceits of love. *Aristotle* told him there were many worlds, and that he hath not conquered one that gapeth for all, galleth *Alexander*. But here he commeth.

Alex. *Parmenio* and *Clytus*, I would have you both readie to goe into *Persia* about an ambassage no lesse profitable to me, than to your selves honourable.

Clytus. Wee are readie at all commands; wishing nothing else, but continually to be commanded.

Alex. Well then, withdraw yourselves, till I have further considered of this matter. [*Exeunt Clytus and Parmenio*.] Now wee will see how *Apelles* goeth forward: I doubt mee that nature hath overcome art, and her countenance his cunning.

Hep. You love, and therefore think any thing.

Alex. But not so farre in love with *Campaspe*, as with *Bucephalus*, if occasion serve either of conflict or of conquest.

Hep. Occasion cannot want, if will doe not. Behold all *Persia* swelling in the pride of their owne power; the *Scythians* carelesse what courage or fortune can do; the *Egyptians* dreaming in the southsayings of their augures, and gaping over the smoake of their beasts intralls. All these *Alexander* are to be subdued, if that world be not slipped out of your head, which you have sworne to conquer with that hand.

Alex. I confesse the labour's fit for *Alexander*, and yet recreation necessarie among so many assaults, bloudie wounds, intolerable troubles: give me leave a little, if not to sit, yet to breath. And doubt not but *Alexander* can, when hee will, throw affections as farre from him as he can cowardise. But behold *Diogenes* talking with one at his tub.

Crysus. One penny *Diogenes*, I am a Cynicke.

Diog. Hee made thee a begger, that first gave thee any thing.

Crysus. Why, if thou wilt give nothing, no bodie will give thee.

Diog. I want nothing, till the springs drie, and the earth perish.

Crysus. I gather for the Gods.

Diog. And I care not for those Gods which want money.

Crysus. Thou art not a right Cynick that wilt give nothing.

Diog. Thou art not, that wilt begge any thing.

Crysus. Alexander, King *Alexander*, give a poore Cynick a groat.

Alex. It is not for a king to give a groat.

Crysus. Then give me a talent.

Alex. It is not for a begger to aske a talent. Away. *Apelles!*

Apel. Here.

Alex. Now gentlewoman? doth not your beautie put the painter to his trumpe?

Camp. Yes my lord, seeing so disordered a countenance, hee feareth hee shall shadow a deformed counterfeite.

Alex. Would he could colour the life with the feature. And mee thinketh *Apelles*, were you as cunning as report saith you are, you may paint flowres as well with sweet smels, as fresh colours, observing in your mixture such things as should draw neere to their savours.

Apel. Your majestie must know, it is no lesse hard to paint savours, than vertues; colours can neither speake, nor thinke.

Alex. Where doe you first begin, when you draw any picture?

Apel. The proportion of the face in just compasse, as I can.

Alex. I would begin with the eye, as a light to all the rest.

Apel. If you will paint, as you are a king, your majestie may beginne where you please; but as you would bee a painter, you must begin with the face.

Alex. Aurelius would in one houre colour foure faces.

Apel. I marvaile in halfe an houre hee did not foure.

Alex. Why, is it so easie?

Apel. No, but he doth it so homely.

Alex. When will you finish *Campaspe?*

Apel. Never finish: for alwayes in absolute beauty there is somewhat above art.

Alex. Why should not I, by labour, be as cunning as *Apelles?*

Apel. God shield you should have cause to be so cunning as *Apelles!*

Alex. Me thinketh foure colours are sufficient to shadow any countenance, and so it was in the time of *Phydias.*

Apel. Then had men fewer fancies, and women not so many favours. For now if the haire of her eye-browes be blacke, yet must the haire of her head be yellow: the attire of her head must bee different from the habit of her bodie, else would the picture seeme like the blazon of ancient armory, not like the sweet delight of new found amiablenesse. For as in garden knots diversitie of odours make a more sweete savour, or as in musique divers strings cause a more delicate consent: so in painting, the more colours, the better counterfeit; observing black for a ground, and the rest for grace.

Alex. Lend me thy pensill *Apelles*, I will paint, and thou shalt judge.

Apel. Here.

Alex. The coale breakes.

Apel. You leane too hard.

Alex. Now it blackes not.

Apel. You leane too soft.

Alex. This is awrie.

Apel. Your eye goeth not with your hand.

Alex. Now it is worse.

Apel. Your hand goeth not with your minde.

Alex. Nay, if all be too hard or soft, so many rules and regards, that one's hand, one's eye, one's minde must all draw together, I had rather bee setting of a battell, than blotting of a boord. But how have I done here?

Apel. Like a king.

Alex. I thinke so: but nothing more unlike a painter. Well *Apelles*, *Campaspe* is finished as I wish, dismisse her, and bring presently her counterfeit after me.

Apel. I will.

Alex. Now *Hephestion*, doth not this matter cotton as I would? *Campaspe* looketh pleasantly, libertie will encrease her beautie, and my love shall advance her honour.

Hep. I will not contrarie your majestie; for time

must weare out that love hath wrought, and reason
weane what appetite nursed.

Alex. How stately shee passeth by, yet how soberly!
a sweete consent in her countenance with a chaste disdaine! desire mingled with coynesse! and I cannot tell
how to terme it, a curst yeelding modesty!

Hep. Let her passe.

Alex. So shee shall for the fairest on the earth.

[*Exeunt.*

ACTUS TERTIUS. SCÆNA QUINTA.

PSYLLUS, MANES, APELLES.

Psyllus. I shall be hanged for tarrying so long.

Manes. I pray God my master be not flowne before
I come.

Psyllus. Away *Manes!* my master doth come.

Apel. Where have you beene all this while?

Psyllus. Nowhere but here.

Apel. Who was here sithens my comming?

Psyllus. Nobodie.

Apel. Ungracious wag, I perceive you have beene
a loytering; was *Alexander* nobodie?

Psyllus. He was a king, I meant no mean bodie.

Apel. I will cudgell your bodie for it, and then will I
say it was no bodie, because it was no honest bodie. Away
in. [*Exit Psyllus.*] Unfortunate *Apelles*, and therefore
unfortunate because *Apelles!* Hast thou by drawing her
beautie, brought to passe that thou canst scarce draw
thine owne breath? And by so much the more hast thou
increased thy care, by how much the more thou hast

shewed thy cunning: was it not sufficient to behold the
fire, and warme thee, but with *Satyrus* thou must kisse
the fire and burne thee? O *Campaspe, Campaspe,* art
must yeeld to nature, reason to appetite, wisdome to
affection! Could *Pigmalion* entreate by prayer to have
his ivory turned into flesh? and cannot *Apelles* obtaine
by plaints to have the picture of his love changed to
life? Is painting so farre inferiour to carving? or dost
thou *Venus* more delight to bee hewed with chizels,
then shadowed with colours? what *Pigmalion* or what
Pyrgoteles, or what *Lysippus* is hee, that ever made thy
face so faire, or spread thy fame so farre as I? unlesse
Venus, in this thou enviest mine art, that in colouring
my sweet *Campaspe,* I have left no place by cunning to
make thee so amiable. But alas! shee is the para-
mour to a prince, *Alexander* the monarch of the earth
hath both her body and affection. For what is it that
kings cannot obtaine by prayers, threats and promises?
Will not shee thinke it better to sit under a cloth of
estate like a queene, than in a poore shop like a huswife?
and esteeme it sweeter to be the concubine of the lord
of the world, than spouse to a painter in Athens? Yes,
yes, *Apelles,* thou maist swimme against the streame
with the crab, and feede against the winde with the
deere, and peck against the steele with the cockatrice:
starres are to be looked at, not reached at: princes to
be yeelded unto, not contended with: *Campaspe* to be
honoured, not obtained: to be painted, not possessed of
thee. O faire face! O unhappy hand! and why didst
thou drawe it so faire a face? O beautifull countenance,
the expres image of *Venus,* but somwhat fresher: the

only patterne of that eternitie which *Jupiter* dreaming
asleepe, could not conceive againe waking. Blush *Venus,*
for I am ashamed to ende thee.　Now must I paint
things unpossible for mine art, but agreeable with my
affections : deepe and hollow sighes, sad and melancholie
thoughtes, woundes and slaughters of conceits, a life
posting to death, a death galloping from life, a wavering constancie, an unsetled resolution, and what not,
Apelles? And what but *Apelles?* But as they that are
shaken with a feaver are to be warmed with cloathes,
not groanes, and as he that melteth in a consumption is
to be recured by colices, not conceits : so the feeding
canker of my care, the never dying worme of my heart,
is to be killed by counsell, not cries ; by applying of
remedies, not by replying of reasons.　And sith in cases
desperate there must be used medicines that are ex-
treame, I will hazard that little life that is left, to restore the greater part that is lost ; and this shall be my
first practise : for wit must worke where authoritie is
not.　As soone as *Alexander* hath viewed this portrai-
ture, I will by devise give it a blemish, that by that
meanes she may come againe to my shop ; and then as
good it were to utter my love, and die with deniall, as
conceale it, and live in dispaire.

SONG BY APELLES.

Cupid and my Campaspe playd,
At cardes for kisses, Cupid payd ;
He stakes his quiver, bow, and arrows,
His mother's doves, and teeme of sparows ;
Looses them too ; then, downe he throwes
The corrall of his lippe, the rose

Growing on's cheek, (but none knows how)
With these, the cristall of his brow,
And then the dimple of his chinne;
All these did my Campaspe winne.
At last, hee set her, both his eyes;
Shee won, and Cupid blind did rise.
   O love! has shee done this to thee?
   What shall (alas!) become of mee?

ACTUS QUARTUS. SCÆNA PRIMA.

SOLINUS, PSYLLUS, GRANICHUS, MANES,
DIOGENES, POPULUS.

Solinus.

THIS is the place, the day, the time, that *Diogenes* hath appointed to flie.

Psyllus. I will not loose the flight of so faire a foule as *Diogenes* is, though my master cudgell my no body, as he threatened.

Gran. What *Psyllus*, will the beast wag his wings to day?

Psyllus. Wee shall heare: for here commeth *Manes*: *Manes* will it be?

Manes. Be! he were best be as cunning as a bee, or else shortly he will not bee at all.

Gran. How is hee furnished to flie, hath he—

Manes. Thou art an asse! capons, geese, have feathers. He hath found *Dedalus* wings, and hath beene peecing them this mo— so broad in the shoulders. O you shall see h— ayre even like a tortoys.

Sol. Me thinkes so wise a man should not bee so mad, his body must needs be too heavie.

Manes. Why, hee hath eaten nothing this seven night but corke and feathers.

Psyllus. Touch him *Manes.*

Manes. Hee is so light that hee can scarce keepe him from flying at midnight.

Populus intrat.

Manes. See they begin to flocke, and behold my master bustels himselfe to flie.

Diog. You wicked and bewitched Athenians, whose bodies make the earth to groane, and whose breathes infect the ayre with stench. Come ye to see *Diogenes* flie? *Diogenes* commeth to see you sinke: yea call me dogge, so I am, for I long to gnaw the bons in your skins. Yee tearme mee an hater of men: no, I am a hater of your manners. Your lives dissolute, not fearing death, will prove your deaths desperat, not hoping for life. What do you else in Athens but sleepe in the day, and surfeit in the night: backe-gods in the morning with pride, in the evening belly-gods with gluttony! You flatter kings, and call them gods, speak truth of your selves, and confesse you are divels! From the bee you have taken not the honey, but the wax, to make your religion; framing it to the time, not to the truth. Your filthy lust you colour under a courtly colour of love, injuries abroad under the title of policies at home, and secret malice creepeth under the name of publike justice. You have caused *Alexander* to drie up springs and plant vines, to sow rocket and weed

endiff, to sheare sheepe, and shrine foxes. All conscience is sealed at Athens. Swearing commeth of a
hot mettle: lying of a quick wit: flattery of a flowing
tongue: undecent talke of a merry disposition. All
things are lawfull at Athens. Either you think there
are no gods, or I must think ye are no men. You
build as though you should live for ever, and surfeit as
though you should die to morrowe. None teacheth
true philosophie but *Aristotle*, because hee was the kings
schoole-master! O times! O men! O corruption in
manners! Remember that greene grasse must turne to
drie hay. When you sleepe, you are not sure to wake;
and when you rise, not certaine to lie downe. Looke
you never so high, your heads must lie level with your
feet. Thus have I flowne over your disordered lives,
and if you will not amend your manners, I will studie to
flie further from you, that I may bee neerer to honestie.

Sol. Thou ravest *Diogenes*, for thy life is different
from thy words. Did not I see thee come out of a
brothell house? was it not a shame?

Diog. It was no shame to goe out, but a shame to
goe in.

Gran. It were a good deede *Manes*, to beate thy
master.

Manes. You were as good eate my master.

One of the people. Hast thou made us all fooles, and
wilt thou not flie?

Diog. I tell thee, unlesse thou be honest, I will flie.

People. Dog! dog! take a bone!

Diog. Thy father need feare no dogs, but dogs thy
father.

People. We will tell *Alexander*, that thou reprovest him behinde his back.

Diog. And I will tell him, that you flatter him before his face.

People. Wee will cause all the boyes in the streete to hisse at thee.

Diog. Indeede I thinke the Athenians have their children readie for any vice, because they bee Athenians.

Manes. Why master, meane you not to flie?

Diog. No, *Manes*, not without wings.

Manes. Every body will account you a lyar.

Diog. No, I warrant you; for I will alwayes say the Athenians are mischevous.

Psyllus. I care not, it was sport enough for mee to see these old huddles hit home.

Gran. Nor I.

Psyllus. Come, let us goe! and hereafter when I meane to rayle upon any body openly, it shall bee given out, I will flie.   [*Exeunt.*

ACTUS QUARTUS. SCÆNA SECUNDA.

CAMPASPE, APELLES.

Campaspe sola. Campaspe, it is hard to judge whether thy choyce be more unwise, or thy chance unfortunate. Doest thou preferre—but stay, utter not that in wordes, which maketh thine eares to glow with thoughts. Tush! better thy tongue wagge, than thy heart breake! Hath a painter crept further into thy minde than a prince? *Apelles*, than *Alexander?* Fond

wench! the basenes of thy minde bewraies the meannesse of thy birth.   But alas! affection is a fire, which
kindleth as well in the bramble as in the oake; and
catcheth hold where it first lighteth, not where it may
best burne.   Larkes that mount aloft in the ayre, build
their neasts below in the earth; and women that cast
their eyes upon kings, may place their hearts upon vas-
sals.   A needle will become thy fingers better than a
lute, and a distaffe is fitter for thy hand than a scepter.
Antes live safely, till they have gotten wings, and juniper is not blowne up till it hath gotten an high top.
The meane estate is without care as long as it continueth without pride.   But here commeth *Apelles*, in
whom I would there were the like affection.

Apel. Gentlewoman, the misfortune I had with your
picture, will put you to some paines to sit againe to be
painted.

Camp. It is small paines for mee to sit still, but
infinite for you to draw still.

Apel. No madame! to painte *Venus* was a pleasure,
but to shadow the sweete face of *Campaspe* it is a heaven!

Camp. If your tongue were made of the same flesh
that your heart is, your words would bee as your
thoughts are: but such a common thing it is amongst
you to commend, that oftentimes for fashion sake you
call them beautifull, whom you know blacke.

Apel. What might men doe to be beleeved?

Camp. Whet their tongue on their hearts.

Apel. So they doe, and speake as they thinke.

Camp. I would they did!

Apel. I would they did not!

Camp. Why, would you have them dissemble?

Apel. Not in love, but their love. But will you give mee leave to aske you a question without offence?

Camp. So that you will answere mee another without excuse.

Apel. Whom doe you love best in the world?

Camp. He that made me last in the world.

Apel. That was a god.

Camp. I had thought it had beene a man: But whom doe you honour most, *Apelles?*

Apel. The thing that is likest you, *Campaspe.*

Camp. My picture?

Apel. I dare not venture upon your person. But come, let us go in: for *Alexander* will thinke it long till we returne.   [*Exeunt.*

ACTUS QUARTUS. SCÆNA TERTIA.

CLYTUS, PARMENIO.

Clytus. We heare nothing of our embassage; a colour belike to bleare our eyes, or tickle our eares, or inflame our hearts. But what doth *Alexander* in the meane season; but use for tantara—sol, fa, la—for his hard couch, downe beds; for his handfull of water, his standing cup of wine?

Par. *Clytus,* I mislike this new delicacie and pleasing peace: for what else do we see now than a kind of softnes in every mans minde; bees to make their hives in souldiers helmets, our steeds furnished with footclothes of gold, insteede of sadles of steele: more time to be required to scowre the rust of our weapons, than there was wont to be in subduing the countries of our enemies. Sithence *Alexander* fell from his hard armour to his soft robes, behold the face of his court; youths that were wont to carry devises of victory in their shields, engrave now posies of love in their ringes: they that were accustomed on trotting horses to charge the enemie with a launce, now in easie coches ride up and down to court ladies; in steade of sword and target to hazard their lives, use pen and paper to paint their loves. Yea, such a feare and faintnesse is growne in court, that they wish rather to heare the blowing of a horne to hunt, than the sound of a trumpet to fight. O Philip, wert thou alive to see this alteration, thy men turned to women, thy souldiers to lovers, gloves worne in velvet caps, in stead of plumes in graven helmets, thou wouldest either dye among them for sorrow, or counfound them for anger.

Clytus. Cease *Parmenio*, least in speaking what becommeth thee not, thou feele what liketh thee not: truth is never without a scracht face, whose tongue although it cannot be cut out, yet must it be tied up.

Par. It grieveth me not a little for *Hephestion*, who thirsteth for honour not ease; but such is his fortune and neernesse in friendship to *Alexander*, that hee must lay a pillow under his head, when hee would put a target in his hand. But let us draw in, to see how well it becomes them to tread the measures in a daunce, that were wont to set the order for a march. [*Exeunt.*

ACTUS QUARTUS. SCÆNA QUARTA.

APELLES, CAMPASPE.

Apel. I have now, *Campaspe*, almost made an ende.

Camp. You told mee, *Apelles*, you would never end.

Apel. Never end my love: for it shal be eternall.

Camp. That is, neither to have beginning nor ending.

Apel. You are disposed to mistake, I hope you do not mistrust.

Camp. What will you say if *Alexander* perceive your love?

Apel. I will say it is no treason to love.

Camp. But how if hee will not suffer thee to see my person?

Apel. Then will I gaze continually on thy picture.

Camp. That will not feede thy heart.

Apel. Yet shall it fill mine eye: besides the sweet thoughts, the sure hopes, thy protested faith, wil cause me to embrace thy shadow continually in mine armes, of the which by strong imagination I will make a substance.

Camp. Wel, I must be gone: but this assure your selfe, that I had rather be in thy shop grinding colours, than in *Alexander's* court, following higher fortunes. [*Campaspe alone.*] Foolish wench, what hast thou done? that, alas! which cannot be undone, and therefore I feare me undone. But content is such a life, I care not for aboundance. O *Apelles*, thy love commeth from the heart, but *Alexander's* from the mouth. The

love of kings is like the blowing of winds, which whistle
sometimes gently among the leaves, and straight waies
turne the trees up by the rootes; or fire which warmeth
afarre off, and burneth neere hand; or the sea, which
maketh men hoise their sailes in a flattering calme, and
to cut their mastes in a rough storme. They place
affection by times, by policy, by appoyntment; if they
frowne, who dares call them unconstant? if bewray
secrets, who will tearme them untrue? if fall to other
loves, who trembles not, if hee call them unfaithfull?
In kings there can bee no love, but to queenes: for
as neere must they meete in majestie, as they doe in
affection. It is requisite to stand aloofe from kings
love, *Jove*, and lightening.   [*Exit.*

ACTUS QUARTUS. SCÆNA QUINTA.

APELLES, PAGE.

Apel. Now *Apelles* gather thy wits together: *Campaspe* is no lesse wise then faire, thy selfe must be no
lesse cunning then faithfull. It is no small matter to
be rivall with *Alexander.*

Page. *Apelles*, you must come away quickly with the
picture; the king thinketh that now you have painted
it, you play with it.

Apel. If I would play with pictures, I have enough
at home.

Page. None perhaps you like so well.

Apel. It may be I have painted none so well.

Page. I have knowen many fairer faces.

Apel. And I many better boyes.   [*Exeunt.*

ACTUS QUINTUS. SCÆNA PRIMA.

D<small>IOGENES</small>, S<small>YLVIUS</small>, P<small>ERIM</small>, M<small>ILO</small>, T<small>RICO</small>, M<small>ANES</small>.

Sylvius.

HAVE brought my sons, *Diogenes,* to be taught of thee.

Diog. What can thy sonnes do?

Syl. You shall see their qualities: Dance, sirha! [*Then Perim danceth.*] How like you this: doth he well?

Diog. The better, the worser.

Syl. The musicke very good.

Diog. The musitions very bad; who onely study to have their strings in tune, never framing their manners to order.

Syl. Now shall you see the other: tumble, sirha! [*Milo tumbleth.*] How like you this? why do you laugh?

Diog. To see a wagge that was borne to breake his neck by destinie, to practise it by art.

Milo. This dogge will bite me, I will not be with him.

Diog. Feare not boy, dogges eate no thistles.

Perim. I marvell what dogge thou art, if thou be a dogge.

Diog. When I am hungry, a mastife; and when my belly is full, a spannell.

Syl. Dost thou beleeve that there are any gods, that thou art so dogged?

Diog. I must needs beleeve there are gods: for I thinke thee an enemie to them.

Syl. Why so?

Diog. Because thou hast taught one of thy sonnes to rule his legges, and not to follow learning; the other to bend his bodie every way, and his minde no way.

Perim. Thou doest nothing but snarle, and barke like a dogge.

Diog. It is the next way to drive away a theefe.

Syl. Now shall you heare the third, who sings like a nightingale.

Diog. I care not: for I have a nightingale to sing her selfe.

Syl. Sing, sirha!

[*Trico singeth.*]

Song.

What bird so sings, yet so does wayle?
  O t'is the ravish'd nightingale.
Jug, jug, jug, jug, tereu, shee cryes,
And still her woes at midnight rise.
Brave prick song! who is't now we heare?
None but the larke so shrill and cleare;
How at heavens gates she claps her wings,
The morne not waking till shee sings.
Heark, heark, with what a pretty throat
Poore Robin red-breast tunes his note;
Heark how the jolly cuckoes sing
Cuckoe, to welcome in the spring;
Cuckoe, to welcome in the spring.

Syl. Loe *Diogenes!* I am sure thou canst not doe so much.

Diog. But there is never a thrush but can.

Syl. What hast thou taught *Manes* thy man?

Diog. To be as unlike as may be thy sons.

Manes. He hath taught me to fast, lie hard, and run away.

Syl. How sayest thou *Perim*, wilt thou bee with him?

Perim. I, so he will teach me first to runne away.

Diog. Thou needest not be taught, thy legges are so nimble.

Syl. How sayest thou *Milo*, wilt thou be with him?

Diog. Nay hold your peace, hee shall not.

Syl. Why?

Diog. There is not roome enough for him and me to tumble both in one tub.

Syl. Well *Diogenes*, I perceive my sonnes brooke not thy manners.

Diog. I thought no lesse, when they knew my vertues.

Syl. Farewell *Diogenes*, thou neededst not have scraped rootes, if thou would'st have followed *Alexander*.

Diog. Nor thou have followed *Alexander*, if thou hadst scraped rootes.   [*Exeunt.*

ACTUS QUINTUS. SCÆNA SECUNDA.

Apel. [*alone.*] I feare mee *Apelles*, that thine eyes have blabbed that which thy tongue durst not. What little regard hadst thou, whilest *Alexander* viewed the counterfeit of *Campaspe!* thou stoodest gazing on her countenance. If he espie or but suspect, thou must needs twice perish, with his hate, and thine owne love. Thy pale lookes, when he blushed; thy sad countenance, when he smiled; thy sighes, when he questioned; may breed in him a jelousie, perchance a frenzie. O love! I never before knew what thou wert, and now hast thou made me that I know not what my selfe am! onely this I know, that I must endure intolerable passions, for unknowne pleasures. Dispute not the cause, wretch, but yeeld to it: for better it is to melt with desire, than wrastle with love. Cast thy selfe on thy carefull bed, be content to live unknown, and die unfound. O *Campaspe*, I have painted thee in my heart: painted? nay, contrary to mine arte, imprinted; and that in such deepe characters, that nothing can rase it out, unlesse it rubbe my heart out.   [*Exit.*

ACTUS QUINTUS. SCÆNA TERTIA.

MILECTUS, PHRYGIUS, LAIS, DIOGENES.

Mil. It shall goe hard, but this peace shall bring us some pleasure.

Phry. Downe with armes, and up with legges, this is a world for the nonce.

Lais. Sweet youths, if you knew what it were to save your sweet blood, you would not so foolishly go about to spend it. What delight can there be in gashing, to make foule scarres in faire faces, and crooked maimes in streight legges? as though men being borne goodly by nature, would of purpose become deformed by folly; and all forsooth for a new found tearme, called *valiant*, a word which breedeth more quarrels than the sense can commendation.

Mil. It is true Lais, a feather-bed hath no fellow,

good drinke makes good blood, and shall pelting words spill it?

Phry. I meane to enjoy the world, and to draw out my life at the wire-drawers, not to curtall it off at the cutlers.

Lais. You may talke of warre, speake bigge, con-quer worlds with great words: but stay at home, where in steade of alarums you shall have dances; for hot battailes with fierce men, gentle skirmishes with faire women. These pewter coates can never sit so well as satten doublets. Beleeve me, you cannot conceive the pleasure of peace, unlesse you despise the rudenes of warre.

Mil. It is so. But see *Diogenes* prying over his tub: *Diogenes* what sayest thou to such a morsell?

Diog. I say, I would spit it out of my mouth, because it should not poyson my stomacke.

Phry. Thou speakest as thou art, it is noe meate for dogges.

Diog. I am a dogge, and philosophy rates me from carrion.

Lais. Uncivil wretch, whose maners are answerable to thy calling; the time was thou wouldest have had my company, had it not beene, as thou saidst, too deare.

Diog. I remember there was a thing that I repented mee of, and now thou hast tolde it; indeed it was too deare of nothing, and thou deare to no bodie.

Lais. Downe, villaine! or I will have thy head broken.

Mil. Will you couch?

Phry. Avant, curre! Come sweet *Lais*, let us goe to some place, and possesse peace. But first let us sing, there is more pleasure in tuning of a voyce, than in a volly of shot.

Mil. Now let us make hast, least *Alexander* finde us here.   [*Exeunt.*

ACTUS QUINTUS. SCÆNA QUARTA.

ALEXANDER, HEPHESTION, PAGE, DIOGENES, APELLES, CAMPASPE.

Alex. Me thinketh, *Hephestion*, you are more melancholy than you were accustomed; but I perceive it is all for *Alexander*. You can neither brooke this peace, nor my pleasure; bee of good cheare, though I winke, I sleepe not.

Hep. Melancholy I am not, nor well content: for I know not how, there is such a rust crept into my bones with this long ease, that I feare I shall not scowre it out with infinite labours.

Alex. Yes, yes, if all the travailes of conquering the world will set either thy bodie or mine in tune, we will undertake them. But what thinke you of *Apelles*? Did yee ever see any so perplexed? Hee neither answered directly to any question, nor looked stedfastly upon any thing. I hold my life the painter is in love.

Hep. It may be: for commonly we see it incident in artificers to be enamoured of their owne workes, as *Archidamus* of his wooden dove, *Pygmalion* of his ivorie image, *Arachne* of his wooden swanne; especially painters, who playing with their owne conceits, now coveting to draw a glancing eie, then a rolling, now a winking, still mending it, never ending it, till they be caught with it; and then poore soules they kisse the colours with their lips, with which before they were loth to taint their fingers.

Alex. I will find it out.   Page goe speedily for *Apelles*, will him to come hither, and when you see us earnestly in talke, sodainly crie out, *Apelles shop is on fire!*

Page. It shall be done.

Alex. Forget not your lesson.

Hep. I marvell what your devise shal be.

Alex. The event shall prove.

Hep. I pittie the poore painter if he be in love.

Alex. Pitie him not, I pray thee; that severe gravity set aside, what doe you thinke of love?

Hep. As the *Macedonians* doe of their hearbe *beet*, which looking yellow in the ground, and blacke in the hand, thinke it better seene than toucht.

Alex. But what doe you imagine it to be?

Hep. A word by superstition thought a god, by use turned to an humour, by selfe-will made a flattering madnesse.

Alex. You are too hard hearted to thinke so of love. Let us goe to *Diogenes*.   *Diogenes*, thou may'st thinke it somewhat that *Alexander* commeth to thee againe so soone.

Diog. If you come to learne, you could not come soone enough; if to laugh, you be come too soone.

Hep. It would better become thee to be more courteous, and frame thy self to please.

Diog. And you better to bee lesse, if you durst displease.

Alex. What doest thou thinke of the time we have here?

Diog. That we have little, and lose much.

Alex. If one be sicke what wouldst thou have him doe?

Diog. Bee sure that hee make not his physician his heire.

Alex. If thou mightest have thy will how much ground would content thee?

Diog. As much as you in the end must be contented withall.

Alex. What, a world?

Diog. No, the length of my bodie.

Alex. *Hephestion,* shall I bee a little pleasant with him?

Hep. You may: but hee will be very perverse with you.

Alex. It skils not, I cannot be angry with him. *Diogenes,* I pray thee what doest thou thinke of love?

Diog. A little worser than I can of hate.

Alex. And why?

Diog. Because it is better to hate the things which make to love, than to love the things which give occasion of hate.

Alex. Why, bee not women the best creatures in the world?

Diog. Next men and bees.

Alex. What doest thou dislike chiefly in a woman?

Diog. One thing.

Alex. What?

Diog. That she is a woman.

VOL. I.   L

Alex. In mine opinion thou wert never borne of a woman, that thou thinkest so hardly of women; but now commeth *Apelles*, who I am sure is as farre from thy thoughts, as thou art from his cunning. *Diogenes*, I will have thy cabin removed neerer to my court, because I will be a philosopher.

Diog. And when you have done so, I pray you remove your court further from my cabin, because I will not be a courtier.

Alex. But here commeth *Apelles*. *Apelles*, what peece of work have you now in hand?

Apel. None in hand, if it like your majestie: but I am devising a platforme in my head.

Alex. I thinke your hand put it in your head. Is it nothing about *Venus*?

Apel. No, but some thing above *Venus*.

Page. *Apelles*, *Apelles*, looke aboute you, your shop is on fire!

Apel. Aye mee! if the picture of *Campaspe* be burnt, I am undone!

Alex. Stay *Apelles*, no haste; it is your heart is on fire, not your shop; and if *Campaspe* hang there, I would shee were burnt. But have you the picture of *Campaspe?* Belike you love her well, that you care not though all be lost, so she be safe.

Apel. Not love her: but your majestie knowes that painters in their last workes are said to excell themselves, and in this I have so much pleased my selfe, that the shadow as much delighteth mee being an artificer, as the substance doth others that are amorous.

Alex. You lay your colours grosly; though I could

not paint in your shop, I can spie into your excuse. Be not ashamed *Apelles*, it is a gentleman's sport to be in love. Call hither *Campaspe*. Methinkes I might have beene made privie to your affection; though my counsell had not bin necessary, yet my countenance might have beene thought requisite. But *Apelles*, forsooth, loveth under hand, yea and under *Alexanders* nose, and—but I say no more.

Apel. *Apelles* loveth not so: but hee liveth to doe as *Alexander* will.

Alex. *Campaspe*, here is newes. *Apelles* is in love with you.

Camp. It pleaseth your majestie to say so.

Alex. *Hephestion*, I will trie her too. *Campaspe*, for the good qualities I know in *Apelles*, and the vertue I see in you, I am determined you shall enjoy one another. How say you *Campaspe*, would you say I?

Camp. Your hand-maid must obey, if you command.

Alex. Thinke you not *Hephestion*, that shee would faine be commanded?

Hep. I am no thought-catcher, but I ghesse unhappily.

Alex. I will not enforce marriage, where I cannot compell love.

Camp. But your majestie may move a question, where you be willing to have a match.

Alex. Beleeve me, *Hephestion*, these parties are agreed, they would have mee both priest and witnesse. *Apelles*, take *Campaspe*; why move yee not? *Campaspe*, take *Apelles*; will it not be? If you be ashamed one of the other, by my consent you shall never come

together.   But dissemble not *Campaspe*, doe you love
Apelles?

Camp. Pardon my lord, I love *Apelles!*

Alex. Apelles, it were a shame for you, being loved
so openly of so faire a virgin, to say the contrarie. Doe
you love *Campaspe?*

Apel. Onely *Campaspe!*

Alex. Two loving wormes, *Hephestion!* I perceive
Alexander cannot subdue the affections of men, though
he conquer their countries.   Love falleth like a dew
as well upon the low grasse, as upon the high cedar.
Sparkes have their heate, ants their gall, flies their
spleene.   Well, enjoy one another, I give her thee
frankly, *Apelles*. Thou shalt see that *Alexander* maketh
but a toy of love, and leadeth affection in fetters; using
fancie as a foole to make him sport, or a minstrell to
make him merry.   It is not the amorous glance of an
eye can settle an idle thought in the heart; no, no, it
is childrens game, a life for seamsters and schollers;
the one pricking in clouts have nothing else to thinke
on; the other picking fancies out of books, have little
else to marvaile at.   Go *Apelles*, take with you your
Campaspe, Alexander is cloyed with looking on that
which thou wond'rest at.

Apel. Thankes to your majestie on bended knee, you
have honoured *Apelles*.

Camp. Thankes with bowed heart, you have blessed
Campaspe.   [*Exeunt.*

Alex. Page, goe warne *Clytus* and *Parmenio* and the
other lords to be in a readinesse, let the trumpet sound,
trike up the drumme, and I will presently into *Persia.*

How now *Hephestion,* is *Alexander* able to resist love as he list?

Hep. The conquering of *Thebes* was not so honourable as the subduing of these thoughts.

Alex. It were a shame *Alexander* should desire to command the world, if he could not command himselfe. But come let us goe, I will trie whether I can better beare my hand with my heart, than I could with mine eye. And good *Hephestion,* when all the world is wonne, and every country is thine and mine, either find me out another to subdue, or on my word I will fall in love.   [*Exeunt.*

THE EPILOGUE AT THE BLACKE
FRIERS.

WHERE the rain-bow toucheth the tree, no caterpillars will hang on the leaves: where the gloworme creepeth in the night, no adder will goe in the day. Wee hope in the eares where our travailes be lodged, no carping shall harbour in those tongues. Our exercises, must be as your judgement is, resembling water, which is alwayes of the same colour into what it runneth. In the *Troyan* horse lay couched souldiers, with children; and in heapes of many words we feare divers unfit, among some allowable. But as *Demosthenes* with often breathing up the hill amended his stammering; so wee hope with sundrie labours against the haire, to correct our studies. If the tree be blasted that blossomes, the fault is in the winde, and not in the root; and if our pastimes bee misliked, that have beene allowed, you must impute it to the malice of others, and not our endevour. And so we rest in good case, if you rest well content.

THE EPILOGUE AT THE COURT.

WE cannot tell whether wee are fallen among *Diomedes* birdes or his horses; the one received some men with sweet notes, the other bit all men with sharpe teeth. But as *Homer's* gods conveyed them into cloudes, whom they would have kept from curses; and as *Venus*, least *Adonis* should be pricked with the stings of adders, covered his face with the wings of swans: so wee hope, being shielded with your Highnesse countenance, wee shall, though wee heare the neighing, yet not feele the kicking of those jades; and receive, though no prayse (which wee cannot deserve) yet a pardon, which in all humilitie we desire. As yet we cannot tell what we should tearme our labours, iron or bullion; only it belongeth to your Majestie to make them fit either for the forge, or the mynt; currant by the stampe, or counterfeit by the anvill. For as nothing is to be called white, unlesse it had beene named white by the first creator, so can there be nothing thought good in the opinion of others, unlesse it be christened good by the judgement of your selfe. For our selves againe, we are like these torches of waxe, of which being in your Highnesse hands, you may make doves or vultures, roses or nettles, laurell for a garland, or ealder for a disgrace.

SAPHO AND PHAO.

PLAYED BEFORE THE QUEENES MAJESTIE ON SHROVE
TUESDAY: BY HER MAJESTIES CHILDREN,
AND THE CHILDREN OF PAULES.

DRAMATIS PERSONÆ.

VULCAN.
CUPID.
PHAO, *a young Ferryman.*
TRACHINUS, *a Courtier.*
PANDION, *a Scholar.*
CRYTICUS, *Page to Trachinus.*
MOLUS, *Servant to Pandion.*
CALYPHO, *one of the Cyclops.*

VENUS.
SAPHO, *Princess of Syracuse.*
MILETA,
LAMIA,
FAVILLA,
ISMENA, } *Ladies of Sapho's Court.*
CANOPE,
EUGENUA,
SYBILLA, *an aged Soothsayer.*

SCENE—*Syracuse.*

THE PROLOGUE AT THE BLACKE
FRIERS.

WHERE the bee can sucke no honey, shee leaveth her sting behind; and where the beare cannot finde *Origanum* to heale his griefe, hee blasteth all other leaves with his breath. Wee feare it is like to fare so with us, that seeing you cannot draw from our labours sweet content, you leave behinde you a sowre mislike: and with open reproach blame our good meanings because you cannot reape your wonted mirths. Our intent was at this time to move inward delight, not outward lightnesse; and to breed (if it might be) soft smiling, not loud laughing: knowing it to the wise to be as great pleasure to heare counsell mixed with wit, as to the foolish to have sport mingled with rudenesse. They were banished the theater of *Athens*, and from *Rome* hissed, that brought parasites on the stage with apish actions, or fooles with uncivill habits, or curtizans with immodest words. We have endevoured to be as farre from unseemely speeches, to make your eares glow, as we hope you will be free from unkind reports to make our cheekes blush. The gryffon never spreadeth her wings in the sunne, when she hath any sicke feathers: yet have we ventured to present our exercise before your judgments, when we know them full of weake matter; yeelding rather our selves to the curtesie, which wee have ever found, than to the precisenesse, which we ought to feare.

THE PROLOGUE AT THE COURT.

THE *Arabians* being stuffed with perfumes, burn hemlocke, a ranke poyson: and in *Hybla* being cloid with honie, they account it daintie to feed on wax. Your Highnesse eyes whom variety hath fild with faire showes, and whose eares pleasure hath possessed with rare sounds; will (we trust) at this time resemble the princely eagle, who fearing to surfet on spices, stoopeth to bite on worme-wood. Wee present no conceits nor wars, but deceits and loves, wherein the truth may excuse the plainenesse: the necessitie, the length: the poetry, the bitternesse. There is no needles point so small, which hath not his compasse: nor haire so slender, that hath not his shadow: nor sport so simple, which hath not his shew. Whatsoever we present, whether it be tedious (which wee feare) or toyish (which we doubt) sweet or sowre, absolute or imperfect, or whatsoever: in all humblenesse we all, and I on knee for all, intreat, that your Highnesse imagine your selfe to be in a deepe dreame, that staying the conclusion, in your rising your Majesty vouchsafe but to say, *and so you awakt.*

SAPHO AND PHAO.

ACTUS PRIMUS. SCÆNA PRIMA.

PHAO, VENUS, CUPID.

Phao.

THOU art a ferriman, *Phao*, yet a freeman; possessing for riches content, and for honours quiet. Thy thoughts are no higher than thy fortunes, nor thy desires greater than thy calling. Who climbeth, standeth on glasse, and falleth on thorne. Thy hearts thirst is satisfied with thy hands thrift, and thy gentle labours in the day, turne to sweete slumbers in the night. As much doth it delight thee to rule thine oare in a calme streame, as it doth *Sapho* to sway the scepter in her brave court. Envie never casteth her eye low, ambition pointeth alwayes upward, and revenge barketh only at starres. Thou farest delicately, if thou have a fare to buy anything. Thine angle is readie, when thine oare is idle; and as sweet is the fish which thou gettest in the river, as the foule which other buy in the market; thou needest not feare poyson in thy glasse, nor treason in thy gard. The wind is thy greatest enemy, whose might is withstood with pollicie. O sweet life, seldome found under a golden covert, often under a thatched cottage. But here commeth one, I will withdraw myselfe aside, it may be a passenger.

Venus. It is no lesse unseemely than unwholsome for *Venus*, who is most honoured in princes courts, to sojourne with *Vulcan* in a smiths forge ; where bellowes blow in steed of sighes, darke smoakes rise for sweete perfumes, and for the panting of loving hearts, is onely heard the beating of steeled hammers. Unhappy *Venus*, that carrying fire in thine owne brest, thou shouldest dwell with fire in his forge. What doth *Vulcan* al day but endevour to be as crabbed in manners, as hee is crooked in body ? driving nailes, when he should give kisses, and hammering hard armours, when he should sing sweet amours. It came by lot, and not love, that I was linked with him. Hee gives thee bolts, *Cupid*, in steed of arrowes, fearing belike (jealous foole that he is) that if he should give thee an arrow head, hee should make himselfe a broad head. But come, wee will to *Syracusa*, where thy deitie shall be showne, and my dis-daine. I will yoke the necke, that yet never bowed, at which, if *Jove* repine, *Jove* shall repent. *Sapho* shall know, be shee never so faire, that there is a *Venus*, which can conquer, were shee never so fortunate.

Cupid. If *Jove* espie *Sapho*, hee will devise some new shape to entertaine her.

Venus. Strike thou *Sapho*, let *Jove* devise what shape he can.

Cupid. Mother, they say she hath her thoughts in a string ; that she conquers affections, and sendeth love

up and downe upon errands; I am afraid she will yerke
me, if I hit her.

Venus. Peevish boy, can mortall creatures resist that,
which the immortall gods cannot redresse?

Cupid. The gods are amorous: and therefore willing to be pierced.

Venus. And shee amiable, and therefore must be
pierced.

Cupid. I dare not!

Venus. Draw thine arrow to the head, else I wil
make thee repent it at the heart! Come away, and behold the ferry boy readie to conduct us. Pretie youth,
doe you keepe the ferry that bendeth to *Syracusa?*

Phao. The ferry, faire ladie, that bendeth to *Syracusa.*

Venus. I feare, if the water should begin to swell,
thou wilt want cunning to guide.

Phao. These waters are commonly as the passengers
be; and therefore carrying one so faire in shew, there
is no cause to feare a rough sea.

Venus. To passe the time in thy boate, canst thou
devise any pastime?

Phao. If the winde be with mee, I can angle, or tell
tales: if against mee, it will be pleasure for you to see
me take paines.

Venus. I like not fishing: yet was I borne of the sea.

Phao. But he may blesse fishing, that caught such
an one in the sea.

Venus. It was not with an angle, my boye, but with
a nette.

Phao. So was it said, that *Vulcan* caught *Mars* with
Venus.

Venus. Didst thou heare so? It was some tale.

Phao. Yea madam, and that in the boate I did meane to make my tale.

Venus. It is not for a ferrie man to talke of the gods loves: but to tell how thy father could dig, and thy mother spinne. But come, let us away.

Phao. I am readie to waite.   [*Exeunt.*

ACTUS PRIMUS. SCÆNA SECUNDA.

Trachinus, Pandion, Cryticus, Molus.

Trachi. *Pandion,* since your comming from the universitie to the court, from *Athens* to *Syracusa,* how doe you feele yourselfe altered either in humor or opinion?

Pandi. Altered *Trachinus,* I say no more, and shame that any should know much.

Trachi. Here you see as great vertue, far greater braverie, the action of that which you contemplate. *Sapho* faire by nature, by birth royall, learned by education, by government politicke, rich by peace: insomuch as it is hard to judge, whether shee bee more beautifull or wise, vertuous or fortunate. Besides, doe you not looke on faire ladies instead of good letters, and behold faire faces instead of fine phrases? In universities vertues and vices are but shadowed in colours, white and blacke; in courts shewed to life, good and bad. There times past are read of in old books, times present set downe by new devises, times to come conjectured at by aime, by prophesie, or chance: here are times in perfection; not by devise, as fables; but in execution, as truths. Beleeve me *Pandion,* in *Athens* you have but tombs, we in court the bodies ; you the pictures of *Venus* and the wise goddesses, wee the persons and the vertues. What hath a scholler found out by study, that a courtier hath not found out by practise. Simple are you that thinke to see more at the candle snuffe than the sunne beames; to saile further in a little brooke, than in the maine ocean; to make a greater harvest by gleaning than reaping. How say you, *Pandion*, is not all this true ?

Pandi. *Trachinus*, what would you more, all true.

Trachi. Cease then to lead thy life in a studie pinned with a few boards, and endeavour to be a courtier to live in emboste roofes.

Pandi. A labour intolerable for *Pandion.*

Trachi. Why?

Pandi. Because it is harder to shape a life to dissemble, than to goe forward with the libertie of truth.

Trachi. Why, doe you thinke in court any use to dissemble ?

Pandi. Doe you know in court any that meane to live ?

Trachi. You have no reason for it, but an old report.

Pandi. Report hath not alwaies a blister on her tongue.

Trachi. I, but this is the court of *Sapho*, natures miracle, which resembleth the tree *Salurus*, whose roote is fastned upon knotted steel, and in whose top bud leaves of pure gold.

Pandi. Yet hath *Salurus* blasts and water boughes, wormes and caterpillers.

Trachi. The vertue of the tree is not the cause, but

the easterly wind; which is thought commonly to bring cankers and rottennesse.

Pandi. Nor the excellencie of *Sapho* the occasion, but the iniquitie of flatterers; who alwayes whisper in princes eares suspition and sowrenesse.

Trachi. Why, then you conclude with mee, that *Sapho* for vertue hath no co-partner.

Pandi. Yea, and with the judgement of the world, that shee is without comparison.

Trachi. We will thither straight.

Pandi. I would I might returne streight.

Trachi. Why, there you may live still.

Pandi. But not still.

Trachi. How like you the ladies, are they not passing faire?

Pandi. Mine eye drinketh neither the colour of wine nor women.

Trachi. Yet am I sure that in judgement you are not so severe, but that you can be content to allow of beauty by day or by night.

Pandi. When I behold beautie before the sunne, his beames dimme beauty: when by candle, beauty obscures torch light; so as no time I can judge, because at any time I cannot discerne; being in the sunne a brightnes to shadow beauty, and in beauty a glistering to extinguish light.

Trachi. Schollerlike said; you flatter that, which you seeme to mislike; and seek to disgrace that, which you most wonder at. But let us away.

Pandi. I follow. And you sir boye, go to *Syracusa* about by land, where you shall meete my stuffe; pay for the cariage, and convay it to my lodging.

Trachi. I thinke all your stuffe are bundles of paper,
but now must you learne to turne your library to a
wardrope, and see whether your rapier hang better by
your side, than the penne did in your eare.	[*Exeunt.*

ACTUS PRIMUS. SCÆNA TERTIA.

CRYTICUS, MOLUS.

Cryti. *Molus,* what oddes betweene thy commons in
Athens and thy diet in court? a pages life and a schollers?

Molus. This difference; there of a little I had somewhat, here of a great deale nothing; there I did weare
pantophles on my leggs, here doe I beare them in my
hands.

Cryti. Thou maist bee skilled in thy logick, but not
in thy lerypoope: belike no meate can downe with you,
unlesse you have a knife to cut it: but come among us,
and you shall see us once in a morning have a mouse
at a bay.

Molus. A mouse? unproperly spoken.

Cryti. Aptly understoode, a mouse of beefe.

Molus. I thinke, indeed, a peece of beefe as big as a
mouse, serves a great company of such cattes. But
what else?

Cryti. For other sports, a square die in a pages pocket,
is as decent as a square cap on a graduates head.

Molus. You courtiers be mad fellowes! we silly soules
are only plodders at *Ergo,* whose witts are claspt up with
our bookes; and so full of learning are wee at home,
that wee scarse know good manners when we come
abroad. Cunning in nothing but in making sm-

great by figures, pulling on with the sweate of our
studies a great shooe upon a little foote; burning out
one candle in seeking for another; raw worldlings in
matters of substance, passing wranglers about shadowes.

Cryti. Then is it time lost to bee a scholler.   Wee
pages are Politians, for looke what wee heare our masters talke of, we determine of, and where we suspect,
we undermine: and where we mislike for some particular grudge, there wee picke quarrels for a generall
griefe.   Nothing among us but instead of good morrow,
what newes? we fall from cogging at dice, to cogge
with states: and so forward are meane men in those
matters, that they would be cocks to tread downe others,
before they be chickens to rise themselves.   Youths are
verie forward to stroake their chinnes, though they have
no beards, and to lie as loud as he that hath lived longest.

Molus. These be the golden dayes!

Cryti. Then be they very darke dayes: for I can see
no gold.

Molus. You are grosse witted, master courtier.

Cryti. And you master scholler slender witted.

Molus. I meant times which were prophesied golden
for plentie of all things, sharpnesse of wit, excellencie
in knowledge, pollicie in government, for—

Cryti. Soft *Scholaris*, I denie your argument.

Molus. Why, it is no argument.

Cryti. Then I denie it, because it is no argument.
But let us goe and follow our masters.   [*Exeunt.*

ACTUS PRIMUS. SCÆNA QUARTA.

MILETA, LAMIA, FAVILLA, ISMENA, CANOPE,
EUGENUA.

Mileta. Is it not strange that Phao on the sodaine should be so faire?

Lamia. It cannot be strange sith Venus was disposed to make him faire. That cunning had beene better bestowed on women, which would have deserved thanks of nature.

Isme. Haply she did it in spite of women, or scorne of nature.

Canope. Proud elfe! how squeamish hee is become already; using both disdainefull lookes, and imperious words; insomuch that hee galleth with ingratitude. And then ladies, you know how it cutteth a woman to become a wooer.

Euge. Tush! children and fooles, the fairer they are, the sooner they yeeld; an apple will catch the one; a baby the other.

Isme. Your lover I thinke bee a faire foole: for you love nothing but fruit and puppets.

Mileta. I laugh at that you all call love, and judge it onely a word called love. Methinks liking, a curtesie, a smile, a becke, and such like, are the very quintessence of love.

Favilla. I, Mileta, but were you as wise as you would bee thought faire; or as faire, as you thinke yourselfe wise; you would bee as ready to please men, as you are coy to pranke yourselfe; and as carefull to to be accounted amorous, as you are willing to be thought discreete.

Mileta. No, no, men are good soules (poore soules) who never enquire but with their eyes, loving to father the cradle, though they but mother the childe. Give mee their gifts, not their vertues; a graine of their golde weigheth downe a pound of their witte; a dramme of *give mee*, is heavier than an ounce of *heare mee*. Beleeve mee ladies, *give* is a pretie thing.

Isme. I cannot but oftentimes smile to myselfe to heare men call us weake vessels, when they prove themselves broken hearted; us fraile, when their thoughts cannot hang together; studying with words to flatter, and with bribes to allure; when wee commonly wish their tongues in their purses, they speake so simplie; and their offers in their bellies, they doe it so peevishly.

Mileta. It is good sport to see them want matter: for then fall they to good maners, having nothing in their mouthes but *sweet mistres*, wearing our hands out with courtly kissings, when their wits faile in courtly discourses. Now rufling their haires, now setting their ruffes; then gazing with their eyes, then sighing with a privie wring by the hand; thinking us like to bee wooed by signes and ceremonies.

Euge. Yet wee, when we sweare with our mouthes we are not in love; then we sigh from the heart, and pine in love.

Canope. Wee are mad wenches, if men marke our words: for when I say, I would none cared for love more than I, what meane I, but I would none loved but I; where we cry *away*, doe wee not presently say, *go to :* and when men strive for kisses, wee exclaime, *let us alone,* as though we would fall to that ourselves.

Favilla. Nay, then *Canope,* it is time to goe,—and behold *Phao !*

Isme. Where ?

Favilla. In your head *Ismena,* nowhere else : but let us keepe on our way.

Isme. Wisely.   [*Exeunt.*

ACTUS SECUNDUS. SCÆNA PRIMA.

PHAO, SYBILLA.

Phao.

PHAO, thy meane fortune causeth thee to use an oare, and thy sodaine beautie a glasse : by the one is seene thy neede, in the other thy pride.   O *Venus !* in thinking thou hast blest me, thou hast curst me ; adding to a poore estate, a proud heart ; and to a disdained man, a disdaining mind. Thou dost not flatter thyselfe *Phao,* thou art faire : faire ? I feare mee faire bee a word too foule for a face so passing faire.   But what availeth beauty ? hadst thou all things thou wouldest wish, thou mightst die to morrow ; and didst thou want all things thou desirest, thou shalt live till thou diest.   Tush ! *Phao,* there is growne more pride in thy minde, than favour in thy face.   Blush foolish boy, to thinke on thine owne thoughts ; cease complaints, and crave counsell.   And loe ! behold *Sybilla,* in the mouth of her cave ; I will salute her.   Ladie, I feare me I am out of my way, and so benighted withall, that I am compelled to aske your direction.

Sybi. Faire youth, if you will be advised by me, you
shall for this time seeke none other inne, than my cave:
for that it is no lesse perilous to travaile by night, than
uncomfortable.

Phao. Your courtesie offred, hath prevented what my
necessitie was to intreate.

Sybi. Come neere, take a stoole, and sit downe.
Now for that these winter nights are long, and that
children delight in nothing more than to heare old wives
tales, wee will beguile the time with some storie. And
though you behold wrinckles and furrows in my tawnie
face, yet may you happily finde wisdome and counsell
in my white haires.

Phao. Lady, nothing can content me better than a
tale, neither is there anything more necessary for me
than counsell.

Sybi. Were you borne so faire by nature.

Phao. No, made so faire by *Venus.*

Sybi. For what cause?

Phao. I feare me for some curse.

Sybi. Why, doe you love, and cannot obtaine?

Phao. No, I may obtaine, but cannot love.

Sybi. Take heed of that my childe!

Phao. I cannot chuse, good madame.

Sybi. Then hearken to my tale, which I hope shal
be as a streight thread to lead you out of those crooked
conceits, and place you in the plaine path of love.

Phao. I attend.

Sybi. When I was young, as you now are, I speake
it without boasting, I was as beautifull: for *Phœbus* in
his godhead sought to get my maidenhead: but I fonde

wench, receiving a benefit from above, began to waxe squemish beneath; not unlike to *Asolis*, which being made greene by heavenly drops, shrinketh into the ground when there fall showers: or the *Syrian* mudde, which being made white chalke by the sunne, never ceaseth rolling, till it lie in the shadow. Hee to sweete prayers added great promises; I, either desirous to make triall of his power, or willing to prolong mine owne life; caught up my handfull of sand, consenting to his sute, if I might live as many yeares as there were graines. *Phœbus* (for what cannot the gods doe, and what for love will they not do) granted my petition. And then, I sigh and blush to tell the rest, I recalled my promise.

Phao. Was not the god angrie to see you so unkind?

Sybi. Angrie my boy, which was the cause that I was unfortunate.

Phao. What revenge for such rigor used the gods?

Sybi. None, but suffring us to live, and know we are no gods.

Phao. I pray tell on.

Sybi. I will. Having received long life by *Phœbus*, and rare beauty by nature, I thought all the yeare would have beene May; that fresh colours would alwaies continue, that time and fortune could not weare out, what gods and nature had wrought up: not once imagining that white and red should returne to blacke and yellow; juniper, the longer it grew, the crookeder it wexed; or that in a face without blemish, there should come wrinkles without number. I did as you doe, goe with my glasse, ravished with the pride of mine ow￼￼ ￼￼tie; and you shall doe, as I doe, loath to see ￼￼ ￼￼

daining deformitie.   There was none that heard of **my**
fault, but shunned my favour; insomuch as I **stooped**
for age before I tasted of youth; sure to be long li**ved,**
uncertaine to be beloved.   Gentlemen that used to **sigh**
from their hearts for my sweet love, began to point **with**
their fingers at my withered face; and laughed to **see**
the eyes, out of which fire seemed to sparkle, to be **suc-**
coured being old with spectacles.   This causeth me **to**
withdraw myselfe to a solitarie cave, where I must **lead**
six hundred yeares in no lesse pensiveness of **crabbed**
age, than griefe of remembred youth.   Only this **com-**
fort, that being ceased to be faire, I studie to be wise ;
wishing to be thoght a grave matron, since I cannot **re-**
turne to be a yong maid.

Phao.   Is it not possible to die before you become *so*
old ?

Sybi.   No more possible than to return as you **are,**
to be so young.

Phao.   Could not you settle your fancie upon **any, or**
would not destinie suffer it ?

Sybi.   Women willingly ascribe that to fortune, **which**
wittingly was committed by frowardnesse.

Phao.   What will you have me doe ?

Sybi.   Take heed you doe not as I did.   Make **not**
too much of fading beautie, which is faire in the **cradle,**
and foule in the grave ; resembling *Polyon*, whose **leaves**
are white in the morning, and blue before night ; or
Anyta, which being a sweet flowre at the rising of **the**
sun, becommeth a weede, if it be not pluckt before **the**
setting.   Faire faces have no fruites, if they have no
witnesses.   When you shall behold over this tender

flesh a tough skinne; your eyes which were wont to glance at others faces, to be sunke so hollow that you can scarce look out of your owne head; and when all your teeth shall wagge as fast as your tongue; then will you repent the time which you cannot recall, and bee enforced to beare what most you blame. Loose not the pleasant time of your youth, than the which there is nothing swifter, nothing sweeter. Beautie is a slipperie good, which decreaseth whilest it is increasing; resembling the medlar, which in the moment of his full ripenes, is knowen to be in a rottennesse. Whiles you looke in the glasse it waxeth old with time; if on the sun, parcht with heate; if on the winde, blasted with colde. A great care to keepe it, a short space to enjoy it, a sodaine time to loose it. Bee not coy when you are courted; Fortunes wings are made of Time's feathers, which stay not whilest one may measure them. Be affable and curteous in youth, that you may be honoured in age. Roses that lose their colours, keepe their savours; and pluckt from the stalke, are put to the stil. *Cotonea* because it boweth when the sun riseth, is sweetest, when it is oldest: and children, which in their tender yeares sow curtesie, shall in their declining states reap pitie. Bee not proud of beauties painting, whose colours consume themselves, because they are beauties painting.

Phao. I am driven by your counsell into divers conceipts, neither knowing how to stand, or where to fall: but to yeeld to love is the onely thing I hate.

Sybi. I commit you to fortune, who is like to play such prankes with you, as your tender yeares can scarse

beare, nor your greene wits understand. But repaire
unto mee often, and if I cannot remove the effects, yet
will I manifest the causes.

Phao. I goe readie to returne for advice, before I am
resolved to adventure.

Sybi. Yet hearken to my words, thou shalt get
friendship by dissembling, love by hatred ; unlesse thou
perish, thou shalt perish ; in digging for a stone, thou
shalt reach a starre ; thou shalt be hated most, because
thou art loved most : thy death shal be feared and
wished. So much for prophecie, which nothing can
prevent : and this for counsell, which thou maist follow.
Keepe not company with antes that have winges, nor
talke with any neere the hille of a mowle ; where thou
smellest the sweetnes of serpents breath, beware thou
touch no part of the body. Be not merry among those
that put buglosse in their wine, and suger in thine. If
any talke of the eclipse of the sun, say thou never sawest it. Nourish no conies in thy vaults, nor swallows
in thine eves. Sow. next thy vines *Mandrage,* and ever
keepe thine eares open, and thy mouth shut, thine eyes
upward, and thy fingers downe : so shalt thou doe better
than otherwise, though never so well as I wish.

Phao. Alas ! madame, your prophecie threateneth
miseries, and your counsell warneth impossibilities.

Sybi. Farewell I can answer no more. [*Exit.*

ACTUS SECUNDUS. SCÆNA SECUNDA.

PHAO, SAPHO, TRACHINUS, PANDION,
CRYTICUS, MOLUS.

Phao. Unhappy *Phao!*—But soft, what gallant troupe is this? what gentlewoman is this?

Cryti. Sapho, a ladie here in *Sicily.*

Sapho. What faire boy is that?

Trachi. Phao, the ferriman of *Syracusa.*

Phao. I never saw one more brave: be all ladies of such majestie?

Cryti. No, this is shee that all wonder at and worship.

Sapho. I have seldome seene a sweeter face; be all ferrimen of that fairnesse?

Trachi. No, madam, this is he that *Venus* determined among men to make the fairest.

Sapho. Seeing I am only come forth to take the ayre, I will crosse the ferrie, and so the fields, then going in thorough the parke, I thinke the walke wil be pleasant.

Trachi. You will much delight in the flattering greene, which now beginneth to be in his glorie.

Sapho. Sir boy, will yee undertake to carie us over the water? Are you dumb, can you not speake?

Phao. Madame, I crave pardon, I am spurblind, I could scarce see.

Sapho. It is pittie in so good a face there should be an evill eye.

Phao. I would in my face there were never an eye.

Sapho. Thou canst never bee rich in a trade of life of all the basest.

Phao. Yet content madame, which is a kinde of life of all the best.

Sapho. Wilt thou forsake thy ferrie, and follow the court as a page?

Phao. As it pleaseth fortune madame, to whom I am a prentice.

Sapho. Come, let us goe.

Trachi. Will you goe *Pandion.*

Pandi. Yea.   [*Exeunt.*

ACTUS SECUNDUS. SCÆNA TERTIA.

MOLUS, CRYTICUS, CALYPHO.

Molus. *Cryticus* comes in good time, I shall not be alone. What newes *Cryticus?*

Cryti. I taught you that lesson to aske what newes, and this is the newes: to morrow there shall a desperate fray bee betweene two, made at all weapons, from the browne bill to the bodkin.

Molus. Now thou talkest of fraies, I pray thee what is that, wherof they talke so commonly in court, valour, the stab, the pistoll, for the which every man that dareth is so much honoured?

Cryti. O *Molus*, beware of valour! he that can looke big, and weare his dagger pomel lower than the point, that lyeth at a good ward, and can hit a button with a thrust, and will into the field man to man for a bout or two; he *Molus* is a shrewd fellow, and shal be well folowed.

Molus. What is the end?

Cryti. Danger or death.

Molus. If it bee but death that bringeth all this commendation, I account him as valiant that is killed with a surfet, as with a sword.

Cryti. How so?

Molus. If I venture upon a full stomack to eate a rasher on the coales, a carbonado, drinke a carouse, swallow all things that may procure sicknesse or death; am not I as valiant to die so in an house, as the other in a field? Meethinkes that epicures are as desperate as souldiours, and cookes provide as good weapons as cutlers.

Cryti. O valiant knight!

Molus. I will die for it, what greater valor?

Cryti. Schollers fight, who rather seeke to choake their stomakes, then see their bloud.

Molus. I will stand upon this point, if it bee valour to dare die, he is valiant howsoever he dieth.

Cryti. Well, of this hereafter: but here commeth *Calypho*, wee will have some sport.

Caly. My mistresse, I thinke, hath got a gadfly, never at home, and yet none can tell where abroade. My master was a wise man, when hee matcht with such a woman. When shee comes in, we must put out the fire, because of the smoake; hang up our hammers, because of the noyse; and doe no work, but watch what shee wanteth. She is faire, but by my troth I doubt of her honestie. I must seeke her, that I feare *Mars* hath found.

Cryti. Whom dost thou seeke?

Caly. I have found those I seeke not.

Molus. I hope you have found those, which are honest.

Caly. It may be: but I seeke no such.

Molus. *Cryticus,* you shall see me by learning to prove *Calypho* to be the divell.

Cryti. Let us see: but I pray thee prove it better than thou didst thyselfe to be valiant.

Molus. *Calypho,* I will prove thee to be a divell.

Caly. Then will I sweare thee to be a god.

Molus. The divell is blacke.

Caly. What care I?

Molus. Thou art black.

Caly. What care you?

Molus. Therefore thou art the divell.

Caly. I deny that.

Molus. It is the conclusion, thou must not denie it.

Caly. In spite of all conclusions, I will denie it.

Cryti. *Molus,* the smith holds you hard.

Molus. Thou seest he hath no reason.

Cryti. Trie him againe.

Molus. I will reason with thee now from a place.

Caly. I meane to answere you in no other place.

Molus. Like master, like man.

Caly. It may be.

Molus. But thy master hath hornes.

Caly. And so mayest thou.

Molus. Therefore thou hast hornes, and *ergo* a devill.

Caly. Bee they all devils that have hornes?

Molus. All men that have hornes are.

Caly. Then are there moe devils on earth than in hell.

Molus. But what doest thou answere?

Caly. I deny that.

Molus. What?

Caly. Whatsoever it is, that shall prove me a devill. But hearest thou scholler, I am a plaine fellow, and can fashion nothing but with the hammer. What wilt thou say, if I prove thee a smith?

Molus. Then will I say thou art a scholler.

Cryti. Proove it *Calypho,* and I will give thee a good *Colaphum.*

Caly. I will prove it, or else—

Cryti. Or else what?

Caly. Or else I will not prove it. Thou art a smith: therefore thou art a smith. The conclusion, you say, must not bee denied: and therefore it is true, thou art a smith.

Molus. I, but I denie your antecedent.

Caly. I, but you shall not. Have I not toucht him, *Cryticus?*

Cryti. You have both done learnedly: for as sure as hee is a smith, thou art a devill.

Caly. And then hee a devill, because a smith: for that it was his reason to make me a devill, being a smith.

Molus. There is no reasoning with these mechanicall dolts, whose wits are in their hands, not in their heads.

Cryti. Bee not cholericke, you are wise: but let us take up this matter with a song.

Caly. I am content, my voice is as good as my reason.

Molus. Then shall wee have sweet musique. But come, I will not breake off.   [*Exeunt.*

SONG.

Cryti. Merry knaves are we three-a.
Molus. When our songs do agree-a.
Caly. O now I well see-a,
    What anon we shall be-a.
Cryti. If we ply thus our singing.
Molus. Pots then must be flinging.
Caly. If the drinke be but stinging.
Molus. I shall forget the rules of grammer.
Caly. And I the pit-apat of my hammer.

Chor. { To the tap-house then let's gang, and rore,
Cal hard, 'tis rare to vamp a score,
Draw dry the tub, be it old or new,
And part not till the ground looke blew.

ACTUS SECUNDUS. SCÆNA QUARTA.

PHAO, SYBILLA.

Phao. What unacquainted thoughts are these *Phao*, far unfit for thy thoughts, unmeete for thy birth, thy fortune, thy yeares; for *Phao*, unhappy, canst thou not be content to behold the sunne, but thou must covet to build thy nest in the sunne? Doth *Sapho* bewitch thee, whom all the ladies in *Sicily* could not wooe? Yea, poore *Phao*, the greatnesse of thy minde is farre above the beautie of thy face, and the hardnesse of thy fortune beyond the bitternesse of thy words. Die *Phao*, *Phao* die: for there is no hope if thou be wise; nor safetie, if thou be fortunate. Ah *Phao*, the more thou seekest to suppresse those mounting affections, they soare the loftier; and the more thou wrestlest with them, the stronger they waxe; not unlike unto a ball, which the harder it is throwne against the earth, the higher it

boundeth into the ayre: or our *Sycilian* stone, which
groweth hardest by hammering.   O divine love! and
therefore divine, because love; whose deitie no conceit
can compasse, and therefore no authoritie can constraine;
as miraculous in working as mightie, and no more to
bee suppressed than comprehended.   How now *Phao*,
whether art thou carried? committing idolatry with that
God, whom thou hast cause to blaspheme.   O *Sapho!*
faire *Sapho!* peace miserable wretch, enjoy thy care in
covert, weare willow in thy hat, and bayes in thy heart.
Leade a lambe in thy hand, and a fox in thy head, a dove
on the backe of thy hand, and a sparrow in the palme.
Gold boyleth best, when it bubleth least; water runneth
smoothest, where it is deepest.   Let thy love hang at
thy hearts bottome, not at the tongues brimme. Things
untold, are undone; there can be no greater comfort,
than to know much; nor any lesse labour, then to say
nothing.   But ah! thy beautie *Sapho*, thy beautie!
Beginnest thou to blab? I, blab it *Phao*, as long as
thou blabbest her beautie. Bees that die with honie,
are buried with harmonie. Swannes that end their
lives with songs, are covered when they are dead with
flowers: and they that till their later gaspe commend
beautie, shall be ever honored with benefits.   In these
extremities I will goe to none other oracle, than *Sybilla;*
whose olde yeares have not beene idle in these young
attempts; and whose sound advice may mitigate (though
the heavens cannot remove) my miseries.   O *Sapho!*
sweet *Sapho! Sapho:—Sybilla!*

Sybi. Who is there?

Phao. One, not worthy to bee one.

Sybi. Faire *Phao?*

Phao. Unfortunate *Phao!*

Sybi. Come in.

Phao. So I will; and quite thy tale of *Phœbus,* with one whose brightnesse darkeneth *Phœbus.* I love *Sapho, Sybilla, Sapho!*—ah *Sapho, Sybilla!*

Sybi. A short tale *Phao,* and sorrowful; it asketh pitie rather than counsell.

Phao. So it is *Sybilla:* yet in those firme yeeres mee thinketh there should harbour such experience, as may deferre though not take away, my destinie.

Sybi. It is hard to cure that by words, which cannot be eased by hearbs; and yet if thou wilt take advice, be attentive.

Phao. I have brought mine eares of purpose, and will hang at your mouth, till you have finished your discourse.

Sybi. Love, faire childe, is to bee governed by art, as thy boat by an oare: for fancie, though it commeth by hazard, is ruled by wisdome. If my precepts may perswade, (and I pray thee let them perswade) I would wish thee first to be diligent: for that women desire nothing more than to have their servants officious. Be alwayes in sight, but never slothfull. Flatter, I meane lie; little things catch light minds, and fancie is a worme, that feedeth first upon fennell. Imagine with thyselfe all are to bee wonne, otherwise mine advice were as unnecessary as thy labour. It is unpossible for the brittle mettle of women to withstand the flattering attempts of men: only this, let them bee asked; their sex requireth no losse, their modesties are to bee allowed so much.

Bee prodigall in prayses and promises, beautie must have
a trumpet, and pride a gift.   Peacockes never spread
their feathers, but when they are flattered; and gods
are seldome pleased, if they be not bribed.   There is
none so foule, that thinketh not herselfe faire.   In com-
mending thou canst loose no labour: for of every one
thou shalt be beleeved.   Oh simple women! that are
brought rather to beleeve what their eares heare of flattering men, than what their eyes see in true glasses.

Phao. You digresse, onely to make mee beleeve that
women doe so lightly beleeve.

Sybi. Then to the purpose.   Chuse such times to
breake thy suite as thy lady is pleasant.   The wooden
horse entred *Troy*, when the souldiers were quaffing;
and *Penelope* forsooth, whom fables make so coy, among
the pots wrung her woers by the fists, when she lowred
on their faces, grapes minde glasses.   *Venus* worketh
in *Bacchus* presse, and bloweth fire upon his liquour.
When thou talkest with her, let thy speech bee pleasant,
but not incredible.   Chuse such words as may (as many
may) melt her minde: honey rankleth, when it is eaten
for pleasure; and faire words wound, when they are
heard for love.   Write, and persist in writing; they
reade more than is written to them, and write lesse than
they thinke.   In conceit studie to be pleasant; in attire
brave, but not too curious; when shee smileth, laugh
out-right; if rise, stand up; if sit, lie downe; loose all
thy time to keepe time with her.   Can you sing, shew
your cunning; can you dance, use your legges; can
you play upon any instrument, practise your fingers to
please her fancie; seek out qualities.   If shee seeme at

the first cruell, bee not discouraged. I tell thee a
strange thing, women strive, because they would bee
overcome: force they call it, but such a welcome force
they account it, that continually they studie to bee enforced.   To faire words joyne sweete kisses, which if
they gently receive, I say no more, they will gently
receive.   But bee not pinned alwayes on her sleeves,
strangers have greene rushes, when daily guests are not
worth a rush.   Looke pale, and learne to be leane, that
who so seeth thee, may say, the gentleman is in love.
Use no sorcerie to hasten thy successe.   Wit is a witch;
Ulisses was not faire, but wise; not cunning in charmes,
but sweete in speech; whose filed tongue made those
inamoured that sought to have him inchanted.   Bee not
coy, beare, sooth, sweare, die to please thy ladie: these
are rules for poore lovers, to others I am no mistresse.
He hath wit enough, that can give enough.   Dumbe
men are eloquent, if they be liberall.   Beleeve me great
gifts are little gods.   When thy mistresse doth bend
her brow, doe not thou bend thy fist.   Camockes must
bee bowed with sleight, not strength; water to bee trained
with pipes, not stopped with sluces; fire to bee quenched
with dust, not with swords.   If thou have a rivall, bee
patient; arte must winde him out, not malice; time,
not might; her change, and thy constancie.   Whatsoever shee weareth, sweare it becomes her.   In thy love
be secret; *Venus* coffers, though they bee hollow never
sound; and when they seeme emptiest, they are fullest.
Olde foole that I am! to doe thee good, I begin to
doate, and counsell that, which I would have concealed.
Thus, *Phao*, have I given thee certaine regards, no

rules,—only to set thee in the way,—not to bring thee home.

Phao. Ah *Sybilla*, I pray goe on, that I may glut myselfe in this science.

Sybi. Thou shalt not surfet *Phao*, whilst I diet thee. Flies that die on the honiesuckle become poyson to bees. A little in love is a great deale.

Phao. But all that can bee said not enough.

Sybi. White silver draweth black lines, and sweete words will breed sharpe torments.

Phao. What shall become of me?

Sybi. Goe dare.

Phao. I goe! *Phao*, thou canst but die; and then as good die with great desires, as pine in base fortunes.

[*Exit.*

ACTUS TERTIUS. SCÆNA PRIMA.

TRACHINUS, PANDION, MILETA, ISMENA,
EUGENUA.

Trachi.

APHO is falne sodainly sicke, I cannot ghesse the cause.

Mileta. Some cold belike, or else a womans qualme.

Pandi. A strange nature of cold to drive one into such an heate.

Mileta. Your physicke sir, I thinke be of the second sort; else would you not judge it rare, that hot fevers are ingendred by cold causes.

Pandi. Indeed, lady, I have no more physicke than

will purge choller, and that if it please you, I will practise upon you. It is good for women that be waspish.

Isme. Faith, sir, no, you are best purge your owne
melancholy : belike you are a male content.

Pandi. It is true, and are not you a female content?

Trachi. Soft! I am not content, that a male and
female content, should go together.

Mileta. Ismena is disposed to bee merrie.

Isme. No, it is *Pandion* would faine seeme wise.

Trachi. You shall not fall out: for pigeons after
biting fall to billing, and open jarres make the closest
jests.

Euge. *Mileta! Ismena! Mileta!* come away, my
ladie is in a sowne!

Mileta. Aye me!

Isme. Come let us make haste.

Trachi. I am sorrie for *Sapho*, because shee will
take no physicke; like you *Pandion*, who being sicke
of the sullens, will seeke no friend.

Pandi. Of men wee learne to speake, of gods to hold
our peace. Silence shall disgest what folly hath swal-
lowed, and wisdome weane what fancie hath noursed.

Trachi. Is it not love?

Pandi. If it were, what then?

Trachi. Nothing, but that I hope it be not.

Pandi. Why, in courts there is nothing more common. And as to be bald among the *Mycanians* it was
accounted no shame, because they were all bald; so to
bee in love among courtiers it is no discredit; for that
they are all in love.

Trachi. Why, what doe you thinke of our ladies?

Pandi. As of the *Seres* wooll, which being whitest and softest, fretteth soonest and deepest.

Trachi. I will not tempt you in your deepe melancholy, least you seeme sowre to those which are so sweet. But come, let us walke a little into the fields, it may be the open ayre will disclose your close conceits.

Pandi. I will goe with you: but send our pages away. [*Exeunt.*

ACTUS TERTIUS. SCÆNA SECUNDA.

Cryticus, Molus, Calypho.

Cryti. What browne studie art thou in *Molus*, no mirth? no life?

Molus. I am in the depth of my learning driven to a muse, how this Lent I shall scamble in the court, that was woont to fast so oft in the universitie.

Cryti. Thy belly is thy god.

Molus. Then is he a deafe god.

Cryti. Why?

Molus. For *venter non habet aures.* But thy backe is thy god.

Cryti. Then it is a blind god.

Molus. How prove you that?

Cryti. Easie. *Nemo videt manticæ, quod in tergo est.*

Molus. Then would the sachell that hangs at your god, *id est*, your backe, were full of meate to stuffe my god, *hoc est*, my belly.

Cryti. Excellent. But how canst thou studie, when thy minde is onely in the kitchen?

Molus. Doth not the horse travaile best, that sleepeth with his head in the maunger?

Cryti. Yes, what then?

Molus. Good wits will apply.   But what cheere is there here this Lent?

Cryti. Fish.

Molus. I can eate none, it is windie.

Cryti. Egges.

Molus. I must eate none, they are fire.

Cryti. Cheese.

Molus. It is against the old verse, *Caseus est nequam.*

Cryti. Yea, but it disgesteth all things except itselfe.

Molus. Yea, but if a man hath nothing else to eate, what shall it disgest?

Cryti. You are disposed to jest.   But if your silken throate can swallow no packthred, you must picke your teeth, and play with your trencher.

Molus. So shall I not incurre the fulsome and un-mannerly sinne of surfeting.   But here commeth *Ca-lypho.*

Cryti. What newes?

Caly. Since my being here, I have sweat like a dogge to prove my master a devill; hee brought such reasons to refell me, as I promise you I shal thinke the better of his wit, as long as I am with him.

Molus. How?

Caly. Thus, I alwayes arguing that he had hornes, and therefore a devill: hee said, foole, they are things like hornes, but no hornes; for once in the senate of gods being holden a solemne session, in the midst of their talke, I put in my sentence, which was so indif-

ferent, that they all concluded it might as well have
beene left out, as put in, and so placed on each side of
my head things like hornes, and called me a *Parenthesis.* Now my masters, this may be true, for I have
seen it myselfe about divers sentences.

Molus. It is true, and the same time did *Mars* make
a ful point, that *Vulcans* head was made a *Parenthesis.*

Cryti. This shall goe with me: I trust in *Syracusa*
to give one or other a *Parenthesis.*

Molus. Is *Venus* yet come home?

Caly. No, but were I *Vulcan*, I would by the gods.

Cryti. What wouldst thou?

Caly. Nothing, but as *Vulcan*, halt by the gods.

Cryti. I thought you would have hardly entreated
Venus.

Caly. Nay, *Venus* is easily entreated: but let that
goe by.

Cryti. What?

Caly. That which maketh so many *Parenthesis.*

Molus. I must goe by too, or else my master will not
goe by me, but meete me full with his fist. Therefore, if wee shall sing, give me my part quickly: for if
I tarrie long, I shall cry my part wofully.   [*Exeunt.*

SONG.

Omnes. Arme, arme, the foe comes on apace.
Caly. What's that red nose, and sulphury face?
Molus. Tis the hot leader.
Cryti. What's his name?
Molus. Bacchus, a captaine of plumpe fame:
A goat the beast on which he rides,
Fat grunting swine run by his sides,
His standerd-bearer feares no knockes,

For he's a drunken butter-box,
Who when i' th' red field thus he revels,
Cryes out, "ten towsan tunne of tivells!"
   Caly. What's he so swaggers in the van?
   Molus. O! that's a roring Englishman,
Who in deepe healths do's so excell,
From *Dutch* and *French* he beares the bel.
   Cryti. What victlers follow *Bacchus* campes?
   Molus. Fooles, fidlers, panders, pimpes, and rampes.
   Caly. See, see, the battaile now growes hot,
Here legs flye, here goes heads to th' pot,
Here whores and knaves tosse broken glasses,
Here all the souldiers looke like asses.
   Cryti. What man ere heard such hideous noyse?
   Molus. O! that's the vintners bawling boyes.
Anon, Anon, the trumpets are,
Which call them to the fearefull barre.
   Caly. Rush in, and lets our forces try.
   Molus. O no, for see they flie, they flie!
   Cryti. And so will I.
   Caly. And I.
   Molus. And I.
   Omnes. 'Tis a hot day, in drinke to die.

ACTUS TERTIUS. SCÆNA TERTIA.

SAPHO *in her bed*, MILETA, ISMENA, CANOPE,
EUGENUA, FAVILLA, LAMIA.

Sapho. Hey ho: I know not which way to turne me.
Ah! ah! I faint, I die!

Mileta. Madame, I thinke it good you have more
clothes, and sweat it out.

Sapho. No, no, the best ease I find is to sigh it out.

Isme. A strange disease that should breed such a
desire.

Sapho. A strange desire that hath brought such a
disease.

Canope. Where, ladie, do you feele your most paine?

Sapho, Where no bodie else can feele it, *Canope.*

Canope. At the heart?

Sapho. In the heart,

Canope. Will you have any *Mithrydate?*

Sapho. Yea, if for this disease there were any *Mithry-date.*

Mileta. Why? what disease is it madame, that phy-sicke cannot cure?

Sapho. Onely the disease, *Mileta,* that I have.

Mileta, Is it a burning ague?

Sapho. I thinke so, or a burning agonie.

Euge. Will you have any of this syrope to moysten your mouth?

Sapho. Would I had some locall things to dry my braine.

Favilla. Madame, will you see if you can sleepe?

Sapho. Sleepe, *Favilla?* I shall then dreame.

Lamia. As good dreame sleeping, as sigh waking.

Euge. Phao is cunning in all kinde of simples, and it is hard, if there be none to procure sleepe,

Sapho. Who?

Euge. Phao.

Sapho. Yea, *Phao! Phao!*—ah *Phao!* let him come presently.

Mileta. Shall wee draw the curtaines, whilest you give yourselfe leave to slumber?

Sapho. Doe, but depart not; I have such starts in my sleepe, disquieted I know not how. [*In a slumber.*] *Phao! Phao!*

Isme. What say you, madame?

Sapho. Nothing, but if I sleepe not now, you send for *Phao.* Ah gods! [*She falleth asleepe. The curtaines drawne.*]

Mileta. There is a fish called *Garus*, that healeth all sicknesse, so as whilest it is applied one name not *Garus.*

Euge. An evill medicine for us women: for if wee should bee forbidden to name *Garus*, we should chat nothing but *Garus.*

Canope. Well said, *Eugenua*, you know yourselfe.

Euge. Yea, *Canope*, and that I am one of your sexe.

Isme. I have heard of an hearbe called *Lunarie*, that being bound to the pulses of the sick, cause nothing but dreames of weddings and dances.

Favilla. I thinke, *Ismena*, that hearbe bee at thy pulses now: for thou art ever talking of matches and merriments.

Canope. It is an unluckie signe in the chamber of the sicke to talke of marriages: for my mother said, it foresheweth death.

Mileta. It is very evill to *Canope* to sit at the beds feet, and foretelleth danger: therefore remove your stoole, and sit by mee.

Lamia. Sure it is some cold shee hath taken.

Isme. If one were burnt, I thinke wee women would say hee died of a colde.

Favilla. It may be some conceit.

Mileta. Then is there no feare: for yet did I never heare of a woman that died of a conceit.

Euge. I mistrust her not: for that the owle hath not shrikt at the window, or the night raven croked, both being fatall.

Favilla. You are all superstitious, for these be but fancies of doting age: who by chance observing it in some, have set it downe as a religion for all.

Mileta. *Favilla*, thou art but a girle; I would not have a weesell cry, nor desire to see a glasse, nor an old wife come into my chamber; for then though I lingred in my disease, I should never escape it.

Sapho. Ah, who is there? what sodaine affrights be these? Methought *Phao* came with simples to make me sleepe. Did no bodie name *Phao*, before I beganne to slumber?

Mileta. Yes, we told you of him.

Sapho. Let him be here to-morrow.

Mileta. He shall, will you have a little broth to comfort you?

Sapho. I can relish nothing.

Mileta. Yet a little you must take to sustaine nature.

Sapho. I cannot *Mileta*, I will not. Oh which way shall I lie? what shall I doe? Heigh ho! O *Mileta*, helpe to reare mee up, my bed, my head lies too low. You pester mee with too many clothes. Fie, you keepe the chamber too hot!—avoide it! it may bee I shall steale a nap when all are gone.

Mileta. We will.

Sapho sola. Ah! impatient disease of love, and goddesse of love thrice unpitifull. The eagle is never striken with thunder, nor the olyve with lightning, and may great ladies bee plagued with love? O *Venus*, have I not strawed thine altars with sweete roses? kept thy swannes in cleare rivers? fed thy sparrowes with ripe corne, and harboured thy doves in faire houses? Thy

tortoys have I nourished under my fig tree, my chamber
have I sieled with thy cockleshels, and dipped thy sponge
into the freshest waters.   Didst thou nurse me in my
swadling clouts with wholsome hearbes, that I might
perish in my flowring yeares by fancie?   I perceive,—
but too late I perceive, and yet not too late, because at
last,—that straines are caught as wel by stooping too
low, as reaching too high : that eyes are bleared as soone
with vapours that come from the earth, as with beames
that proceed from the sun.   Love lodgeth sometimes in
caves : and thou, *Phœbus*, that in the pride of thy heate
shinest all day in our horizon, at night dippest thy head
in the ocean.   Resist it, *Sapho*, whilest it is yet tender.
Of acornes comes oakes, of drops flouds, of sparkes
flames, of atomies elements.   But alas, it fareth with
me as with waspes, who feeding on serpents, make their
stings more venemous : for glutting myself on the face
of *Phao*, I have made my desire more desperate.   Into
the neast of an *Alcyon* no bird can enter but the *Alcyon* ;
and into the hart of so great a ladie, can any creepe but
a great lord ?   There is an hearbe (not unlike unto my
love) which the farther it groweth from the sea, the
salter it is ; and my desires the more they swarve from
reason, the more seeme they reasonable.   When *Phao*
commeth, what then ? wilt thou open thy love ? Yea ?
No ! *Sapho :* but staring in his face till thine eyes
dazell, and thy spirits faint, die before his face ; then
this shall be written on thy tomb, that though thy love
were greater than wisdome could endure, yet thine
honour was such, as love could not violate : *Mileta !*

    Mileta. I come.

Sapho. It wil not be, I can take no rest, which way soever I turne.

Mileta. A strange maladie!

Sapho. *Mileta,* if thou wilt, a martyrdome. But give me my lute, and I will see if in song I can beguile mine owne eyes.

Mileta. Here, madame.

Sapho. Have you sent for *Phao?*

Mileta. Yea.

Sapho. And to bring simples that will procure sleepe?

Mileta. No.

Sapho. Foolish wench, what should the boy doe here, if he bring not remedies with him? you thinke belike I could sleepe, if I did but see him. Let him not come at all: yes, let him come: no, it is no matter: yet will I trie, let him come: doe you heare?

Mileta. Yea, madame, it shall be done. Peace, no noise: she beginneth to fall asleepe. I will goe to *Phao.*

Isme. Goe speedily: for if she wake, and finde you not here, she will be angry. Sicke folkes are testie, who though they eate nothing, yet they feede on gall.

SONG.

Sapho. O cruell Love! on thee I lay
My curse, which shall strike blinde the day;
Never may sleepe with velvet hand
Charme thine eyes with sacred wand;
Thy jaylours shal be hopes and feares;
Thy prison-mates, grones, sighes, and teares;
Thy play to weare out weary times,
Phantasticke passions, vowes, and rimes;
Thy bread bee frownes; thy drinke bee gall;
Such as when you *Phao* call,

The bed thou lyest on by despaire;
Thy sleepe, fond dreames; thy dreames long care;
Hope (like thy foole) at thy beds head,
Mockes thee, till madnesse strike thee dead;
As *Phao*, thou dost mee, with thy proud eyes;
In thee poore *Sapho* lives, for thee shee dies.

ACTUS TERTIUS. SCÆNA QUARTA.

MILETA, PHAO, ISMENA, SAPHO, VENUS.

Mileta. I would either your cunning *Phao*, or your fortune, might by simples provoke my ladie to some slumber.

Phao. My simples are in operation as my simplicitie is, which if they doe little good, assuredly they can doe no harme.

Mileta. Were I sicke, the very sight of thy faire face would drive me into a sound sleepe.

Phao. Indeede gentlewomen are so drowsie in their desires, that they can scarse hold up their eyes for love.

Mileta. I meane the delight of beauty would so bind my senses, as I should bee quickly rocked into a deepe rest.

Phao. You women have an excuse for an advantage, which must be allowed, because onely to you women it was allotted.

Mileta. *Phao*, thou art passing faire, and able to draw a chaste eie not only to glance, but to gaze on thee. Thy young yeares, thy quicke wit, thy stayed desires, are of force to control those which should command.

Phao. Lady, I forgot to commend you first: and

least I should have overslipped to praise you at all, you
have brought in my beauty, which is simple, that in
curtesie I might remember yours, which is singular.

Mileta. You mistake of purpose, or misconster of
malice.

Phao. I am as farre from malice, as you from love;
and to mistake of purpose were to mislike of peevishnes.

Mileta. As farre as I from love? Why, thinke you
mee so dull I cannot love, or so spitefull I will not?

Phao. Neither, lady: but how should men imagine
women can love, when in their mouthes there is nothing
rifer, than *in faith I doe not love.*

Mileta. Why, will you have women's love in their
tongues?

Phao. Yea, else do I thinke there is none in their
hearts.

Mileta. Why?

Phao. Because there was never any thing in the bottome of a womans heart, that commeth not to her tongues
ende.

Mileta. You are too young to cheapen love.

Phao. Yet old enough to talke with market folkes. ·

Mileta. Well, let us in.

Isme. Phao is come.

Sapho. Who? *Phao?* *Phao,* let him come neere:
but who sent for him?

Mileta. You, madame.

Sapho. I am loath to take any medicines: yet must
I rather than pine in these maladies. *Phao,* you may
make me sleep, if you will.

Phao. If I can, I must, if you will.

Sapho. What hearbs have you brought, *Phao*?

Phao. Such as will make you sleepe, madame, though they cannot make me slumber.

Sapho. Why, how can you cure mee, when you cannot remedie yourselfe?

Phao. Yes, madame, the causes are contrarie. For it is onely a drinesse in your braines, that keepeth you from rest. But—

Sapho. But what?

Phao. Nothing,—but mine is not so.

Sapho. Nay, then I despaire of helpe, if our disease be not all one.

Phao. I would our diseases were all one.

Sapho. It goes hard with the patient, when the phisition is desperate.

Phao. Yet *Medea* made the ever-waking dragon to snort, when shee poore soule could not winke.

Sapho. *Medea* was in love, and nothing could cause her rest but *Jason*.

Phao. Indeede I know no herb to make lovers sleepe, but hearts-ease; which because it groweth so high, I cannot reach for.

Sapho. For whom?

Phao. For such as love.

Sapho. It stoopeth very low, and I can never stoop to it, that—

Phao. That what?

Sapho. That I may gather it: but why doe you sigh so, *Phao*?

Phao. It is mine use, madame.

Sapho. It will doe you harme, and me too: for I never heare one sigh, but I must sigh also.

Phao. It were best then that your ladyship give me leave to be gone: for I can but sigh.

Sapho. Nay stay, for now I begin to sigh, I shall not leave though you bee gone. But what doe you thinke best for your sighing to take it away?

Phao. Yew, madame.

Sapho. Mee?

Phao. No, madame, yew of the tree.

Sapho. Then will I love yew the better. And indeed I thinke it would make me sleepe too, therefore all other simples set aside, I will simply use only yew.

Phao. Do, madame: for I thinke nothing in the world so good as yew.

Sapho. Farwell for this time.

Venus. Is not your name *Phao?*

Phao. *Phao,* faire *Venus,* whom you made so faire.

Venus. So passing faire! O faire *Phao,* O sweete *Phao:* what wilt thou doe for *Venus?*

Phao. Any thing that commeth in the compasse of my poore fortune.

Venus. *Cupid* shall teach thee to shoote, and I will instruct thee in dissembling.

Phao. I will learne any thing but dissembling.

Venus. Why my boy?

Phao. Because then I must learne to be a woman.

Venus. Thou heardest that of a man.

Phao. Men speake truth.

Venus. But truth is a *shee,* and so alwaies painted.

Phao. I thinke a painted truth.

Venus. Wel, farwell for this time: for I must visit *Sapho.*   [*Phao exit.*

ACTUS QUARTUS. SCÆNA PRIMA.

VENUS, SAPHO, CUPID.

Venus.

APHO, I have heard thy complaints, and pittied thine agonies.

Sapho. O *Venus,* my cares are onely knowne to thee, and by thee onely came the cause. *Cupid,* why didst thou wound me so deepe?

Cupid. My mother bad mee draw mine arrow to the head.

Sapho. Venus, why didst thou prove so hatefull?

Venus. Cupid tooke a wrong shaft.

Sapho. O *Cupid,* too unkind to make me so kind, that almost I transgresse the modesty of my kinde.

Cupid. I was blinde, and could not see mine arrow.

Sapho. How came it to passe, thou didst hit my heart?

Cupid. That came by the nature of the head, which being once let out of the bow, can finde none other lighting place but the heart.

Venus. Bee not dismaid, *Phao* shall yeeld.

Sapho. If he yeelde, then shall I shame to embrace one so meane,—if not die; because I cannot embrace one so meane.   Thus doe I finde no meane.

Venus. Well, I will worke for thee.   Farwell.

Sapho. Farwell sweete *Venus,* and thou *Cupid,* which art sweetest in thy sharpnesse.   [*Exit Sapho.*

ACTUS QUARTUS.   SCÆNA SECUNDA.

Venus, Cupid.

Venus. *Cupid,* what hast thou done? put thine arrowes in *Phao's* eyes, and wounded thy mothers heart.

Cupid. You gave him a face to allure, then why
should not I give him eyes to pearce?

Venus. O *Venus!* unhappie *Venus!* who in bestow-
ing a benefit upon a man, hast brought a bane unto a
goddesse. What perplexities dost thou feele? O faire
Phao! and therefore made faire to breed in mee a
frenzie. O would that when I gave thee golden locks
to curle thy head, I had shackled thee with yron locks
on thy feete. And when I noursed thee, *Sapho,* with
lettice, would it had turned to hemlocke. Have I brought
a smooth skin over thy face, to make a rough scarre in
my heart? And given thee a fresh colour like the damask
rose, to make mine pale like the stained turkis? O
Cupid, thy flames with *Psyche's* were but sparkes, and
my desires with *Adonis* but dreames, in respect of these
unacquainted torments. Laugh, *Juno!* *Venus* is in love;
but *Juno* shall not see with whom, least she be in love.
Venus belike is become stale: *Sapho* forsooth because
she hath many vertues, therefore shee must have all
the favours. *Venus* waxeth old: and then she was a
pretie wench, when *Juno* was a yong wife; now crowes
foote is on her eye, and the black oxe hath trod on her
foot. But were *Sapho* never so vertuous, doth she think
to contend with *Venus* to be as amorous? Yeeld, *Phao!*
but yeeld to me, *Phao;* I intreat where I may com-

mand; command thou, where thou shouldst intreat. In this case, *Cupid*, what is thy counsell ? *Venus* must both play the lover and the dissembler ; and therefore the dissembler, because the lover.

Cupid. You will ever be playing with arrowes, like children with knives ; and then when you bleed, you cry : go to *Vulcan*, intreat by prayers, threaten with blowes, wooe with kisses, ban with curses, trie all meanes to rid these extremities.

Venus. To what end ?

Cupid. That he might make me new arrowes : for nothing can roote out the desires of *Phao*, but a new shaft of inconstancie, nor any thing turne *Sapho's* heart, but a new arrow of disdaine. And then they disliking one the other, who shall enjoy *Phao* but *Venus?*

Venus. I will follow thy counsell. For *Venus*, though she be in her latter age for yeares : yet is she in her nonage for affections. When *Venus* ceaseth to love let love cease to rule. But come let us to *Vulcan*.

[*Exeunt.*

ACTUS QUARTUS. SCÆNA TERTIA.

SAPHO, MILETA, ISMENA, EUGENUA,
LAMIA, FAVILLA, CANOPE.

Sapho. What dreames are these, *Mileta?* And can there be no truth in dreams ? yea dreames have their truth. Methought I saw a stockdove or woodquist, (I know not how to tearme it) that brought short strawes to build his nest in a tall cedar, where, whilst with his

bil he was framing his building, he lost as many feathers
from his wings, as he laid strawes in his nest: yet
scambling to catch hold to harbor in the house he had
made, he sodainely fell from the bough where he stood.
And then pittifully casting up his eyes, he cryed in such
tearmes (as I imagined) as might either condemne the
nature of such a tree, or the daring of such a mind.
Whilest he lay quaking upon the ground, and I gazing
on the cedar, I might perceive antes to breed in the
rinde, coveting only to hoord; and caterpillers to cleave
to the leaves, labouring only to suck; which caused
moe leaves to fall from the tree, than there did feathers
before from the dove.   Methought, *Mileta,* I sighed in
my sleepe, pittying both the fortune of the bird and the
misfortune of the tree: but in this time quils began to
bud againe in the bird, which made him looke as though
he would flie up; and then wished I that the body of
the tree would bow, that he might but creep up the tree;
then, and so—Hey ho!

Mileta. And so what?

Sapho. Nothing, *Mileta:* but and so I waked. But
did nobody dreame but I?

Mileta. I dreamed last night (but I hope dreames are
contrarie), that holding my head over a sweete smoake,
all my haire blazd on a bright flame.   Methought *Ismena* cast water to quench it: yet the sparkes fel on my
bosom, and wiping them away with my hand, I was all
in a goare bloud, till one with a few fresh flowers stanched
it.   And so stretching myselfe as stiffe, I started, it was
but a dream.

Isme. It is a signe you shall fall in love with hearing

faire words. Water signifieth counsell, flowers death.
And nothing can purge your loving humor but death.

Mileta. You are no interpreter, but an interprater,
harping alwaies upon love, till you be as blind as a harper.

Isme. I remember last night but one, I dreamed
mine eye-tooth was loose, and that I thrust it out with
my tongue.

Mileta. It fortelleth the losse of a friend : and I ever
thought thee so ful of prattle, that thou wouldest thrust
out the best friend with thy tatling.

Isme. Mileta, but it was loose before! and if my
friend bee loose, as good thrust out with plaine words
as kept in with dissembling.

Euge. Dreames are but dotings, which come either
by things we see in the day, or meates that we eate, and
so the common sense preferring it to be imaginative.

Isme. Soft *Philosofatrix,* well seene in secrets of art,
and not seduced with the superstitions of nature.

Sapho. Ismenaes tongue never lyeth still, I thinke
all her teeth will be loose, they are so often jogged
against her tongue. But say on, *Eugenua.*

Euge. There is all.

Sapho. What did you dreame, *Canope?*

Canope. I seldome dreame, madam : but sithence
your sicknes I cannot tell whether with our watching,
but I have had many phantasticall visions : for even
now slumbring by your beds side, meethought I was
shadowed with a cloud, where laboring to unwrap myselfe, I was more intangled. But in the midst of my
striving it seemed to myselfe gold, with faire drops ; I
filled my lap, and running to shew it my fellowes, it

turned to dust: I blushed, they laughed; and then I waked, being glad it was but a dreame.

Isme. Take heede, *Canope*, that gold tempt not your lap, and then you blush for shame.

Canope. It is good lucke to dreame of gold.

Isme. Yea, if it had continued gold.

Lamia. I dreame every night, and the last night this. Methought that walking in the sunne, I was stung with the flie *Tarantula*, whose venom nothing can expell but the sweet consent of musick. I tried all kinde of instruments, but found no ease, till at the last two lutes tuned in one key so glutted my thirsting eares, that my griefe presentlie ceased: for joy whereof as I was clapping my hands, your ladyship called.

Mileta. It is a signe that nothing shall asswage your love but marriage: for such is the tying of two in wedlocke, as is the tuning of two lutes in one key: for striking the strings of the one, strawes will stirre upon the strings of the other, and in two minds linked in love, one cannot be delighted, but the other rejoiceth.

Favilla. Methought going by the sea side among pebels, I saw one playing with a rounde stone, ever throwing it into the water, when the sunne shined; I asked the name, he saide, it was called *Abeston*, which being once hot, would never be cold; he gave it me, and vanished. I forgetting myselfe, delighted with the faire show, would alwaies shew it by candlelight, pull it out in the sunne, and see how bright it would looke in the fire, where catching heate, nothing could coole it: for anger I threw it against the wall, and with the heaving up of mine arme I waked.

Mileta. Beware of love, *Favilla:* for women's hearts are such stones, which warmed by affection, cannot be cold by wisdome.

Favilla. I warrant you: for I never credit men's words.

Isme. Yet be warie: for women are scorched sometimes with men's eyes, though they had rather consume than confesse.

Sapho. Cease your talking: for I would faine sleep, to see if I can dream, whether the bird hath feathers, or the ant wings. Draw the curtaine.

ACTUS QUARTUS. SCÆNA QUARTA.

VENUS, VULCAN, CUPID.

Venus. Come, *Cupid, Vulcan's* flames must quench *Venus'* fires. *Vulcan?*

Vulcan. Who?

Venus. Venus.

Vulcan. Ho, ho! *Venus.*

Venus. Come sweet *Vulcan,* thou knowest how sweet thou hast found *Venus;* who being of all the goddesses the most faire, hath chosen thee of all the gods the most foule; thou must needes then confesse I was most loving. Enquire not the cause of my suit by questions: but prevent the effects by curtesie. Make me six arrow heads, it is given thee of the gods by permission to frame them to any purpose, I shall request them by prayer. Why lowrest thou *Vulcan?* wilt thou have a kisse? hold up thy head, *Venus* hath young thoughts, and fresh affections. Rootes have strings, when boughes have no leaves. But harken in thine eare, *Vulcan :* how sayest thou ?

Vulcan. Vulcan is a god with you, when you are disposed to flatter. A right woman, whose tongue is like a bees sting, which pricketh deepest, when it is fullest of hony ; because you have made mine eyes drunke with faire lookes, you will set mine eares on edge with sweet words. You were wont to say that the beating of hammers made your head ake, and the smoake of the forge your eyes water, and every coale was a block in your way. You weepe rose water, when you aske ; and spit vineger, when you have obtained. What would you now with new arrowes ? belike *Mars* hath a tougher skin on his heart, or *Cupid* a weaker arme, or *Venus* a better courage. Well, *Venus*, there is never a smile in your face but hath made a wrinckle in my forhead ; *Ganymedes* must fill your cup, and you wil pledge none but *Jupiter*. But I will not chide *Venus*. Come, *Cyclops*, my wife must have her will ; let us doe that in earth, which the gods cannot undoe in heaven.

Venus. Gramercie sweet *Vulcan !* to your worke.

[*The* Song, *in making of the Arrowes.*]

Vulcan. My shag-haire *Cyclops*, come, let's ply
Our *Lemnion* hammers lustily ;
By my wifes sparrowes,
I sweare these arrowes,
Shall singing fly
Through many a wantons eye.
These headed are with golden blisses.
These silver-ones feathered with kisses.
  But this of lead
  Strikes a clowne dead,

When in a dance
Hee fals in a trance,
To se his black-brow lasse not busse him,
And then whines out for death t' untrusse him.
So, so, our worke being don lets play,
Holliday (boyes) cry holliday.

Vulcan. Here, *Venus*, I have finished these arrowes
by art, bestow them you by wit: for as great advise
must he use that hath them, as he cunning that made
them.

Venus. *Vulcan*, now you have done with your forge,
let us alone with the fancie: you are as the fletcher, not
the archer, to medle with the arrows, not the aime.

Vulcan. I thought so: when I have done working,
you have done wooing. Where is now sweet *Vulcan?*
Well, I can say no more, but this, which is enough,
and as much as any can say, *Venus* is a woman.

Venus. Be not angry, *Vulcan*, I will love thee againe,
when I have either busines, or nothing else to doe.

Cupid. My mother will make much of you, when
there are no more men than *Vulcan*.

ACTUS QUINTUS. SCÆNA PRIMA.

Venus, Cupid.

Venus.

OME, *Cupid*, receive with thy father's instruments thy mother's instructions: for
thou must bee wise in conceit, if thou wilt
be fortunate in execution. This arrow is feathered with
the wings of *Ægitus*, which never sleepeth for feare of

his hen : the head toucht with the stone *Perillus*, which
causeth mistrust and jealousie.   Shoote this, *Cupid*, at
men that have faire wives, which will make them rub
the browes, when they swell in the braines.   This shaft
is headed with *Lydian* steel, which striketh a deepe
daine of that which wee most desire ; the feathers are of
Turtle, but dipped in the bloud of a *Tigresse ;* draw this
up close to the head at *Sapho*, that she may despise,
where now shee doates.   Good, my boy, gall her on the
side, that for *Phao's* love shee may never sigh.   This
arrow is feathered with the *Phœnix* wing, and headed
with the *Eagle's* bill ; it maketh men passionate in desires, in love constant, and wise in conveyance, melting
as it were their fancies into faith : this arrow, sweet
childe, and with as great aime as thou canst, must *Phao*
be striken withal ; and cry softly to thyself in the very
loose, *Venus!* Sweete *Cupid*, mistake it not, I will make
a quiver for that by itselfe.   The fourth hath feathers
of the *Peacok*, but glewed with the gumme of the *Mirtle*
tree, headed with fine golde, and fastned with brittle
Chrysocoll : this shoot at dainty and coy ladies, at amiable and yong nymphes, chuse no other white but women : for this will worke liking in their mindes, but not
love ; affabilitie in speech, but no faith ; courtly favours
to bee mistresses over many, but constant to none :
sighes to be fetcht from the lungs, not the heart ; and
teares to be wrung out with their fingers, not their eyes ;
secret laughing at men's pale looks and neate attire ;
open rejoycing at their owne comelinesse and men's
courting. Shoote this arrow among the thickest of them,
whose bosomes lie open, because they would bee striken

with it. And seeing men terme women *Jupiter's* fooles, women shall make men *Venus'* fooles. This shaft is lead in the head, and whose feathers are of the night *Raven*, a deadly and poysoned shaft, which breedeth hate only against those which sue for love. Take heede, *Cupid*, thou hit not *Phao* with this shaft: for then shall *Venus* perish. This last is an old arrow, but newly mended, the arrow which hit both *Sapho* and *Phao*, working onely in meane minds an aspiring to superiours, and in high estates a stooping to inferiours: with this, *Cupid*, I am galled myselfe, till thou have galled *Phao* with the other.

Cupid. I warrant you I will cause *Phao* to languish in your love, and *Sapho* to disdaine his.

Venus. Goe, loyter not, nor mistake your shaft. Now, *Venus*, hast thou playd a cunning part, though not currant. But why should *Venus* dispute of unlawfulnesse in love, or faith in affection; being both the goddesse of love and affection; knowing there is as little truth to be used in love, as there is there reason. No, sweet *Phao*, *Venus* will obtaine, because she is *Venus*. Not thou, *Jove*, with thunder in thy hand, shalt take him out of my hands. I have new arrowes now for my body, and fresh flames, at which the gods shall tremble, if they begin to trouble me. But I will expect the event, and tarrie for *Cupid* at the forge.

ACTUS QUINTUS. SCÆNA SECUNDA.

SAPHO, CUPID, MILETA, VENUS.

Sapho. What hast thou done, *Cupid?*

Cupid. That my mother commanded, *Sapho.*

Sapho. Methinkes, I feele an alteration in my minde, and as it were a withdrawing in myselfe of mine owne affections.

Cupid. Then hath mine arrow his effect.

Sapho. I pray thee tell me the cause?

Cupid. I dare not.

Sapho. Feare nothing : for if *Venus* fret, *Sapho* can frowne, thou shalt be my sonne. *Mileta,* give him some sweete meates ; speake, good *Cupid,* and I will give thee many pretie things.

Cupid. My mother is in love with *Phao,* shee willed mee to strike you with disdaine of him, and him with desire of her.

Sapho. O spitefull *Venus ; Mileta,* give him some of that. What else, *Cupid ?*

Cupid. I could bee even with my mother : and so I will, if I shall call you mother.

Sapho. Yes, *Cupid,* call mee any thing, so I may be even with her.

Cupid. I have an arrow, with which if I strike *Phao,* it will cause him to loath only *Venus.*

Sapho. Sweet *Cupid,* strike *Phao* with it. Thou shalt sit in my lap, I will rocke thee asleepe, and feed thee with all fine knackes.

Cupid. I will about it. [*Exit Cupid.*

Sapho. But come quickly againe. Ah unkind *Venus,* is this thy promise to *Sapho ?* But if I get *Cupid* from thee, I myselfe will be the Queene of Love. I will direct these arrowes with better ayme, and conquer mine owne affections with greater modestie. *Venus'* heart shall flame, and her love bee as common as her craft. O *Mileta*, time hath disclosed that, which my temperance hath kept in: but sith I am rid of the disease, I will not bee ashamed to confesse the cause; I loved *Phao*, *Mileta*, a thing unfit for my degree, but forced by my desire.

Mileta. Phao?

Sapho. Phao, Mileta—of whom now *Venus* is ena-moured.

Mileta. And doe you love him still?

Sapho. No, I feele relenting thoughts, and reason not yeelding to appetite. Let *Venus* have him,—no, shee shall not have him. But here comes *Cupid:* How now, my boy, hast thou done it?

Cupid. Yea, and left *Phao* rayling on *Venus*, and cursing her name: yet still sighing for *Sapho*, and blasing her vertues.

Sapho. Alas poore *Phao!* thy extreme love should not be requited with so mean a fortune, thy faire face deserved greater favours: I cannot love, *Venus* hath hardned my heart.

Venus. I marvaile *Cupid* commeth not all this while. How now, in *Saphoes* lap?

Sapho. Yea, *Venus*, what say you to it? in *Saphoes* lap!

Venus. Sir boy, come hither.

Cupid. I will not.

Venus. What now? will you not? hath *Sapho* made you so sawcie?

Cupid. I will bee *Sapho's* sonne, I have as you com-manded striken her with a deepe disdaine of *Phao*, and

Phao as she entreated mee, with a great despite of you.

Venus. Unhappy wag, what hast thou done? I will make thee repent it every vaine in thy heart.

Sapho. Venus, be not cholericke; *Cupid* is mine, he hath given me his arrowes, and I will give him a new bow to shoote in. You are not worthy to bee the ladie of love, that yeeld so often to the impressions of love. Immodest *Venus!* that to satisfie the unbridled thoughts of thy heart, transgressest so farre from the stay of thine honour! How sayest thou, *Cupid,* wilt thou be with me?

Cupid. Yes.

Sapho. Shall not I be on earth the goddesse of affections?

Cupid. Yes.

Sapho. Shall not I rule the fancies of men, and lead *Venus* in chaines like a captive?

Cupid. Yes.

Sapho. It is a good boy!

Venus. What have wee here, you the goddesse of love? and you her sonne, *Cupid?* I will tame that proud heart, else shall the gods say, they are not *Venus'* friends. And as for you, sir boy, I will teach you how to run away: you shall be stript from top to toe, and whipt with nettles, not roses; I will set you to blow *Vulcan's* coales, not to beare *Venus'* quiver; I will handle you for this geere—well, I say no more. But as for the new mistris of love, or lady, I cry you mercie; I thinke you would be called a goddesse, you shall know what it is to usurpe the name of *Venus!* I will pull

those plumes, and cause you to cast your eyes on your
feete, not your feathers: your soft haire will I turne to
hard bristles, your tongue to a sting, and those alluring
eyes to unluckinesse: in which if the gods aide mee not,
I will curse the gods.

Sapho. *Venus,* you are in a vaine answerable to your
vanitie, whose high words neither become you, nor feare
mee.   But let this suffice, I will keepe *Cupid* in despight of you, and yet with the content of the gods.

Venus. Will you? Why then we shall have pretie
gods in heaven, when you take gods prisoners on earth.
Before I sleepe you shall both repent, and finde what it
is but to thinke unreverently of *Venus.* Come, *Cupid,*
shee knowes not how to use thee; come with me, you
know what I have for you,—will you not?

Cupid. Not I!

Venus. Well, I will be even with you both, and that
shortly.   [*Exit.*

Sapho. *Cupid,* feare not, I will direct thine arrowes
better: every rude asse shal not say hee is in love.   It
is a toye made for ladies, and I will keepe it onely for
ladies.

Cupid. But what will you doe for *Phao?*

Sapho. I will wish him fortunate.   This will I doe
for *Phao,* because I once loved *Phao:* for never shall
it be said that *Sapho* loved to hate, or that out of love
shee could not be as courteous, as shee was in love
passionate.   Come, *Mileta,* shut the doore. [*Exeunt.*

ACTUS QUINTUS. SCÆNA TERTIA.

Phao, Sybilla.

Phao. Goe to *Sybilla*, tell the beginning of thy love, and the end of thy fortune. And loe how happily shee sitteth in her cave. *Sybilla?*

Sybi. *Phao*, welcome, what newes?

Phao. *Venus*, the goddesse of love, I loath, *Cupid* caused it with a new shaft. *Sapho* disdaineth me, *Venus* caused it for a new spite. O *Sybilla!* if *Venus* be unfaithfull in love, where shall one flie for truth? She useth deceit, is it not then likely shee will dispense with subtiltie? And being carefull to commit injuries, will shee not be carelesse to revenge them; I must now fall from love to labour, and endevour with mine oare to get a fare, not with my pen to write a fancie. Loves are but smokes, which vanish in the seeing, and yet hurt whilest they are seene. A ferrie, *Phao*, no the starres cannot call it a worser fortune. Range rather over the world, forsweare affections, entreate for death. O *Sapho!* thou hast *Cupid* in thine armes, I in my hart; thou kissest him for sport; I must curse him for spite: yet wil I not curse him, *Sapho*, whom thou kissest. This shall bee my resolution, where ever I wander to be as I were ever kneeling before *Sapho;* my loyaltie unspotted, though unrewarded. With as little malice will I goe to my grave, as I did lie withall in my cradle. My life shall be spent in sighing and wishing, the one for my bad fortune, the other for *Saphoes* good.

Sybi. Doe so, *Phao :* for destinie calleth thee as well

from *Sicily* as from love. Other things hang over thy head, which I must neither tell, nor thou enquire. And so farewell.

Phao. Farewell, *Sybilla*, and farewell *Sicily*. Thoughts shall be thy food, and in thy steps shall be printed behind thee, that there was none so loyall left behinde thee. Farewel *Syracusa*, unworthy to harbour faith, and when I am gone, unlesse *Sapho* be here, unlikely to harbour any.

THE EPILOGUE.

THEY that tread in a maze, walke oftentimes in one path, and at the last come out where they entred in. Wee feare wee have lead you all this while in a labyrinth of conceits, divers times hearing one device, and have now brought you to an end, where we first began. Which wearisome travaile you must impute to the necessitie of the historie, as *Theseus* did his labour to the art of the labyrinth. There is nothing causeth such giddinesse, as going in a wheele; neither can there any thing breed such tediousnesse, as hearing many words uttered in a small compasse. But if you accept this dance of a farie in a circle, wee will hereafter at your wils frame our fingers to all formes. And so wee wish every one of you a thread, to lead you out of the doubts wherewith wee leave you intangled, that nothing be mistaken by our rash oversights, nor misconstrued by your deepe insights.

GALLATHEA.

PLAYED BEFORE THE QUEENES MAJESTIE AT GREEN-WICH, ON NEW-YEERES DAY AT NIGHT.

BY THE CHILDREN OF PAULS,

DRAMATIS PERSONÆ.

NEPTUNE.
CUPID.
FAIRIES.
TYTERUS. } aged Shepherds.
MELEBEUS.
ERICTHINIS.
ALCHEMIST.
ASTRONOMER.
AUGUR.
MARINER.
RALPH.
ROBIN.
DICK.
PETER, *the Alchemist's Boy.*

VENUS.
DIANA.
TELUSA.
EUROTA.
RAMIA. } *Diana's Nymphs.*
LARISSA.
GALLATHEA, *Daughter to Tyterus.*
PHILLIDA, *Daughter to Melebeus.*
HÆBE.

SCENE—*Lincolnshire.*

THE PROLOGUE.

IOS and *Smyrna* were two sweet cities, the first named of the *Violet*, the latter of the *Myrrhe*: *Homer* was borne in the one, and buried in the other; Your Majesties judgement and favour, are our sunne and shadow, the one comming of your deepe wisdome, the other of your wonted grace. Wee in all humilitie desire, that by the former, receiving our first breath, we may in the latter, take our last rest.

Augustus Cæsar had such piercing eyes, that whoso looked on him, was constrained to winke. Your Highnesse hath so perfit a judgement, that whatsoever wee offer, wee are enforced to blush; yet as the *Athenians* were most curious, that the lawne, wherewith *Minerva* was covered, should be without spot or wrinkle; so have we endevoured with all care, that what we present your Highnesse, should neither offend in scene nor syllable; knowing that as in the ground where gold groweth, nothing will prosper but gold; so in your Majesties mind, where nothing doth harbour but vertue, nothing can enter but vertue.

GALLATHEA.

ACTUS PRIMUS. SCÆNA PRIMA.

TYTERUS, GALLATHEA.

Tyterus.

THE sunne doth beate upon the plain fields, wherefore let us sit down, *Gallathea*, under this faire oake, by whose broad leaves being defended from the warme beames, wee may enjoy the fresh aire, which softly breathes from *Humber* flouds.

Galla. Father, you have devised wel; and whilst our flocke doth roame up and downe this pleasant greene, you shall recount to mee, if it please you, for what cause this tree was dedicated unto *Neptune*, and why you have thus disguised me.

Tyte. I doe agree thereto, and when thy state and my care be considered, thou shalt know this question was not asked in vaine.

Galla. I willingly attend.

Tyte. In times past, where thou seest a heape of small pyble, stood a stately temple of white marble, which was dedicated to the God of the Sea, (and in right being

so neere the sea) hither came all such as either ventured by long travell to see countries, or by great traffique
to use merchandise, offering sacrifice by fire, to get safetie
by water; yeelding thankes for perils past, and making
prayers for good successe to come; but fortune, constant
in nothing but inconstancie, did change her copie, as
the people their custome; for the land being oppressed
by *Danes*, who instead of sacrifice committed sacrilege;
instead of religion, rebellion; and made a prey of that
in which they should have made their prayers, tearing
downe the temple even with the earth, being almost
equall with the skies; enraged so the god, who binds
the winds in the hollowes of the earth, that he caused
the seas to breake their bounds, sith men had broke
their vowes, and to swell as farre above their reach, as
men had swerved beyond their reason: then might you
see ships sayle where sheepe fed, anchors cast where
ploughes goe, fishermen throw their nets, where hus-
bandmen sow their corne, and fishes throw their scales
where fowles doe breed their quils: then might you
gather froth where now is dew, rotten weeds for sweete
roses, and take view of monstrous maremaides, instead
of passing faire maides.

Galla. To heare these sweet marvailes I would mine
eyes were turned also into eares.

Tyte. But at the last our countrymen repenting, and
not too late because at last, *Neptune* either weary of his
wroth, or wary to doe them wrong, upon condition con-
sented to ease their miseries.

Galla. What condition will not miserable men accept?

Tyte. The condition was this, that at every five yeeres day, the fairest and chastest virgin in all the countrey, should be brought unto this tree, and heere being bound, (whom neither parentage shall excuse for honour, nor vertue for integrity) is left for a peace offering unto *Neptune.*

Galla. Deere is the peace that is bought with guilt-lesse bloud.

Tyte. I am not able to say that, but hee sendeth a monster called the *Agar,* against whose comming the waters roare, the fowles flie away, and the cattell in the field for terrour shunne the bankes.

Galla. And shee bound to endure that horrour?

Tyte. And shee bound to endure that horror.

Galla. Doth this monster devoure her?

Tyte. Whether shee bee devoured of him, or conveyed to *Neptune,* or drowned betweene both, it is not permitted to know, and incurreth danger to conjecture: Now, *Gallathea,* heere endeth my tale, and beginneth thy tragedie.

Galla. Alas! father, and why so?

Tyte. I would thou hadst beene lesse faire, or more fortunate, then shouldest thou not repine that I have disguised thee in this attire, for thy beautie will make thee to be thought worthy of this god; to avoide therefore destinie (for wisdome ruleth the starres) I thinke it better to use an unlawfull meanes (your honour preserved) then intolerable griefe, both life and honour hazarded, and to prevent (if it be possible) thy constellation by my craft. Now hast thou heard the custome of this countrey, the cause why this tree was dedicated unto *Neptune,* and the vexing care of thy fearefull father.

Galla. Father, I have beene attentive to heare, and by your patience am readie to answere. Destinie may bee deferred, not prevented : and therefore it were better to offer myselfe in triumph then to be drawne to it with dishonour. Hath nature (as you say) made mee so faire above all, and shall not vertue make mee as famous as others? Doe you not know (or doth overcarefulnesse make you forget) that an honorable death is to bee preferred before an infamous life. I am but a childe, and have not lived long, and yet not so childish, as I desire to live ever : vertues I meane to carry to my grave, not gray haires. I would I were as sure that destiny would light on mee, as I am resolved it could not feare me. Nature hath given me beautie, Vertue courage ; Nature must yeeld me death, Vertue honour. Suffer me therefore to die, for which I was borne, or let mee curse that I was borne, sith I may not die for it.

Tyte. Alasse! *Gallathea,* to consider the causes of change, thou art too young, and that I should find them out for thee too too fortunate.

Galla. The destinie to mee cannot be so hard, as the disguising hatefull.

Tyte. To gaine love the gods have taken shapes of beasts, and to save life art thou coy to take the attire of men?

Galla. They were beastly gods, that lust could make them seeme as beasts.

Tyte. In health it is easie to counsell the sicke, but

it's hard for the sicke to follow wholesome counsaile.
Well let us depart, the day is far spent.   [*Exeunt.*

ACTUS PRIMUS. SCÆNA SECUNDA.

CUPID, NYMPH OF DIANA.

Cupid. Faire Nymph, are you strayed from your company by chance, or love you to wander solitarily on purpose?

Nymph. Faire boy, or god, or whatever you bee; I
would you knew these woods are to me so well knowne,
that I cannot stray though I would; and my minde so
free, that to bee melancholy I have no cause. There
is none of *Dianaes* traine that any can traine, either out
of their way, or out of their wits.

Cupid. What is that *Diana?* a goddesse? What
her nymphs, virgins? What her pastimes, hunting?

Nymph. A goddesse? who knowes it not? Virgins?
Who thinkes it not? Hunting? Who loves it not?

Cupid. I pray thee, sweete wench, amongst all your
sweet troupe, is there not one that followeth the sweetest
thing, sweet love?

Nymph. Love? good sir, what meane you by it? or
what doe you call it?

Cupid. A heate full of coldnesse, a sweet full of bitternesse, a paine full of pleasantnesse; which maketh
thoughts have eyes, and hearts eares; bred by desire,
nursed by delight, weaned by jelousie, kilde by dissembling, buried by ingratitude; and this is love, faire
lady, will you any?

Nymph. If it be nothing else, it is but a foolish thing.

Cupid. Try, and you shall find it a pretie thing.

Nymph. I have neither will nor leysure, but I will follow *Diana* in the chace, whose virgins are all chaste, delighting in the bow that wounds the swift hart in the forrest, not fearing the bowe that strikes the soft heart in the chamber. This difference is betweene my mistris *Diana*, and your mother (as I ghesse) *Venus*, that all her nymphes are amiable and wise in their kind, the other amorous and too kind for their sexe; and so farewell, little god.   [*Exit.*

Cupid. *Diana*, and thou, and all thine, shall know that *Cupid* is a great god; I will practise a while in these woodes, and play such pranckes with these nymphes, that while they ayme to hit others with their arrowes, they shall bee wounded themselves with their owne eyes.   [*Exit.*

ACTUS PRIMUS. SCÆNA TERTIA.

MELEBEUS, PHILLIDA.

Meleb. Come, *Phillida*, faire *Phillida*, and I feare me too faire being my *Phillida*, thou knowest the custome of this country, and I the greatnes of thy beautie, we both the fiercenes of the monster *Agar.* Every one thinketh his owne child faire, but I know that which I most desire, and would least have, that thou art fairest. Thou shalt therefore disguise thyselfe in attire, least I should disguise myselfe in affection, in suffering thee to perish by a fond desire, whom I may preserve by a sure deceipt.

Phil. Deare father, Nature could not make me so

faire as she hath made you kinde, nor you more kinde then me dutifull. Whatsoever you command I will not refuse, because you command nothing but my safetie, and your happinesse. But how shall I be disguised?

Meleb. In mans apparell.

Phil. It will neither become my bodie, nor my mind.

Meleb. Why, *Phillida?*

Phil. For then I must keepe company with boyes, and commit follies unseemelie for my sexe; or keepe company with girles, and bee thought more wanton then becommeth. Besides I shall be ashamed of my long hose and short coate, and so unwarilie blabbe out something by blushing at every thing.

Meleb. Feare not, *Phillida,* use wil make it easie, feare must make it necessarie.

Phil. I agree, since my father will have it so, and fortune must.

Meleb. Come let us in, and when thou art disguised, roame about these woods till the time be past, and *Neptune* pleased. [*Exeunt.*

ACTUS PRIMUS. SCÆNA QUARTA.

MARINER, RAFFE, ROBIN, *and* DICKE.

Robin. Now, *Mariner,* what callest thou on the sea?

Mar. It is called a wracke.

Raffe. I take no pleasure in it. Of would not bee drowned, ones clothes wil when he is taken up.

Dicke. What cal'st thou the thing wee were bound to?

Mar. A raughter.

Raffe. I will rather hang myselfe on a raughter in the house, then be so haled in the sea, there one may have a leape for his life; but I marvaile how our master speedes.

Dicke. Ile warrant by this time he is wetshod. Did you ever see water bubble as the sea did? But what shall we doe?

Mar. You are now in Lyncolnshire, where you can want no foule, if you can devise meanes to catch them, there bee woods hard by, and at every miles end houses: so that if you seeke on the land, you shall speed better than on the sea.

Robin. Sea? nay I will never saile more! I brooke not their diet: their bread is so hard, that one must carie a whetstone in his mouth to grinde his teeth: the meate so salt, that one would thinke after dinner his tongue had beene powdred ten daies.

Raffe. O! thou hast a sweet life, *Mariner*, to be pin'd in a few boords, and to be within an inch of a thing bottomlesse. I pray thee how often hast thou beene drowned?

Mar. Foole thou seest I am yet alive.

Robin. Why bee they dead that bee drownd, I had thought they had bin with the fish, and so by chance bin caught up with them in a net againe. It were a shame a little cold water should kill a man of reason, when you shall see a poore mynow lie in it that hath no understanding.

Mar. Thou art wise from the crowne of thy head up-

wards: seeke you new fortunes now, I will follow mine
olde. I can shift the moone and the sun, and know by
one carde, what all you cannot do by a whole paire.
The load-stone that alwaies holdeth his nose to the north,
the two and thirty points for the winde, the wonders I
see would make all you blind: you be but boyes, I feare
the sea no more then a dish of water. Why, fooles, it
is but a liquid element. Farewell.

Robin. It were good we learned his cunning at the
cardes, for we must live by cosenage; wee have neither
lands nor wit, nor masters, nor honestie.

Raffe. Nay I would faine have his thirty two, that
is, his three dozen lacking foure points, for you see betwixt us three there is not two good points.

Dicke. Let us call him a little back that we may
learne those points. Sirra, a word: I pray thee shew
us thy points.

Mar. Will you learne?

Dicke. I.

Mar. Then as you like this I will instruct you in all
our secrets: for there is not a clowte nor carde, nor
boord, nor post, that hath not a speciall name, or singular nature.

Dicke. Well begin with your points, for I lacke only
points in this world.

Mar. North. North and by east. North north-east.
North-east and by north, north-east. North-east and
by east. East north-east, east and by north-east.

Dicke. Ile say it. North, north-east, north-east,
nore-nore and by nore-east. I shall never doe it!

Mar. This is but one quarter.

Robin. I shall never learne a quarter of it. I will try. North, north-east, is by the west side, north and by north.

Dicke. Passing ill!

Mar. Hast thou no memorie? Try thou.

Raffe. North north and by north. I can goe no further!

Mar. O dullard! is thy head lighter then the wind, and thy tongue so heavie it will not wagge? I will once againe say it.

Raffe. I will never learne this language, it will get but small living, when it will scarce be learned till one be olde.

Mar. Nay then farwell; and if your fortunes exceed not your wits, you shall starve before ye sleepe. [*Exit.*

Raffe. Was there ever such cosening? Come let us to the woods, and see what fortune wee may have before they bee made shippes: as for our master hee is drownd.

Dicke. I will this way.

Robin. I this.

Raffe. I this, and this day twelvemounth let us all meete heere againe: it may bee we shall either beg together, or hang together.

Dicke. It skils not so we be together. But let us sing now, though wee cry heereafter. [*Exeunt.*

SONG.

Omnes. Rocks, shelves, and sands, and seas, farewell.
　　　Fie! who would dwell
　　　In such a hell

> As is a ship, which (drunke) does reele,
> Taking salt healths from deck to keele.
> *Robin.* Up were we swallowed in wet graves,
> *Dicke.*   All sowc't in waves,
> *Raffe.*   By *Neptune's* slaves.
> *Omnes.* What shall wee doe being toss'd to shore?
> *Robin.* Milke some blinde taverne, and (there) roare.
> *Raffe.* Tis brave (my boyes) to saile on land,
>   For being well man'd,
>   We can cry stand,
> *Dicke.* The trade of pursing neare shal faile,
>   Until the hangman cryes strike saile.
> *Omnes.* Rove then no matter whither,
>   In faire or stormy wether.
>   And as wee live, lets dye together,
>   One hempen caper, cuts a feather.

ACTUS SECUNDUS. SCÆNA PRIMA.

GALLATHEA *alone.*

BLUSH, *Gallathea,* that must frame thy affection fit for thy habit, and therefore be thought immodest, because thou art unfortunate. Thy tender yeares cannot dissemble this deceipt, nor thy sexe beare it. O would the gods had made mee as I seeme to bee, or that I might safely bee what I seeme not. Thy father doteth, *Gallathea,* whose blinde love corrupteth his fond judgement, and jealous of thy death, seemeth to dote on thy beauty; whose fond care carrieth his partiall eye as farre from trueth, as his hart is from falshood. But why dost thou blame him, or blab what thou art, when thou shouldest onely counterfet what thou art not. But whist! heere commeth a lad: I will learne of him how to behave myselfe.

Enter PHILLIDA *in man's attire.*

Phil. I neither like my gate, nor my garments; the one untoward, the other unfit; both unseemely. O *Phillida!* but yonder staieth one, and therefore say nothing; but O *Phillida!*

Galla. I perceive that boyes are in as great disliking of themselves as maides, therefore though I weare the apparell, I am glad I am not the person.

Phil. It is a pretty boy and a faire, he might well have beene a woman; but because he is not, I am glad I am, for now under the colour of my coate, I shall de-cipher the follies of their kind.

Galla. I would salute him, but I feare I should make a curtesie instead of a legge.

Phil. If I durst trust my face as well as I doe my habite, I would spend some time to make pastime, for say what they will of a man's wit, it is no second thing to be a woman.

Galla. All the bloud in my body would bee in my face, if he should aske me (as the question among men is common) are you a maide?

Phil. Why stand I still? boyes should be bolde; but heere commeth a brave traine that will spill all our talke.

Enter DIANA, TELUSA, *and* EUROTA.

Diana. God speed, faire boy.

Galla. You are deceived, lady.

Diana. Why, are you no boy?

Galla. No faire boy.

Diana. But I see an unhappy boy.

Tel. Saw you not the deare come this way, hee flew downe the wind, and I beleeve you have blancht him.

Galla. Whose deare was it, ladie?

Tel. Diana's deare.

Galla. I saw none but mine owne deare.

Tel. This wagge is wanton or a foole! Aske the other, *Diana.*

Galla. I know not how it commeth to passe, but yonder boy is in mine eye too beautifull; I pray the gods the ladies thinke him not their deare.

Diana. Prettie lad, doe your sheepe feed in the forrest, or are you straied from your flocke, or on purpose come yee to marre *Diana's* pastime?

Phil. I understand not one word you speake.

Diana. What, art thou neither lad nor shepheard?

Phil. My mother said I could be no lad till I was twentie yeare old, nor keepe sheepe till I could tell them; and therefore, lady, neither lad nor shephard is heere.

Tel. These boyes are both agreed, either they are verie pleasant or too perverse: you were best, lady, make them tuske these woodes, whilest we stand with our bowes, and so use them as beagles since they have so good mouthes.

Diana. I wil. Follow me without delay, or excuse, and if you can doe nothing, yet shall you hallow the deare.

Phil. I am willing to goe, not for these ladies companie, because myselfe am a virgine, but for that fayre boyes favour, who I thinke be a god.

Diana. You, sir boy, shall also goe.

Galla. I must if you command, and would if you bad not. [*Exeunt.*

ACTUS SECUNDUS. SCÆNA SECUNDA.

Cupid *alone in Nymphes apparell, and* Neptune *lystning.*

Cupid. Now, *Cupid,* under the shape of a silly girle shew the power of a mightie god. Let *Diana* and all her coy nymphes know, that there is no heart so chaste but thy bow can wound; nor eyes so modest, but thy brandes can kindle; nor thoughts so staied, but thy shafts can make wavering, weake and wanton : *Cupid,* though he bee a child, is no babie. I will make their paines my pastimes, and so confound their loves in their owne sexe, that they shall dote in their desires, delight in their affections, and practise onely impossibilities. Whilest I trewant from my mother, I will use some tyranny in these woodes, and so shall their exercise in foolish love, bee my excuse for running away. I wil see whether faire faces be alwaies chast, or *Diana's* virgins onely modest, else wil I spende both my shafts and shifts, and then, ladies, if you see these daintie dames intrapt in love, say softly to yourselves, we may all love. [*Exit.*

Nept. Doe silly shepheards goe about to deceive great *Neptune,* in putting on man's attire upon women : and *Cupid* to make sport deceive them all, by using a woman's apparell upon a god ; then *Neptune* that hast taken sundry shapes to obtaine love, sticke not to practise some deceipt to shew thy deity ; and having often thrust thyselfe into the shape of beastes to deceive men, be not coy to use the shape of a shepheard, to shew thyselfe a god. *Neptune* cannot be over-reached by swaines, himselfe is subtile, and if *Diana* be over-taken by craft, *Cupid* is wise. I will into these woodes and marke all, and in the end wil marre all.   [*Exit.*

ACTUS SECUNDUS. SCÆNA TERTIA.

Enter RAFFE *alone.*

Raffe. Call you this seeking of fortunes when one can finde nothing but birds nestes? would I were out of these woods, for I shall have but woodden lucke; here's nothing but the skreeking of owles, croking of frogs, hissing of adders, barking of foxes, walking of hagges. But what be these? [*Enter Fairies dauncing and playing and so, Exeunt.*] I will follow them, to hel I shall not goe, for so faire faces never can have such hard fortunes. What black boy is this?

Enter the Alcumist's boy PETER.

Peter. What a life doe I lead with my master, no-thing but blowing of bellowes, beating of spirits, and scraping of croslets? it is a very secret science, for none almost can understand the language of it. Sublimation, almigation, calcination, rubification, encorporation, circi-nation, sementation, albification, and frementation; with as many termes unpossible to be uttered, as the arte to bee compassed.

Raffe. Let mee crosse myselfe, I never heard so many great devils in a little monkies mouth.

Peter. Then our instruments, croslets, sublivatories,

cucurbits, limbecks, decensores, violes, manuall and murall, for enbibing and conbibing; bellowes, molificative and endurative.

Raffe. What language is this? doe they speak so?

Peter. Then our metals; saltpeeter, vitrioll, sal tartar, sal perperat, argoll, resagar, sal armonick, egrimony, lumany, brimstone, valerian, tartar alam, breeme-worte, glasse, unsleked lyme, chalke, ashes, hayre, and what not; to make I know not what.

Raffe. My haire beginneth to stand upright, would the boy would make an end!

Peter. And yet such a beggerly science it is, and so strong on multiplication, that the end is to have neither gold, wit, nor honestie.

Raffe. Then am I just of thy occupation. What fellow, well met.

Peter. Fellow! upon what acquaintance?

Raffe. Why thou saist, the end of thy occupation is to have neither wit, money nor honestie; and methinks at a blush, thou shouldest be one of my occupation.

Peter. Thou art deceived, my master is an alcumist.

Raffe. What's that, a man?

Peter. A little more than a man, and a haires bredth lesse than a god. Hee can make of thy cap gold, and by multiplication of one grote three old angels. I have knowne him of the tagge of a point, to make a silver boule of a pint.

Raffe. That makes thee have never a point, they be al turned to pots: but if he can do this, he shall be a god altogether.

Peter. If thou have any gold to worke on, thou art

then made for ever : for with one pound of golde, hee will goe neere to pave tenne akers of ground.

Raffe. How might a man serve him and learne his cunning ?

Peter. Easily. First seeme to understand the termes, and specially marke these points. In our art there are four spirits.

Raffe. Nay, I have done if you worke with devils !

Peter. Thou art grosse ; we call those spirits that are the grounds of our arte, and as it were the metals more incorporative for domination. The first spirit is quick-silver.

Raffe. That is my spirit, for my silver is so quicke, that I have much adoe to catch it ; and when I have it, it is so nimble that I cannot hold it ; I thought there was devill in it.

Peter. The second, orpyment.

Raffe. That's no spirit, but a word to conjure a spirit.

Peter. The third, sal armoniack.

Raffe. A proper word.

Peter. The fourth, brimstone.

Raffe. That's a stincking spirit, I thought there was some spirit in it because it burnt so blew. For my mother would often tell me that when the candle burnt blew, there was some ill spirit in the house, and now I per-ceive it was the spirit brimstone.

Peter. Thou canst remember these foure spirits.

Raffe. Let me alone to conjure them.

Peter. Now are there also seaven bodies,—but heere commeth my master.

Enter ALCUMIST.

Raffe. This is a begger.

Peter. No, such cunning men must disguise themselves, as though there were nothing in them, for otherwise they shal be compelled to worke for princes, and so bee constrained to bewray their secrets.

Raffe. I like not his attire, but am enamored of his arte.

Alcum. An ounce of silver limde, as much of crude *Mercury*, of spirits foure, being tempered with the bodies seaven, by multiplying of it ten times, comes for one pound eight thousand pounds, so that I may have onely beechen coales.

Raffe. Is it possible?

Peter. It is more certaine then certainty.

Raffe. Ile tell thee one secret, I stole a silver thimble, dost thou thinke that hee will make it a pottle pot?

Peter. A pottle pot! nay I dare warrant it a whole cupbord of plate! why of the quintessence of a leaden plummet, hee hath framed xx dozen of silver spoones. Looke how hee studies. I durst venture my life hee is now casting about, how of his breath he may make golden bracelets, for often-times of smoke hee hath made silver drops.

Raffe. What doe I heare?

Peter. Didst thou never heare how *Jupiter* came in a golden shower to *Danae?*

Raffe. I remember that tale.

Peter. That shower did my master make of a spoonefull of tartar-alom; but with the fire of bloud, and the

corasive of the ayre, he is able to make nothing infinite,
—but whilest he espieth us.

Alcum. What, *Peter,* doe you loyter, knowing that
every minute increaseth our mine?

Peter. I was glad to take ayre, for the metall came
so fast, that I feared my face would have beene turned
to silver.

Alcum. But what stripling is this?

Peter. One that is desirous to learne your craft.

Alcum. Craft, sir boy! you must call it mystery.

Raffe. All is one, a craftie mystery, and a mysticall
craft.

Alcum. Canst thou take paines?

Raffe. Infinite.

Alcum. But thou must be sworne to bee secret, and
then I will entertaine thee.

Raffe. I can sweare though I be a poore fellow as
well as the best man in the shyre. But, sir, I much
marvaile that you being so cunning, should be so ragged.

Alcum. O my child, grypes make their nests of gold
though their coates are feathers; and wee feather our
nests with diamonds, though our garments be but frize.
If thou knewest the secret of this science the cunning
would make thee so proud that thou wouldest disdaine
the outward pompe.

Peter. My master is so ravisht with his arte that wee
many times goe supperlesse to bed, for he will make
gold of his bread, and such is the drougth of his desire,
that we all wish our very guts were gold.

Raffe. I have good fortune to light upon such a
master.

Alcum. When in the depth of my skill I determine to try the uttermost of mine arte, I am disswaded by the gods; otherwise, I durst undertake to make the fire as it flames, gold; the winde as it blowes, silver; the water as it runnes, lead; the earth as it stands, yron; the skie, brasse; and men's thoughts, firme mettles.

Raffe. I must blesse myselfe, and marvell at you.

Alcum. Come in, and thou shalt see all. [*Exit.*

Raffe. I follow, I runne, I flye; they say my father hath a golden thumbe, you shall see me have a golden body. [*Exit.*

Peter. I am glad of this, for now I shall have leysure to runne away; such a bald arte as never was! let him keepe his new man, for he shall never see his olde againe; god shield me from blowing gold to nothing, with a strong imagination to make nothing any thing.

[*Exit.*

ACTUS SECUNDUS. SCÆNA QUARTA.

GALLATHEA *alone.*

Galla. How now, *Gallathea?* miserable *Gallathea!* that having put on the apparel of a boy, thou canst also put on the minde. O faire *Melebeus!* I, too faire! and therefore I feare, too proud. Had it not bin better for thee to have been a sacrifice to *Neptune*, then a slave to *Cupid?* to die for thy country, then to live in thy fancie? to be a sacrifice, then a lover? O would when I hunted his eye with my heart, hee might have seene my heart with his eyes. Why did Nature to him, a boy, give a face so faire; or to me, a virgine, a fortune so hard? I will now use for the distaffe the bow, and play at quaites abroade that was wont to sow in my sampler at home. It may be, *Gallathea,*—foolish *Gallathea,* what may be?—nothing. Let mee follow him into the woods, and thou, sweet *Venus,* be my guide. [*Exit.*

ACTUS SECUNDUS. SCÆNA QUINTA.

Enter PHILLIDA *alone.*

Phil. Poore *Phillida,* curse the time of thy birth and rarenes of thy beauty, the unaptness of thy apparell, and the untamednes of thy affections. Art thou no sooner in the habite of a boy, but thou must bee enamored of a boy? what shalt thou do when what best liketh thee, most discontenteth thee? Goe into the woods, watch the good times, his best moodes, and transgresse in love a little of thy modestie. I will, I dare not,—thou must, I cannot. Then pine in thine owne peevishnes. I will not, I will. Ah, *Phillida,* doe something, nay any thing rather then live thus. Well, what I will doe, myselfe knowes not, but what I ought I know too well, and so I goe resolute, eyther to bewray my love, or suffer shame. [*Exit.*

ACTUS TERTIUS. SCÆNA PRIMA.

TELUSA *alone.*

Telusa.

OW now? what new conceits, what strange contraries breede in thy minde? is thy *Diana* become a *Venus,* thy chast thoughts

turned to wanton lookes, thy conquering modestie to a
captive imagination? Beginnest thou with *Piralis* to
die in the ayre and live in the fire, to leave the sweet
delight of hunting, and to follow the hote desire of love?
O *Telusa*, these words are unfit for thy sexe being a virgin, but apt for thy affections being a lover. And can
there in yeares so young, in education so precise, in vowes
so holy, and in a heart so chast, enter either a strong
desire or a wish, or a wavering thought of love? Can
Cupid's brands quench *Vesta's* flames, and his feeble
shafts headed with feathers pearce deeper then *Diana's*
arrowes headed with steele? Breake thy bow, *Telusa*,
that seekest to breake thy vow, and let those hands that
aymed to hit the wild hart, scratch out those eyes that
have wounded thy tame hart. O vaine and onely naked
name of chastity, that is made eternal, and perisheth
by time : holy, and is infected by fancy : divine, and is
made mortall by folly. Virgins' harts, I perceive, are
not unlike cotten trees, whose fruit is so hard in the bud,
that it soundeth like steele, and being ripe, poureth
forth nothing but wool ; and their thoughts like the
leaves of lunary, which the further they grow from the
sun, the sooner they are scorched with his beames. O
Melebeus, because thou art faire, must I be fickle, and
falsifie my vow because I see thy vertue? Fond girle
that I am to thinke of love, nay vaine profession that I
follow to disdaine love ; but heere commeth *Eurota*, I
must now put on a red maske and blush, least shee perceive my pale face and laugh.

Enter EUROTA.

Eurota. Telusa, Diana bid mee hunt you out, and saith that you care not to hunt with her, but if you follow any other game then shee hath rowsde, your punishment shall bee to bend all our bowes, and weave all our strings. Why looke yee so pale, so sad, so wildly?

Tel. Eurota, the game I follow is the thing I flie: my strange disease my chiefe desire.

Eurota. I am no *Oedipus* to expound riddles, and I muse how thou canst bee *Sphinx* to utter them. But I pray thee, *Telusa,* tell mee what thou aylest, if thou be sicke, this ground hath leaves to heale: if melancholy, heere are pastimes to use: if peevish, wit must weane it, or time, or counsell. If you bee in love (for I have heard of such a beast called Love) it shall bee cured; why blushest thou, *Telusa?*

Tel. To heare thee in reckoning my paines to recite thine owne. I saw, *Eurota,* how amorously you glanced your eye on the faire boy in the white coate, and how cunningly (now that you would have some talke of love) you hit mee in the teeth with love.

Eurota. I confesse that I am in love, and yet sweare that I know not what it is. I feele my thoughts unknit, mine eyes unstayed, my heart I know not how affected, or infected, my sleepes broken and full of dreames, my wakenesse sad and full of sighes, myselfe in all things unlike myselfe. If this be love, I would it had never beene devised.

Tel. Thou hast told what I am in uttering what thyselfe is: these are my passions, *Eurota,* my unbridled passions, my intolerable passions, which I were as good acknowledge and crave counsell, as to denie and endure perill.

Eurota. How did it take you first, *Telusa?*

Tel. By the eyes, my wanton eyes which conceived the picture of his face, and hanged it on the very strings of my heart. O faire *Melebeus!* O fond *Telusa!* but how did it take you, *Eurota?*

Eurota. By the eares, whose sweete words sunke so deepe into my head, that the remembrance of his wit hath bereaved me of my wisdome; O eloquent *Tyterus!* O credulous *Eurota!* But soft, here commeth *Ramia*, but let her not heare us talke, wee will withdraw our-selves, and heare her talke.

Enter RAMIA.

Ramia. I am sent to seeke others that have lost my-selfe.

Eurota. You shall see *Ramia* hath also bitten on a love leafe.

Ramia. Can there be no heart so chast, but love can wound? nor vowes so holy, but affection can violate. Vaine art thou vertue, and thou chastitie but a by word, when you both are subject to love, of all things the most abject. If Love bee a god, why should not lovers bee vertuous? Love is a god, and lovers are vertuous.

Eurota. Indeed, *Ramia*, if lovers were not vertuous, then wert thou vicious.

Ramia. What are you come so neere me?

Tel. I thinke wee came neere you when we said you loved.

Eurota. Tush, *Ramia!* 'tis too late to recall it, to repent it a shame: therefore I pray thee tell what is love?

Ramia. If myselfe felt onely this infection, I would then take upon me the definition, but being incident to so many, I dare not myselfe describe it, but we will all talke of that in the woods. *Diana* stormeth that sending one to seeke another, shee looseth all. *Servia* of all the nymphes the coyest, loveth deadly, and exclaymeth against *Diana*, honoureth *Venus*, detesteth *Vesta*, and maketh a common scorne of vertue. *Clymene*, whose stately lookes seemed to amaze the greatest lords, stoopeth, yeeldeth, and fauneth on the strange boy in the woods. Myselfe (with blushing I speake it) am thrall to that boy, that faire boy! that beautifull boy!

Tel. What have wee here, all in love? no other food then fancie; no, no, shee shall not have the faire boy.

Eurota. Nor you, *Telusa.*

Ramia. Nor you, *Eurota.*

Tel. I love *Melebeus*, and my deserts shall be answerable to my desires. I will forsake *Diana* for him. I will die for him!

Ramia. So saith *Clymene*, and shee will have him. I care not, my sweet *Tyterus*, though he seeme proud, I impute it to childishnesse: who being yet scarce out of swath-clowtes, cannot understand these deepe conceits; I love him.

Eurota. So doe I, and I will have him!

Tel. Immodest all that we are, unfortunate all that we are like to be; shall virgins beginne to wrangle for love, and become wanton in their thoughts, in their

words, in their actions. O divine Love! which art therefore called divine, because thou over-reachest the wisest,
conquerest the chastest, and doest all things both unlikely and impossible, because thou art Love. Thou
makest the bashfull impudent, the wise fond, the chast
wanton, and workest contraries to our reach, because
thyselfe is beyond reason.

Eurota. Talke no more, *Telusa,* your words wound.
Ah! would I were no woman!

Ramia. Would *Tyterus* were no boy!

Tel. Would *Telusa* were nobodie!   [*Exeunt.*

ACTUS TERTIUS.   SCÆNA SECUNDA.

Phillida *and* Gallathea.

Phil. It is pittie that Nature framed you not a woman,
having a face so faire, so lovely a countenance, so modest a behaviour.

Galla. There is a tree in *Tylos* whose nuts have shels
like fire, and being cracked the kernell is but water.

Phil. What a toy is it to tell mee of that tree, being
nothing to the purpose! I say it is pittie you are not a
woman.

Galla. I would not wish to be a woman unles it were
because thou art a man.

Phil. Nay, I doe not wish to be a woman, for then I
should not love thee, for I have sworne never to love a
woman.

Galla. A strange humour in so prettie a youth, and
according to mine, for myselfe will never a woman.

Phil. It were a shame if a mayden should be a suter,

(a thing hated in that sexe) that thou shouldest deny to bee her servant.

Galla. If it be a shame in mee, it can be no commendation in you, for yourselfe is of that minde.

Phil. Suppose I were a virgin (I blush in supposing myselfe one) and that under the habite of a boy were the person of a maide, if I should utter my affection with sighes, manifest my sweet love by my salt teares, and prove my loyaltie unspotted, and my griefes intolerable, would not then that faire face pittie this true heart?

Galla. Admit that I were, as you would have me suppose that you are; and that I should with intreaties, prayers, oathes, bribes, and whatever can be invented in love, desire your favour,—would you not yeeld?

Phil. Tush! you come in with *admit!*

Galla. And you with *suppose!*

Phil. What doubtfull speeches bee these? I feare mee hee is as I am, a mayden.

Galla. What dread riseth in my mind, I feare the boy to bee as I am a mayden.

Phil. Tush! it cannot bee,—his voice shewes the contrary.

Galla. Yet I doe not thinke it,—for hee would then have blushed.

Phil. Have you ever a sister?

Galla. If I had but one, my brother must needs have two; but I pray have you ever a one?

Phil. My father had but one daughter, and therefore I could have no sister.

Galla. Aye me! hee is as I am, for his speeches be as mine are.

Phil. What shall I doe, either hee is subtill, or my sexe simple.

Galla. I have knowne divers of *Dianaes* nymphes enamoured of him, yet hath hee rejected all, either as too proud to disdaine, or too childish not to understand; or for that he knoweth himselfe to be a virgin.

Phil. I am in a quandarie; *Dianaes* nymphes have followed him, and he despised them, either knowing too well the beautie of his owne face, or that himselfe is of the same mould. I will once againe try him. You promised me in the woods, that you would love mee before all *Dianaes* nymphes.

Galla. I, so you would love me before all *Dianaes* nymphes.

Phil. Can you preferre a fonde boy as I am, before so faire ladies as they are.

Galla. Why should not I as well as you?

Phil. Come let us into the grove, and make much one of another, that cannot tell what to thinke one of another.   [*Exeunt.*

ACTUS TERTIUS. SCÆNA TERTIA.

ALCUMIST, RAFFE.

Alcum. *Raffe,* my boy is run away, I trust thou wilt not run after.

Raffe. I would I had a paire of wings that I might flie after.

Alcum. My boy was the veriest thiefe, the arrantest lyer, and the vilest swearer in the world, otherwise the best boy in the world; hee hath stolne my apparell, all my money, and forgot nothing but to bid me farewell.

Raffe. That will not I forget; farewell, master!

Alcum. Why thou hast not yet seene the end of my art.

Raffe. I would I had not knowne the beginning! Did not you promise mee, of my silver thimble to make a whole cup-board of plate, and that of a *Spanish* needle you would build a silver steeple?

Alcum. I, *Raffe*, the fortune of this art consisteth in the measure of the fire, for if there bee a coale too much, or a sparke too little, if it bee a little too hote, or a thought too soft, all our labour is in vaine; besides, they that blow, must beat time with their breaths, as musicians doe with their breasts; so as there must be of the metals, the fire, and workers, a very harmony.

Raffe. Nay, if you must weigh your fire by ounces, and take measure of a man's blast, you may then make of a dramme of winde a wedge of gold, and of the shadow of one shilling make another, so as you have an organist to tune your temperatures.

Alcum. So is it, and often doth it happen, that the just proportion of the fire and all things concurre.

Raffe. Concurre? condogge! I will away.

Alcum. Then away.   [*Exit Alcumist.*

Enter ASTRONOMER.

Raffe. An arte, quoth you, that one multiplyeth so much all day, that hee wanteth money to buy meate at night? But what have we yonder? What devout man? he will never speake till hee be urged. I will salute him. Sir, there lieth a purse under your feet, if I thought it were not yours, I would take it up.

Astron. Doest thou not know that I was calculating the nativitie of *Alexander's* great horse?

Raffe. Why, what are you?

Astron. An astronomer.

Raffe. What one of those that makes almanackes?

Astron. Ipsissimus. I can tell the minute of thy birth, the moment of thy death, and the manner. I can tell thee what weather shall bee betweene this and *octogessimus octavus mirabilis annus.* When I list I can set a trap for the sun, catch the moone with lyme-twigs, and goe a bat-fowling for stars. I can tell thee things past, and things to come, and with my cunning, measure how many yards of cloudes are beneath the skie, Nothing can happen which I fore-see not,—nothing shall !

Raffe. I hope, sir, you are no more then a god.

Astron. I can bring the twelve signes out of their zodiacks, and hang them up at tavernes.

Raffe. I pray you, sir, tell mee what you cannot doe? for I perceive there is nothing so easie for you to compasse as impossibilities. But what be those signes?

Astron. As a man should say, signes which governe the bodie. The ram governeth the head.

Raffe. That is the worst signe for the head.

Astron. Why?

Raffe. Because it is a signe of an ill ewe.

Astron. Tush, that signe must bee there. Then the bull for the throte, *Capricornus* for the knees.

Raffe. I will heare no more signes, if they be all such desperate signes: but seeing you are, (I know not who to terme you) shall I serve you? I would faine serve.

Astron. I accept thee.

Raffe. Happy am I! for now shall I reach thoughts, and tell how many drops of water goes to the greatest ,showre of raine. You shall see me catch the moone in the 'clips like a cony in a pursnet.

Astron. I will teach thee the golden number, the epact, and the prime,

Raffe. I will meddle no more with numbring of gold, for multiplication is a miserable action; I pray, sir, what weather shall wee have this houre threescore yeere?

Astron. That I must cast by our judicials astrono-micall; therefore come in with me, and thou shall see every wrinkle in my astrologicall wisdome; and I will make the heavens as plaine to thee as the high way, thy cunning shall sit cheeke by jole with the sunnes chariot; then shalt thou see what a base thing it is to have others thoughts creepe on the ground, when as thine shall bee stitched to the starres.

Raffe. Then I shall be translated from this mortality.

Astron. Thy thoughts shall be metamorphosed and made haile fellowes with the gods.

Raffe. O fortune! I feele my very braines moral-lized, and as it were a certaine contempt of earthly actions is crept into my minde, by an aetheriall contemplation. Come let us in.   [*Exeunt.*

ACTUS TERTIUS. SCÆNA QUARTA.

DIANA, TELUSA, EUROTA, RAMIA, LARISSA.

Diana. What newes have we here, ladies! are all in

love? are *Diana's* nymphs become *Venus'* wantons? is it a shame to be chast, because you be amiable? or must you needs be amorous, because you are faire? O *Venus*, if this be thy spight, I will requite it with more then hate! well shalt thou know what it is to drib thine arrowes up and downe *Diana's* leyes! There is an unknowne nymph that straggleth up and downe these woods which I suspect hath beene the weaver of these woes, I saw her slumbring by the brooke side; go search her and bring her; if you find upon her shoulder a burne, it is *Cupid*: if any print on her backe like a leafe, it is *Medea*: if any picture on her left brest like a bird, it is *Calipso*; whoever it bee, bring her hither, and speedily bring her hither.

Tel. I will goe with speed.

Diana. Goe you, *Larissa*, and helpe her.

Larissa. I obey.

Diana. Now, ladies, doth not that make your cheekes blush, that makes mine eares glowe? or can you remember that without sobs, which *Diana* cannot thinke on without sighes? What greater dishonour could happen to *Diana*, or to her nymphes shame, then that there can be any time so idle, that should make their heads so addle? Your chast hearts, my nymphes, should resemble the onix, which is hotest when it is whitest; and your thoughts, the more they are assaulted with desires, the lesse they should be affected. You should thinke love like *Homer's Moly*; a white leafe and a blacke root; a faire shew, and a bitter taste. Of all trees the cedar is greatest, and hath the smallest seedes: of all affections, love hath the greatest name, and the least

vertue. Shall it bee said, and shall *Venus* say it?—nay,
shall it bee seene, and shall wantons see it?—that *Diana* the goddesse of chastitie, whose thoughts are alwayes answerable to her vowes, whose eyes never glanced
on desire, and whose heart abateth the point of *Cupid's*
arrowes, shall have her virgins to become unchast in desires, immoderate in affection, untemperate in love, in
foolish love, in base love! Eagles cast their evill feathers in the sunne, but you cast your best desires upon
a shadow. The birds' *Ibes* lose their sweetnesse when
they lose their sights, and virgins all their vertues with
their unchast thoughts; unchast, *Diana* calleth that,
that hath either any shew or suspicion of lightnesse. O
my deere nymphes! if you knew how loving thoughts
staine lovely faces, you would bee as carefull to have the
one as unspotted, as the other beautifull. Cast before
your eyes the loves of *Venus'* truls, their fortunes, their
fancies, their ends. What are they else but *Silenus'*
pictures; without, lambes and doves; within, apes and
owles; who like *Ixion* imbrace clouds for *Juno*, the
shadowes of vertue in stead of the substance. The eagle's feathers consume the feathers of all others, and
love's desire corrupteth all other vertues. I blush, ladies, that you having beene heretofore patient of labours,
should now become prentises to idlenes; and use the pen
for sonets, not the needle for samplers. And how is
your love placed? upon pelting boyes! perhaps base of
birth, without doubt weake of discretion. I, but they
are faire! O ladies! doe your eyes begin to love colours, whose hearts were wont to loath them? is *Diana's*
chase become *Venus'* court? and are your holy vowes
turned to hollow thoughts?

Ramia. Madame, if love were not a thing beyond reason, we might then give a reason of our doings; but so divine is his force, that it worketh effects as contrarie to that wee wish, as unreasonable against that we ought.

Larissa. Lady, so unacquainted are the passions of love, that wee can neither describe them nor beare them.

Diana. Foolish girles! how willing you are to follow that which you should flie! But heere commeth *Telusa.*

Enter TELUSA *and other with* CUPID.

Tel. We have brought the disguised nymph, and have found on his shoulder *Psiche's* burne, and he confesseth himselfe to be *Cupid.*

Diana. How now, sir! are you caught? are you *Cupid?*

Cupid. Thou shalt see, *Diana*, that I dare confesse myselfe to be *Cupid.*

Diana. And thou shalt see, *Cupid*, that I will shew myselfe to bee *Diana;* that is, conqueror of thy loose and untamed appetites. Did thy mother *Venus* under the colour of a nymph, send thee hither to wound my nymphes? Doth shee adde craft to her malice, and mistrusting her deitie, practise deceit: is there no place but my groves, no persons but my nymphes? Cruell and unkind *Venus*, that spighteth onely chastitie, thou shalt see that *Dianaes* power shall revenge thy policie, and tame this pride. As for thee, *Cupid*, I will breake thy bow, and burne thine arrowes, binde thy hands, clip thy wings, and fetter thy feet. Thou that fattest others with hopes, shalt be fed thyselfe with wishes; and thou that bindest others with golden thoughts, shalt be bound thyselfe with golden fetters ; *Venus'* rods are made of roses, *Dianaes* of bryers. Let *Venus* that great goddesse, ransome *Cupid* that little god. These ladies here whom thou hast infected with foolish love, shall both tread on thee and triumph over thee. Thine owne arrow shal be shot into thine owne bosome, and thou shalt bee inamoured, not on *Psiche's*, but on *Circe's*. I will teach thee what it is to displease *Diana*, distresse her nymphs, or disturbe her game.

Cupid. Diana, what I have done, cannot be undone, but what you meane to doe, shall. *Venus* hath some gods to her friends, *Cupid* shall have all.

Diana. Are you prating ? I will bridle thy tongue and thy power, and in spight of mine owne thoughts, I will set thee a taske every day, which if thou finish not, thou shalt feele the smart. Thou shalt bee used as *Dianaes* slave, not *Venus'* sonne. All the world shall see that I will use thee like a captive, and shew myselfe a conqueror. Come have him in, that wee may devise apt punishments for his proud presumptions.

Eurota. Wee will plague yee for a little god.

Tel. Wee will never pittie thee, though thou be a god.

Ramia. Nor I.

Larissa. Nor I. [*Exeunt.*

ACTUS QUARTUS. SCÆNA PRIMA.

AUGUR, MELEBEUS, TYTERUS, POPULUS.

Augur.

THIS is the day wherein you must satisfie *Neptune* and save yourselves; call together your faire daughters, and for a sacrifice take the fairest; for better it is to offer a virgin then suffer ruine. If you thinke it against nature to sacrifice your children, thinke it also against sense to destroy your countrey. If you imagine *Neptune* pittilesse to desire such a pray, confesse yourselves perverse to deserve such a punishment. You see this tree, this fatall tree, whose leaves though they glister like gold, yet it threatneth to faire virgin's griefe. To this tree must the beautifullest be bound untill the monster *Agar* carrie her away, and if the monster come not, then assure yourselves that the fairest is concealed, and then your countrey shall bee destroyed; therefore consult with yourselves, not as fathers of children, but as favourers of your countrey. Let *Neptune* have his right if you will have your quiet; thus have I warned you to bee carefull, and would wish you to bee wise, knowing that who so hath the fairest daughter, hath the greatest fortune, in loosing one to save all; and so I depart to provide ceremonies for the sacrifice, and command you to bring the sacrifice.   [*Exit Augur.*

Meleb. They say, *Tyterus*, that you have a faire daughter, if it be so, dissemble not, for you shall be a fortunate father. It is a thing holy to preserve ones country, and honourable to be the cause.

Tyte. Indeed, *Melebeus,* I have heard you boast that you had a faire daughter, then the which none was more beautiful. I hope you are not so carefull of a childe, that you will be carelesse of your countrey, or adde so much to nature, that you will detract from wisdome.

Meleb. I must confesse that I had a daughter, and I know you have; but alas! my childes cradle was her grave, and her swath-clowte her winding sheete. I would shee had lived till now, she should willingly have died now; for what could have happened to poore *Melebeus* more comfortable, then to bee the father of a faire childe, and sweet countrey.

Tyte. O *Melebeus!* dissemble you may with men, deceive the gods you cannot, did not I see, (and very lately see) your daughter in your armes, when as you gave her infinite kisses with affection I feare me more then fatherly. You have conveyed her away, that you might cast us all away; bereaving her the honour of her beautie, and us the benefit; preferring a common inconvenience, before a private mischiefe.

Meleb. It is a bad cloth, *Tyterus,* that will take no colour, and a simple father that can use no cunning; you make the people beleeve that you wish well, when you practise nothing but ill; wishing to be thought religious towards the gods, when I know you deceitfull towards men. You cannot overreach mee, *Tyterus,* overshoot yourselfe you may. It is a wily mouse that will breed in the cat's eare, and hee must halt cunningly, that will deceive a cripple. Did you ever see me kisse my daughter? you are deceived, it was my wife. And if you thought so young a piece unfit for so old a person,

and therefore imagined it to be my child, not my spouse,
—you must know that silver haires delight in golden
lockes, and the old fancies crave young nurses, and
frostie yeeres must be thawed by youthfull fires.   But
this matter set aside, you have a faire daughter, *Tyterus*,
and it is pittie you are so fond a father.

Popu. You are both either too fond or too froward :
for whilest you dispute to save your daughters, we
neglect to prevent our destruction.

Alt. Come let us away and seeke out a sacrifice.
We must sift out their cunning, and let them shift for
themselves.   [*Exeunt.*

ACTUS QUARTUS.   SCÆNA SECUNDA.

CUPID, TELUSA, EUROTA, LARISSA, *enter singing.*

> *Tel.* O yes, O yes, if any maid,
> Whom lering *Cupid* has betraid
> To frownes of spite, to eyes of scorne,
> And would in madnes now see torne
> The boy in pieces,—
>   *All three.*   Let her come
> Hither, and lay on him her doome.
>   *Eurota.* O yes, O yes, has any lost
> A heart, which many a sigh hath cost ;
> Is any cozened of a teare,
> Which (as a pearle) disdaine does weare ?
>   *All three.* Here stands the thiefe, let her but come
> Hither, and lay on him her doome.
>   *Larissa.* Is any one undone by fire,
> And turn'd to ashes through desire ?
> Did ever any lady weepe,
> Being cheated of her golden sleepe ?
> Stolne by sicke thoughts !
>   *All three.*   The pirat's found,

And in her teares hee shal be drown'd.
Reade his inditement, let him heare
What hee's to trust to: boy give eare.

Tel. Come, sirra! to your taske. First you must undoe all these lovers knots, because you tyed them.

Cupid. If they be true love knots, 'tis unpossible to unknit them; if false, I never tied them.

Eurota. Make no excuse, but to it.

Cupid. Love-knots are tyde with eyes, and cannot be undone with hands; made fast with thoughts, and cannot be unlosed with fingers; had *Diana* no taske to set *Cupid* to but things impossible, I will to it.

Ramia. Why how now? you tie the knots faster.

Cupid. I cannot chuse, it goeth against my mind to make them loose.

Eurota. Let me see,—now 'tis unpossible to be undone.

Cupid. It is the true love knot of a woman's heart, therefore cannot be undone.

Ramia. That fals in sunder of itselfe.

Cupid. It was made of a man's thought, which will never hang together.

Larissa. You have undone that wel.

Cupid. I, because it was never tide wel.

Tel. To the rest, for shee wil give you no rest. These two knots are finely untide!

Cupid. It was because I never tide them; the one was knit by *Pluto*, not *Cupid*; by money, not love; the other by force, not faith; by appointment, not affection.

Ramia. Why doe you lay that knot aside?

Cupid. For death.

Tel. Why?

Cupid. Because the knot was knit by faith, and must onely be unknit of death.

Eurota. Why laugh you?

Cupid. Because it is the fairest and the falsest; done with greatest arte, and least truth; with best colours, and worst conceits.

Tel. Who tide it?

Cupid. A man's tongue.

Larissa. Why doe you put that in my bosome?

Cupid. Because it is onely for a woman's bosome.

Larissa. Why what is it?

Cupid. A woman's heart.

Tel. Come let us goe in, and tell that *Cupid* hath done his taske; stay you behind, *Larissa*, and see he sleepe not, for love will be idle; and take heede you surfet not, for love will bee wanton.   [*Exit Telusa.*

Larissa. Let mee alone, I will find him somwhat to doe.

Cupid. Lady, can you for pittie see *Cupid* thus punished?

Larissa. Why did *Cupid* punish us without pittie?

Cupid. Is love a punishment?

Larissa. It is no pastime.

Cupid. O *Venus*, if thou sawest *Cupid* as a captive, bound to obey that was wont to command; fearing ladies' threats, that once pearced their hearts; I cannot tell whether thou wouldest revenge it for despight, or laugh at it for disport.   The time may come, *Diana*, and the time shal come, that thou that settest *Cupid* to undoe

knots, shalt intreat *Cupid* to tie knots; and you ladies
that with solace have beheld my paines, shall with sighs
intreat my pittie.   [*Hee offereth to sleepe.*

Larissa. How now, *Cupid*, begin you to nod?

Ramia. Come, *Cupid*, *Diana* hath devised new labours for you that are god of loves, you shall weave
samplers all night, and lackie after *Diana*, all day.
You shall shortly shoote at beastes for men, because you
have made beasts of men; and waite on ladies' traines,
because thou intrappest ladies by traines. All the stories that are in *Diana's* arras, which are of love, you
must picke out with your needle, and in that place sow
Vesta with her nuns, and *Diana* with her nymphes.
How like you this, *Cupid?*

Cupid. I say I will pricke as well with my needle,
as ever I did with mine arrowes.

Tel. *Diana* cannot yeeld, she conquers affection.

Cupid. *Diana* shall yeeld, shee cannot conquer
destiny.

Larissa. Come, *Cupid*, you must to your busines.

Cupid. You shall finde me so busie in your heads,
that you shall wish I had bin idle with your hearts.

ACTUS QUARTUS. SCÆNA TERTIA.

NEPTUNE *alone.*

Neptune. This day is the solemne sacrifice at this
tree, wherein the fairest virgine (were not the inhabitants faithlesse) should bee offered unto me, but so over
carefull are fathers to their children, that they forget
the safety of their countrey, and fearing to become un-

naturall, become unreasonable; their slights may bleere men, deceive me they cannot; I will bee here at the houre, and shew as great crueltie as they have done craft, and well shall they know that *Neptune* should have beene intreated, not cousened.　　　　*[Exit.*

ACTUS QUARTUS. SCÆNA QUARTA.

Enter GALLATHEA *and* PHILLIDA.

Phil. I marvell what virgine the people will present, it is happy you are none, for then it would have falne to your lot, because you are so faire.

Galla. If you had beene a maiden too, I neede not to have feared, because you are fairer.

Phil. I pray thee, sweete boy, flatter not mee, speake truth of thyselfe, for in mine eye of all the world thou art fairest.

Galla. These be faire words, but farre from thy true thoughts, I know mine owne face in a true glasse, and desire not to see it in a flattering mouth.

Phil. O would I did flatter thee, and that fortune would not flatter me. I love thee as a brother, but love not me so.

Galla. No I will not, but love thee better, because I cannot love as a brother.

Phil. Seeing we are both boyes, and both lovers,— that our affection may have some show, and seeme as it were love,—let me call thee mistris.

Galla. I accept that name, for divers before have cald me mistris.

Phil. For what cause?

Galla. Nay there lie the mistrisse.

Phil. Will not you bee at the sacrifice?

Galla. Noe.

Phil. Why?

Galla. Because I dreamt that if I were there, I should bee turned to a virgine, and then being so faire (as thou saist I am) I should be offered as thou knowest one must. But will not you bee there?

Phil. Not unlesse I were sure that a boy might be sacrificed, and not a maiden.

Galla. Why then you are in danger.

Phil. But I would escape it by deceite, but seeing we are resolved to bee both absent, let us wander into these groves till the houre be past.

Galla. I am agreed, for then my feare will be past.

Phil. Why, what dost thou feare?

Galla. Nothing but that you love me not. [*Exit.*

Phil. I will. Poore *Phillida*, what shouldest thou thinke of thyselfe, that lovest one that I feare mee, is as thyselfe is; and may it not bee, that her father practized the same deceit with her, that my father hath with mee, and knowing her to bee faire, feared shee should be unfortunate; if it bee so, *Phillida*, how desperate is thy case? if it be not, how doubtfull? For if she be a mayden, there is no hope of my love; if a boy, a hazard: I will after him or her, and leade a melancholy life that looke for a miserable death. [*Exit.*

ACTUS QUINTUS.   SCÆNA PRIMA.

Enter RAFFE *alone.*

Raffe.

NO more masters now, but a mistresse, if I can light on her.   An astronomer? of all occupations that's the worst; yet wel fare the alcumist, for he keeps good fires though he gets no golde ; the other stands warming himselfe by staring on the starres, which I think he can as soone number as know their vertues.   He told me a long tale of octogessimus octavus, and the meeting of the conjunctions and planets, and the meanetime he fell backeward himselfe into a ponde.   I askt him why he foresaw not that by the starres, he knew it, but contemnd it.   But soft, is not this my brother *Robin?*

Enter ROBIN.

Robin. Yes, as sure as thou art *Raffe.*

Raffe. What, *Robin?* what newes? what fortune?

Robin. Faith I have had but bad fortune, but I priethee tell me thine.

Raffe. I have had two masters, not by arte but by nature ; one said, that by multiplying hee would make of a penny tenne pound.

Robin. I, but could he doe it?

Raffe. Could he doe it, quoth you? why, man, I saw a prettie wench come to his shop, where with puffing, blowing, and sweating, he so plyed her, that hee multiplyed her.

Robin. How?

Raffe. Why he made her of one, two.

Robin. What by fire?

Raffe. No, by the philosopher's stone.

Robin. Why, have philosopher's such stones?

Raffe. I, but they lie in a privie cupboord.

Robin. Why then thou art rich if thou have learned this cunning.

Raffe. Tush! this was nothing! he would of a little fasting spittle make a hose and doublet of cloth of silver.

Robin. Would I had beene with him! for I have had almost no meate but spittle since I came to the woods.

Raffe. How then didst thou live?

Robin. Why, man, I served a fortune-teller, who said I should live to see my father hanged, and both my brothers beg. So I conclude the mill shall be mine, and I live by imagination still.

Raffe. Thy master was an asse, and lookt on the lines of thy hands; but my other master was an astronomer, which could picke my nativitie out of the starres. I should have halfe a dozen starres in my pocket if I have not lost them, but heere they bee, *Sòl, Saturne, Jupiter, Mars, Venus.*

Robin. Why these be but names.

Raffe. I, but by these he gathereth that I was a *Jovalist* borne of a Thursday, and that I should bee a brave *Venerian* and get all my good lucke on a Friday.

Robin. Tis strange that a fish day should be a flesh-day.

Raffe. O *Robin, Venus orta mari, Venus* was borne of the sea, the sea will have fish, fish must have wine,

wine will have flesh, for *Caro carnis genus est muliebre* :
but soft, heere commeth that notable villaine, that once
preferd me to the alcumist.

Enter PETER.

Peter. So I had a master, I would not care what became of me.

Raffe. *Robin*, thou shalt see me fit him. So I had
a servant, I care neither for his conditions, his qualities,
nor his person.

Peter. What *Raffe?* well met. No doubt you had
a warme service of my master the alcumist?

Raffe. 'Twas warme indeed, for the fire had almost
burnt out mine eyes, and yet my teeth still watred with
hunger: so that my service was both too hote and too
cold. I melted all my meate, and made only my slumber thoughts, and so had a full head and an empty belly.
But where hast thou beene since?

Peter. With a brother of thine, I think, for he hath
such a coate, and two brothers (as he saith) seeking of
fortunes.

Robin. 'Tis my brother *Dicke*, I priethee lets goe to
him.

Raffe. Sirra, what was he doing that he came not
with thee?

Peter. Hee hath gotten a master now, that will teach
him to make you both his younger brothers.

Raffe. I, thou passest for devising impossibilities,
that's as true as thy master could make silver pots of
tagges of points.

Peter. Nay, hee will teach him to cozen you both, and so get the mill to himselfe.

Raffe. Nay, if he be both our cozens, I will be his great grandfather, and *Robin* shall be his uncle; but I pray thee bring us to him quickly, for I am great bellied with conceite till I see him.

Peter. Come then and goe with mee, and I will bring yee to him straight.   [*Exeunt.*

ACTUS QUINTUS. SCÆNA SECUNDA.

Augur, Ericthinis.

Augur. Bring forth the virgine, the fatall virgine, the fairest virgine, if you meane to appease *Neptune*, and preserve your countrey.

Erict. Heere shee commeth, accompanied onely with men, because it is a sight unseemely (as all virgins say) to see the misfortune of a maiden, and terrible to behold the fiercenes of *Agar* the monster.

Enter Hæbe *with other to the sacrifice.*

Hœbe. Miserable and accursed *Hœbe*, that being neither faire nor fortunate, thou shouldest bee thought most happy and beautiful. Curse thy birth, thy life, thy death, being borne to live in danger, and having lived, to die by deceite. Art thou the sacrifice to appease *Neptune*, and satisfie the custome, the bloodie custome, ordained for the safety of thy country. I, *Hœbe*, poore *Hœbe*, men will have it so, whose forces command our weake natures; nay the gods will have it so, whose powers dally with our purposes. The *Ægyptians* never cut

their dates from the tree, because they are so fresh and
greene; it is thought wickednes to pull roses from the
stalkes in the garden of Palestine, for that they have
so lively a red: and whoso cutteth the incense tree in
Arabia before it fall, committeth sacriledge. Shall it
onely bee lawfull amongst us in the prime of youth, and
pride of beautie, to destroy both youth and beautie: and
what was honoured in fruits and flowres as a vertue, to
violate in a virgine as a vice? But, alas! destiny
alloweth no dispute; die, *Hœbe, Hœbe* die! wofull *Hœbe!*
and onely accursed *Hœbe!* Farewell the sweete delights of life, and welcome now the bitter pangs of death.
Farewell you chast virgins, whose thoughts are divine,
whose faces faire, whose fortunes are agreeable to your
affections; enjoy, and long enjoy the pleasure of your
curled locks, the amiablenes of your wished looks, the
sweetnesse of your tuned voices, the content of your inward thoughts, the pompe of your outward showes;
onely *Hœbe* biddeth farwell to all the joyes that she
conceived, and you hope for, that shee possessed, and
you shall; farewell the pompe of princes' courts, whose
roofes are imbosst with golde, and whose pavements are
decked with faire ladies, where the dayes are spent in
sweete delights, the nights in pleasant dreames, where
chastitie honoreth affections and commandeth, yeeldeth
to desire and conquereth. Farewell the soveraigne of
all vertue, and goddesse of all virgins, *Diana;* whose
perfections are impossible to bee numbred, and therefore infinite; never to be matched, and therefore immortall. Farewell, sweet parents! yet to be mine, unfortunate parents. How blessed had you beene in

barrennes! how happy had I beene, if I had not bin! Farewell life, vaine life; wretched life! whose sorrowes are long, whose end doubtfull, whose miseries certaine, whose hopes innumirable, whose feares intolerable. Come death, and welcome death whom nature cannot resist, because necessitie ruleth, nor defer because desteny hasteth. Come, *Agar*, thou unsatiable monster of maidens' blood, and devourer of beautie's bowels, glut thyselfe till thou surfet, and let my life end thine. Teare these tender joynts with thy greedy jawes, these yellow lockes with thy blacke feete, this faire face with thy foule teeth. Why abatest thou thy wonted swiftnesse? I am faire, I am a virgine, I am readie. Come, *Agar*, thou horrible monster, and farewell world thou viler monster.

Augur. The monster is not come, and therefore I see *Neptune* is abused, whose rage will I feare me, be both infinite and intolerable: take in this virgine, whose want of beauty hath saved her owne life, and all yours.

Erict. Wee could not finde any fairer.

Augur. Neptune will. Goe deliver her to her father.

Hœbe. Fortunate *Hœbe*, how shalt thou expresse thy joyes? Nay, unhappy girle, that art not the fairest. Had it not beene better for thee to have died with fame, then to live with dishonour, to have preferred the safetie of thy countrey and rarenesse of thy beautie, before sweetnes of life, and vanity of the world? But alas! destiny would not have it so, destiny could not, for it asketh the beautifullest. I would, *Hœbe*, thou hadst beene beautifullest.

Erict. Come, *Hœbe*, heere is no time for us to rea-

son, it had beene best for us thou hadst beene most
beautifull.   [*Exeunt.*

ACTUS QUINTUS. SCÆNA TERTIA.

PHILLIDA, GALLATHEA.

Phil. We met the virgine that should have beene
offered to *Neptune*, belike either the custome is pardoned, or shee not thought fairest.

Galla. I cannot conjecture the cause, but I feare the
event.

Phil. Why should you feare? the god requireth no
boy.

Galla. I would hee did, then should I have no feare.

Phil. I am glad he doth not tho', because if he did,
I should have also cause to feare. But soft, what man
or god is this? Let us closely withdraw ourselves into
the thickets.   [*Exeunt ambo.*

Enter NEPTUNE alone.

Nept. And doe men begin to be equall with gods,
seeking by craft to overreach them that by power over-
see them? Doe they dote so much on their daughters,
that they sticke not to dally with our deities? well shall
the inhabitants see that destinie cannot bee prevented
by craft, nor my anger bee appeased by submission. I
will make havocke of *Diana's* nymphes, my temple shall
bee died with maidens' blood, and there shall be nothing
more vile then to bee a virgine. To bee young and
faire shall be accounted shame and punishment, in so

much as it shall bee thought as dishonorable to bee honest as fortunate to be deformed.

Enter Diana *with her nymphes.*

Diana. O *Neptune*, hast thou forgotten thyselfe, or wilt thou cleane forsake me? Hath *Diana* therefore brought danger to her nymphes, because they be chast? shall vertue suffer both paine and shame, which alwayes deserveth praise and honour?

Enter Venus.

Venus. Praise and honour (*Neptune*) nothing lesse, except it be commendable to be coy, and honorable to be peevish. Sweet *Neptune*, if *Venus* can doe anything, let her try it in this one thing, that *Diana* may finde as small comfort at thy hands, as love hath found courtesie at hers. This is she that hateth sweet delights, envieth loving desires, masketh wanton eyes, stoppeth amorous eares, bridleth youthfull mouthes, and under a name, or a word constancie, entertaineth all kinde of crueltie: shee hath taken my sonne *Cupid*, *Cupid* my lovely sonne, using him like a prentise, whipping him like a slave, scorning him like a beast; therefore, *Neptune*, I intreate thee by no other god then the god of love, that thou evill intreate this goddesse of hate.

Nept. I muse not a little to see you two in this place, at this time, and about this matter; but what say you, *Diana*, have you *Cupid* captive?

Diana. I say there is nothing more vaine, then to dispute with *Venus*; whose untamed affections have bred more brawles in heaven, then is fit to repeate in earth, or possible to recount in number; I have *Cupid*, and will keepe him; not to dandle in my lap, whom I abhorre in my heart; but to laugh him to scorne that hath made in my virgins' hearts such deepe scarres.

Venus. Scarres, *Diana*, call you them that I know to bee bleeding woundes? alas! weake deity, it stretch- eth not so farre, both to abate the sharpnesse of his arrowes, and to heale the hurts. No! love's wounds when they seeme greene, rankle; and having a smooth skin without, fester to the death within. Therefore, *Neptune*, if ever *Venus* stood thee in stead, furthered thy fancies, or shall at all times be at thy command; let either *Diana* bring her virgins to a continuall mas- sacre, or release *Cupid* of his martyrdome.

Diana. It is knowne, *Venus*, that your tongue is as unruly as your thoughts; and your thoughts as unstaied as your eyes; *Diana* cannot chatter, *Venus* cannot chuse.

Venus. It is an honour for *Diana* to have *Venus* meane ill, when she so speaketh well; but you shall see I come not to trifle; therefore once againe, *Neptune*, if that bee not buried, which can never die,—fancie,— or that quenched which must ever burne,—affection;— shew thyselfe the same *Neptune* that I knew thee to be when thou wast a shepheard; and let not *Venus*' words be vaine in thine eares, since thine were imprinted in my heart.

Nept. It were unfit that goddesses should strive, and it were unreasonable that I should not yeeld; and there- fore to please both, both attend; *Diana* I must honour, her vertue deserveth no lesse; but *Venus* I must love, I must confesse so much. *Diana*, restore *Cupid* to

Venus, and I will for ever release the sacrifice of virgins; if therefore you love your nymphs as shee doth her sonne, or preferre not a private grudge before a common griefe; answere what you will doe.

Diana. I account not the choice hard, for had I twentie *Cupids*, I would deliver them all to save one virgine; knowing love to be a thing of all the vainest; virginitie, to bee a vertue of all the noblest. I yeeld! *Larissa* bring out *Cupid:* and now shall it be said, that *Cupid* saved those hee thought to spoile.

Venus. I agree to this willingly: for I will bee wary how my sonne wander againe. But *Diana* cannot forbid him to wound.

Diana. Yes, chastitie is not within the levell of his bow.

Venus. But beautie is a faire marke to hit.

Nept. Well I am glad you are agreed: and say that *Neptune* hath dealt well with beauty and chastitie.

Enter CUPID.

Diana. Here take your sonne.

Venus. Sir boy, where have you beene? alwaies taken, first by *Sapho*, now by *Diana;* how hapneth it, you unhappie elphe?

Cupid. Comming through *Diana's* woods, and seeing so many faire faces with fonde harts, I thought for my sport to make them smart, and so was taken by *Diana*.

Venus. I am glad I have you.

Diana. And I am glad I am rid of him.

Venus. Alas, poore boy! thy winges clypt? thy brandes quencht? thy bow burnt? and thy arrowes broke?

Cupid. I, but it skilleth not! I beare now mine arrowes in my eyes, my winges on my thoughts, my brandes in mine eares, my bowe in my mouth; so as I can wounde with looking, flye with thinking, burne with hearing, shoot with speaking.

Venus. Well you shall up to heaven with me, for on earth thou wilt lose me.

Enter TYTERUS, MELEBEUS, GALLATHEA *and* PHILLIDA.

Nept. But soft, what bee these?

Tyte. Those that have offended thee to save their daughters.

Nept. Why, had you a faire daughter?

Tyte. I, and *Melebeus* a faire daughter.

Nept. Where be they?

Meleb. In yonder woods, and meethinkes I see them comming.

Nept. Well, your deserts have not gotten pardon, but these goddesses' jarres.

Meleb. This is my daughter, my sweet *Phillida.*

Tyte. And this is my faire *Gallathea.*

Galla. Unfortunate *Gallathea*, if this be *Phillida!*

Phil. Accursed *Phillida*, if that bee *Gallathea!*

Galla. And wast thou all this while enamoured of *Phillida*, that sweet *Phillida?*

Phil. And couldest thou doate upon the face of a maiden thyselfe being one, on the face of faire *Gallathea?*

Nept. Doe you both being maidens love one another?

Galla. I had thought the habit agreeable with the sexe, and so burned in the fire of mine owne fancies.

Phil. I had thought that in the attire of a boy there could not have lodged the body of a virgin, and so was inflamed with a sweete desire which now I find a sower deceit.

Diana. Now things falling out as they doe, you must leave these fond affections; nature will have it so, necessitie must.

Galla. I will never love any but *Phillida,* her love is engraven in my heart with her eyes.

Phil. Nor I any but *Gallathea,* whose faith is imprinted in my thoughts by her words.

Nept. An idle choice, strange and foolish, for one virgin to dote on another; and to imagine a constant faith, where there can be no cause of affection. How like you this, *Venus?*

Venus. I like well and allow it, they shall both bee possessed of their wishes, for never shall it bee said that Nature or Fortune shall overthrow Love, and Faith. Is your love unspotted, begunne with truth, continued with constancie, and not to be altered till death?

Galla. Die, *Gallathea,* if thy love be not so!

Phil. Accursed be thou, *Phillida,* if thy love be not so!

Diana. Suppose all this, *Venus,* what then?

Venus. Then shall it be seene, that I can turne one of them to bee a man, and that I will!

Diana. Is it possible?

Venus. What is to Love or the Mistris of Love unpossible? Was it not *Venus* that did the lik

and *Ianthes;* how say yee? are yee agreed? one to be
a boy presently?

Phil. I am content, so I may imbrace *Gallathea.*

Galla. I wish it, so I may enjoy *Phillida.*

Meleb. Soft, daughter, you must know whether I will
have you a sonne.

Tyte. Take me with you, *Gallathea,* I will keepe you
as I begat you, a daughter.

Meleb. *Tyterus,* let yours bee a boy, and if you will,
mine shall not.

Tyte. Nay, mine shall not, for by that meanes my
young sonne shall lose his inheritance.

Meleb. Why then get him to be made a maiden, and
then there is nothing lost.

Tyte. If there bee such changing, I would *Venus*
could make my wife a man.

Meleb. Why?

Tyte. Because she loves alwayes to play with men.

Venus. Well you are both fond, therefore agree to
this changing, or suffer your daughters to endure hard
chance.

Meleb. How say you, *Tyterus,* shall wee referre it to
Venus?

Tyte. I am content, because she is a goddesse.

Venus. *Neptune,* you will not dislike it.

Nept. Not I.

Venus. Nor you, *Diana.*

Diana. Not I.

Venus. *Cupid* shall not.

Cupid. I will not.

Venus. Then let us depart, neither of them shall

know whose lot it shall bee till they come to the church
doore.   One shall be, doth it suffice?

Phil. And satisfie us both, doth it not, *Gallathea?*

Galla. Yes, *Phillida.*

Enter RAFFE, ROBIN, *and* DICKE.

Raffe. Come, *Robin,* I am glad I have met with
thee, for now wee will make our father laugh at these
tales.

Diana. What are these that so malepartly thrust
themselves into our companies?

Robin. Forsooth, madame, we are fortune tellers.

Venus. Fortune-tellers! tell mee my fortune.

Raffe. We doe not meane fortune-tellers, we meane
fortune tellers : we can tel what fortune wee have had
these twelve monthes in the woods.

Diana. Let them alone, they bee but peevish.

Venus. Yet they will bee as good as minstrels at the
marriage, to make us all merrie.

Dicke. I, ladies, we beare a very good consort.

Venus. Can you sing?

Raffe. Basely.

Venus. And you?

Dicke. Meanly.

Venus. And what can you doe?

Robin. If they double it, I will treble it.

Venus. Then shall yee goe with us, and sing *Hymen*
before the marriage.   Are you content?

Raffe. Content? never better content! for there wee
shall be sure to fill our bellies with capons' rumpes, or
some such daintie dishes.

Venus. Then follow us.   [*Exeunt.*

THE EPILOGUE.

GALLATHEA.

GOE all, 'tis I onely that conclude all. You, ladies, may see, that *Venus* can make constancie ficklenesse, courage cowardise, modestie lightnesse; working things impossible in your sexe, and tempering hardest hearts like softest wooll. Yeeld, ladies, yeeld to love, ladies, which lurketh under your eyelids whilest you sleepe, and playeth with your heartstrings whilest you wake: whose sweetnesse never breedeth satietie, labour wearinesse, nor griefe bitternesse. *Cupid* was begotten in a mist, nursed in cloudes, and sucking only upon conceits. Confesse him a conqueror, whom yee ought to regard, sith it is unpossible to resist; for this is infallible, that love conquereth all things but itselfe, and ladies all hearts but their owne.

NOTES.

Prologue, line 5.

 TALE of the Man in the Moone.—This phrase is here used to signify any wild story out of the reach of ordinary rules of criticism. For the popular story of the Man in the Moon, see note to Act 5 of " The Woman in the Moone."

8. *Wee hope in our times none will apply pastimes, because they are fancies.*—An allusion to the dangers actors sometimes encountered from the application of allusions in plays to political and other events, and which sometimes was visited on them with fine and imprisonment. Collier, in his *History of the Stage,* has narrated several instances of this.

Page 5, l. 17. *Sotted.*—Besotted, from *sotie,* folly (Anglo-Norman).

Page 6, l. 6. *Peevish.*—Foolish. Thus in Shakespeare : " Why thou *peevish* sheep," addressed in anger by Antipholus of Ephesus to Dromio of Syracuse, whom he mistakes for his own servant, and who addresses him wrongly. 8. *Sit to her humour.*—An error of the press for " *fit* to her humour," which is the reading of the first edition. 11. *Cease of.*—Leave off.

Page 10, l. 1. *And that shouldest.*—The first edition reads correctly, " and that *thou* shouldest live."

Page 11, l. 20. *Poyson dowe.*—*i. e.* Poison *dough.*

Page 12, l. 7. *Will you see the devill?*—An allusion to the old proverb, " Talk of the devil, and his horns appear." 12. *It tickleth not my liver.*—The seat of love or lust, according to the old authors. In this sense it is used by Shakespeare, " Much Ado about Nothing,"

" If ever love had interest *in his liver;*"

and in the "Merry Wives of Windsor," Pistol declares to Ford
that Sir John Falstaff loves his wife

"—— with *liver* burning hot."

Page 13, l. 3. *Imbroder my bolts.*—i. e. *Embroider;* here used
in the affected style of a pedant. The bird-bolt was a flat-
headed arrow used to knock down small birds.

Page 14, l. 1. *By Mars himselfe had given me.*—The word *had*
in this sentence is not in the first edition or in Blount. I have
added it. In Dilke's edition that editor has read the passage,
"Mars himselfe *was* given me." Of course both readings are
conjectural. 11. *Not onely wound, but also confound.*—I am
answerable for this reading. The line in the first edition, and
also in Blount, reads, "Not onely confound, but also confound;" and in the six vols. of old English plays, 8vo. 1814
(edited by Dilke), sense is endeavoured to be made of the passage by reading: "Not only confound, but *contund.*" This
is explained in a note thus: "'They not only amaze, but *strike
down* those whom they are aimed at;' and it is possible that it
may be intended to resemble a preceding speech of Sir Tophas: 'Why, fool, a *poet* is as much as one should say—*a
poet;*' and I know of no authority for the word contund; but
its derivation from the Latin renders the meaning plain, and
from the character of Sir Tophas, he was likely enough to use
it." But there is no need to thus coin an unknown word to make
the passage clear. Sir Tophas has just declared that his words
wound; and being asked as to his blows, may safely be made to
declare they not only wound but confound. It seems simply
a compositor's error, easily rectified by considering the preli-
minary dialogue. 25. *Wilde mallard.*—The wild drake. There
is an annual merry-making at All Souls' College, Oxford, thus
described in the Rev. J. Pointer's "Oxoniensis Academia,"
1749: "Another custom is that of celebrating their Mallard-
night every year on the 14th of January, in remembrance of
a huge mallard or drake, found (as tradition goes) imprisoned
in a gutter or drain under ground, and grown to a vast big-
ness, at the digging for the foundation of the college."

Page 15, l. 9. *Strowtes.*—Struts. 11. *Simiter.*—Scimiter;
curved swords in the Asiatic style first came into use in England *temp.* Henry VI.

Page 17, l. 25. *Too-too faire Cynthia.*—The commentators
on Shakespeare have written so much on the double use of

this word, as in this instance, for the purpose of giving inten-sity to the expression, that it needs no further note here, than to direct the reader's attention to its frequent use by our author in his other plays.

Page 17, l. 30. *Aslaked.*—Abated. The term is used in Chaucer's " Knight's Tale "—

> " Till at the last *aslaked* was his mood."

Page 21, l. 31. *Recure.*—The word occurs in " The com-plaint of the Black Knight :"

> "—— that I may not attaine
> *Recure* to finde mine adversarie."

frequently in Spenser, and in Act 3, Sc. 7 of " Richard III.," on which Mr. Steevens observes it is used " both as a verb and a substantive in Lilly's ' Endimion.' " (Note by Dilke.)

Page 22, l. 20. *Is not love a lurcher ?—i. e.* A cheater. 24. *Nothing but livers to make nothing but lovers.*—Another allusion to the liver as the seat of love; see note to p. 12, l. 12.

Page 23, l. 13. *Babies.—i. e.* Children's dolls. 16. *Pantables.* —Loose shoes of enriched materials; they are constantly alluded to by the Shakesperian dramatists; thus in Peel's play of King Edward I., Queen Elinor exclaims, " Give me my *pantobles*;" and in Massinger's " Guardian," a lady is described " with pearl embroidered *pantables* on your feet." Stubbs, in the " Anatomy of Abuses," speaks of " corked shoes, puisnets, *pantofles*, and slippers; some of them of black velvet, some of white, some of green, and some of yellow; some of Spanish leather, and some of English ; stitched with silke, and embroi-dered with gold and silver all over the foot, with other gew-gaws innumerable." 28. *How short she was.*—Pettishly abrupt. This use of the word *short* is still common among the pea-santry of England.

Page 24, l. 8. *A strange sight to see water come out of fire.*— " It is evident, from the following speech of Dares, that one of the women was crying, and to this he alludes." (Dilke.)

Page 25, l. 10. *This passeth!*—An exclamation similar in force to the modern " this beats all !" and often used by Shake-speare and other old dramatists to express wonder. In Brewer's *Lingua* we read, " Your traveller's so dote upon me *as passes.*" 16. *Untewed locks.*—Uncombed.

Page 27, l. 3 *That pelting word love.—i. e.* Paltry, contemp-tible.

" Such *pelting* scurvy newes."
> *Two Noble Kinsmen.*

" With here and there a *pelting* scatter'd village,
That yielded mee no charity or pillage."
> *Taylor's Works,* i. 124.

" We have had *pelting* wars, since you refus'd
The Grecians cause."
> *Troilus and Cressida,* Act 4, Sc. 5.

18. *It is a squirrill.*—In the series of Tapestries published by
M. Jubinal is one copied from " the Tapestry of Nancy,"
which curiously illustrates this passage. In it is a lady of
rank seated with a favourite squirrel secured to her wrist by
a chain. This tapestry was found lining the tent of Charles
the Bold, after he was killed at the siege of Nancy, in 1476.
22. *If I feared not to be shent.*—*i. e.* Harshly reproved. Thus
in Shakespeare :

" *Rugby.* Out, alas! here comes my master.
Quickly. We shall be *shent.*"
> *Merry Wives of Windsor.*

" He *shent* our messengers."
> *Troilus and Cressida.*

29. *Digest.*—The old form of the word *digest,* and still used in
the midland counties by the peasantry, those great conserva-
tors of the ancient English language.

Page 28, l. 17. *Ebone.*—*i. e.* Ebony. 21. *Lunary.*—The moon-
wort, to which many superstitious virtues were attached by
our ancestors, and its magical powers particularly esteemed.

Page 30, l. 16. *Yea.*—" Our poet seems to have forgot himself here, as Bagoa has not sung ' the enchantment for sleep.'
The subject is a very fine one, and it is to be regretted that
Lilly did not execute his intention, or that his performance is
lost." (Note in Dilke's edition.) 21. *A dumb shew.*—The
whole of this dumb show, which indicates the action of the rest
of the drama, is omitted in the first edition, and only to be
found in Blount's reprint of 1632.

Page 31, l. 17. *The time was Endimion onely was.*—*i. e. Only,*
or *entirely,* thought of, to the exclusion of all others. Semele
alludes to the former passion of Tellus, and her slight notice
of Endimion at present. 26. *Malepert overthwarts.*—*i. e.* Im-
pertinent wranglings.

Page 32, 1. 24. *A camocke.*—A crooked tree.—Halliwell's *Dictionary.*

Page 33, 1. 1. *Shall she worke stories or poetries.*—In John Taylor's " Needles Excellencie," 1640, is a poem " in prayse of the needle," descriptive of its powers in both these ways :

" —— posies rare and anagrams,
  Signifique searching sentences from names,
  True history, or various pleasant fiction
  In sundry colours mixt, with art's commixion."

2. *It skilleth not.*—It signifieth not.

" It *skills* not greatly who impugns our doom."
  Second Part of Henry VI.

Page 35, 1. 24. *I cannot stand without another.*—Part of this scene is taken from the definition of a noun substantive and a noun adjective, in the beginning of Lilly's grammar. (Note by Dilke.)

Page 36, 1. 4. *Discover mee in all parts.*—Discover is here used in its primitive sense of to *uncover* or *undress*, and accordingly Sir Tophas divests himself of his gun, his sword and shield, and his bow and arrows. (Dilke.) 13. *The bodkin beard.*—Sometimes termed *the stiletto beard;* it was cut to a point on the chin. See further, on beards and their fashions, in the notes to *Midas.* 22. *That bable called love.*—An allusion to the *bauble* carried by the domestic fool of Lilly's era.

Page 37, 1. 9. *In whom there is no waste.*—Shakespeare has the same pun in " Henry IV.," Part 2, Act 1, Sc. 2 :—

" *Ch. Justice.* Your meanes are very slender, and your *waste* great.
  Falstaff. I would it were otherwise; I would my means were greater, and my *waist* slenderer."

Page 38, line 7. *Vaile bonnet.*—To lower the bonnet in token of courtesy.

" Down I vail'd my bonnet low,
  Thinking to show my breeding."
  D'Urfey's Pills to Purge Melancholy.

14. *Without fashion, and quite without favor.*—" Fashion relates to the shape, and favor to the features; and Samias means Dipsas is disagreeable in both." (Dilke.)

Page 39, 1. 6. *The first song.*—This is omitted in the first edition, but appears in Blount's. 22. *Batten.*—To grow fat.

"Could you on this fair mountain leave to feed,
   To *batten* on this moor."   *Hamlet.*

Page 40, l. 10. *Untrusse the points.*—A simile obtained from
the fashions of the day. The *points* were the strings or ribbons, with metal tags attached to them, by which the dress was
tied; to *untruss* was used in the sense of *untie.* 22. *We will
travice.*—*i. e.* Traverse.

Page 41, l. 21. *Recure.*—Recovery.—Halliwell's *Dictionary.*

"But Hector fyrst, of strength most assured,
   His stede agayne hath anonę *recured.*"
                    Lydgate's Troy, 1555.

Page 43, l. 22. *This dissembling passeth.*—See note to p. 25,
l. 10.

Page 51, l. 18. *A pelting chafe.*—An irritable humour.

Page 52, l. 15. *To fodge.*—To move. 21. *Set to the tune of
the black Saunce.*—The black Sanctus, a hymn to St. Satan in
ridicule of the monks; in the "Nugæ Antiquæ" is a very
curious example of the words and music to this profanity.

"Do you think my heart is softened with a *black santis.*"
              Beaumont and Fletcher, Wild Goose Chase.

Page 53, l. 19. *Lusty pugges.*—*i. e.* Strong fellows. The term
pug was used as a jocular term of familiarity.

Page 54, l. 4. *Wambleth.*—*i. e.* Rumbleth.

"Lord, how my stomach wambles!"
                    Wily Beguiled.

5. *Enter the Watch.*—There are many similarities between the
style of arguing adopted by the watch in this scene, and Dog-
berry and his watchmen in Shakespeare. It is not impossible
that this may be the prototype; for the first edition of Endimion was printed in 1591, the first edition of "Much Ado about
Nothing" in 1600, nor is it suspected to have been written before 1599. 25. *Tush, tush, neighbour's, take me with you.*—*i. e.*
Let me understand you; satisfy my mind. A similar phrase
occurs in "Henry IV.," Part 1, Act 2, Sc. 4, where this passage is quoted by Farmer in illustration—

"I would your grace would *take me with you;*
   What means your grace?"

29. *Corance.*—Currants.

Page 55, l. 22. *Rustie as their bils.*—The bill was a broad-
bladed implement on the end of a staff, and so constantly car-

ried by watchmen of the Elizabethan era as to be identified with them. In Dekker's pamphlet *O per se O*, 1612, is a figure of a watchman with his bell, lanthorn, and bill over his shoulder. They are frequently termed "brown bills," from the rust that was allowed to remain on their surfaces; for that these worthies neglected to clean them, we have abundant proof from the constant allusion to that fact by writers of their era. Steel was seldom kept bright even by soldiers, and "brown swords" are as commonly spoken of in the 16th and 17th centuries. 25. *The second song.*—This song is omitted in the first edition of 1591, but here given from Blount.

Page 56, l. 1. *Scabs.*—Low, vulgar fellows; a term of reproach used also by Shakespeare. 4. *A patch.*—*i. e.* A fool. The term originated in the proper name of Wolsey's famous fool, which was Patch. 29. *He tries to lift Endymion.*—In the first edition and in Blount this stage direction is simply conveyed in two words, *he lifts.*

Page 57, l. 7. *Braun-fallen.*—*i. e.* Unnerved. 9. *Lythernesse.* —*i. e.* Flexibility. 26. *Song by Fairies.*—This song is also omitted in the first edition. There is a more than accidental similarity in Shakespeare's Fairies' song in the "Merry Wives of Windsor," which was written several years after Lilly's play had been printed.

Page 58, l. 9. *Heidegeyes.*—Revels, sports.

Page 62, l. 32. *Faire babies.*—*i. e.* The fairies—popularly believed to be very diminutive.

Page 65, l. 9. *Thou hast heere slept fortie yeeres.*—"In Act 3 it was mentioned that he had slept *almost twenty* years; as it is evident but little time had elapsed since, I suspect this to be an error." (Note by Dilke.)

Page 66, l. 2. *To stay thee.*—*i. e.* To support thee.

Page 67, l. 30. *Wolves barking at thee, Cynthia.*—Spenser had already celebrated Queen Elizabeth as Cynthia, and the allusions and compliments of these latter speeches by Endimion are all direct flatteries of the Sovereign who listened to them. See the remarks on this point in our life of Lilly.

Page 68, l. 8. *Tottered.*—*i. e.* Tattered. 27. *Discover this practise.*—*i. e.* Expose the author of the enchantments of Endimion.

Page 69, l. 24. *Lord of Misrule.*—An allusion custom of electing a Lord of Misrule at Chris so common as to be constant at universities s and so general as to be adopted at the palace of the sovereign as well as the hall of the gentleman.

Page 70, l. 25. *A rabbet sucker.—i. e.* Young rabbits who yet suck. Dugdale mentions a feast given in the Inner Temple Hall where many " dishes of rabbit-suckers " appeared. Steevens has quoted the present passage in illustration of the phrase in Shakespeare (1 Henry IV.), " Hang me up by the heels for a rabbit-sucker." 25. *Chicken-peeper.—i. e.* A chicken just peeping from the shell.

Page 73, l. 8. *Watchet.*—A pale blue colour. 9. *Turkis.*—Turquoise.

Page 76, l. 18. *Unacquainted.*—Unknown.

Page 79, l. 1. *Fried myself most in mine affections.* So in Shakespeare :—

> " *Tran.* Gray-beard, thy love doth freeze.
> *Gre.* But thine doth *fry.*"
> *Taming of the Shrew.*

22. *Could not carrie the mind.—i. e.* Could not bear to think.

Page 81, l. 19. *What, young againe?*—From this speech it is evident that, at the conclusion of the preceding one by Cynthia, the youth of Endimion was restored.

Page 82, l. 22. *Speaks the parrat?*—A conventional taunt of an uncomplimentary kind applied to a person's remarks. " Speke Parrot " is used by Skelton as the title to his bitter attack on Cardinal Wolsey; probably as a sort of excuse for such a mass of abuse.

Page 83, l. 20. *A lovely looke.*—The word *lovely* is here used in the sense of *loving.*

Page 84, l. 23. *Nothing resteth.—i. e.* Nothing remains.

Page 86. *The Epilogue.*—It is sufficient to note that this Epilogue is entirely made up from one of Æsop's fables.

Page 93, l. 1. *Campaspe.*—In Dodsley's " Select Collection of Old Plays " the title of this drama is " Alexander and Campaspe." In the first edition, 1584, it is termed " a most excellent comedie of Alexander, Campaspe, and Diogenes ;" but in the second edition, printed by the same publisher in the same year, it is altered simply to " Campaspe ;" and so it continues in the third edition of 1591, and in Blount's reprint of 1632, who terms it on every page " a tragicall comedie of Alexander and Campaspe." It is proper, however, to note that the headline of all previous editions is " Alexander and Campaspe." The subject of the play is taken from Pliny's " Natural History," lib. 35, c. 10.   19. *What could the child receive but singular?*—The word *singular* is here used in the proper sense of the old French *singulier, i. e.* rare or excellent; and it is used alone, in accordance with the common custom of writers of Lilly's era, to leave something unexpressed in a phrase, but which would be understood as necessary to its full completion. 20. *Turkies.*—Turquoise.

Page 94, l. 3. *Happily you conjecture.*—*Happely* in first and second editions; altered to *haply* in Dodsley.

Page 95, l. 10. *Tendreth virtue.*—*i. e.* Loveth virtue; from the old French *tendre.*   24. *Like your Majesty.*—*i. e.* May it please your Majesty.

Page 96, l. 2. *Chyeronte.*—*Chieronie* in first and second editions.

Page 99, l. 19. *Counterfeites.*—Counterfeit was a term formerly used for any kind of picture, but more especially for a portrait. In Dodsley is a long note on this passage, proving the use of the word from authors of our poet's era. Two of his quotations are here selected:—

> " I happen'd on a painter yesternight,
> Sweet Ales he shall draw thy *counterfet.*"
> *Arden of Feversham*, 1592.

> " Prince Edward's lovely *counterfeit*,
> A present to the Castile Elinor."
> *Greene's History of Friar Bacon*, 1630.

Page 100, l. 1. *An old saw of abstinence by Socrates.*—The word *by* is omitted in all the older editions and in Blount's reprint; it is added in Dodsley; and in a copy of the third edition of 1591, among the Garrick plays, it has been inserted in ink by a contemporary hand. 3. *A gallimafray.*—A dish made of several kinds of meat chopped fine and mixed together. From Cotgrave, who uses the word *hachis* for its equivalent, it appears that the Scotch *haggis* and the English *hash* are both derived from that source. In the same way that we use the word, irrespective of cookery, to indicate any confused arrangement of words or things, the authors of our poet's era used this word; and in " Pierce Pennilesse' Supplication to the Devil," 1592, we read, " they mingled them all in one *gallimafry* of glory." 14. *Song.*—This song is, as usual, omitted in all the quartos, but is given by Blount. 17. *Juno's daiery.*—There is a curious instance in Dodsley of the trouble given by a misprint. This word is there spelt " darry," which occasions a note—" I suppose Granichus means *Juno's dairy. S.*"

Now, as the song is only given by Blount, and he spells it as in our text, the error is Dodsley's printer's, which has been perpetuated, together with the explanatory note, in every edition of his work.

Page 102, l. 9. *Apparition is seene in the moone.*—Dodsley omits the word *is*, but it occurs in all the old editions.

Page 103, l. 8. *They are not philosophers, if they know not their duties.*—Dodsley has this passage as given in the first edition —"they were not philosophers if they knewe not their dueties;" but which is evidently wrong, as is also the explanatory note, given in all the editions of Dodsley, to the effect that "the third and Blount's editions read, *these are not;*" the third edition reads, "they are not philosophers, if they knewe not;" the grammar of this speech is properly corrected by Blount, who gives it as in our text.

Page 104, l. 9. *Rules.*—Rulers in Blount; an error not in the old editions.

Page 105, l. 8. *Theban thrall.*—The early editions read *thralls*, as in Dodsley. 16. *Not to be a god.*—The entry of Diogenes is noted in Dodsley after this speech, but not in the old editions or by Blount. In the Garrick copy of the third edition it has been inserted in ink by the hand of a contemporary, one William Neile.

Page 106, l. 8. *To be jump with Alexander.*—To be jump is to agree. So in "Pierce Pennilesse, his Supplication to the Divell," p. 29 : "Not two of them *jump* in one tale." (Note in Dodsley, where other instances are given.) 12. *Furious.*— *i. e.*—Intemperate or raging, used in the sense of the Latin *furor*, or old French *fureur*. Chaucer speaks of "the furial paine of hell," in the Squire's Tale, Canterbury Tales, l. 10762.

Page 107, l. 29. *You are taken tardie.*—This speech is wrongly given to *Manes* in Dodsley.

Page 108, l. 8. *Neither will have ever a man.*—This speech is here printed as in Blount, but all the older editions read, "neither will I have ever a man," which is more correct. 13. *O sweet consent.*—*i. e.* Agreement. In the old musical treatises harmony is frequently termed a *consent of instruments, i. e.* an union of sounds. 13. *A crowde.*—A fiddle.

Page 109, l. 19. *You resemble the lapwing.*—Shakespeare has used this simile. Dodsley remarks that "this simile occurs in our ancient writers perhaps more frequently than any other which can be pointed out." He cites many examples, and others may be seen in the variorum Shakespeare. Here is one :—

> " H'as the lapwing's cunning, I am afraid, my Lord,
> That cries most when she's farthest from the nest."
>
> *Massinger's Old Law.*

Page 110, l. 3. *I love, Hephestion, I love!*—The second exclamation *I love*, which gives greater intensity to Alexander's speech, is omitted by Dodsley, but occurs in all the old editions as well as in Blount. 21. *Warlike sound of drum and trump.*—This paragraph of Hephestion's lengthy speech may be the prototype of that uttered by Shakespeare's Duke of Gloucester—

> " Grim-visaged war hath smooth'd his wrinkled front;
> And now,—instead of mounting barbed steeds
> To fright the souls of fearful adversaries,—
> He capers nimbly in a lady's chamber,
> To the lascivious pleasing of a lute."
>
> *Richard III., Act* 1, *Sc.* 1.

Page 111, l. 9. *Mugill.*—The mugil is the mullet.

" Quosdam mœchos et mujilis intrat."—*Juv. Sat.* 10.

Page 112, l. 3. *Overseene and overtaken.*—*i. e.* Deceived, and intoxicated with unreasoning affection. 25. *Refell.*—*i. e.* Refute. Our author, in his *Euphues*, has the passage :—"I will not *refell* that heere, which shall be confuted hearafter;" and Erasmus, in his *Praise of Folly*, speaks of objections which "by no arguments may be *refelled*." (See note in Dodsley.)

Page 113, l. 22. *Call my page.*—In Dodsley the page's entrance is properly marked after this speech; but it does not occur in the old editions. 27. *See where his tub is.*—The whole of this speech of Alexander's is worthy attention, as curiously indicative of the easy way in which localities were supposed to be changed in the scene according to the desire of the author, as pointed out in the famous passage in Sir Philip Sidney's " Defence of Poesie :"—"Now you shall have three ladies walk to gather flowers, and then we must believe the stage to be a garden. By and by, we heare news of shipwracke in the same place, then are we to blame if we accept it not for a rock !"

Page 114, l. 29. *He is dogged, &c.*—I have pointed this speech anew, in accordance with what I conceive to be its best meaning. Blount has it thus :—" He is dogged,

I cannot tell how sharpe with a kind of sweetness." In Dodsley (last edition, 1825) it is thus :—" He is dogged, but discreet ; I cannot tell how : sharp with a kind of sweetness."

Page 115, l. 4. *Here commeth Apelles.*—The entry of Apelles here is correctly noted in Dodsley, but is not given in the old editions. 6. *Shadowed.—i. e.* Depicted. 19. *Glose with your tongue.*—To *glose* is to *flatter.* Our author, in his *Euphues,* declares of the ladies, that "in extolling their beauties, they give more credite to their owne glasses, than men's *gloses.*"

Page 116, l. 15. *Make me to stay.*—The word *to* is omitted in Dodsley, but occurs in all the old editions.

Page 117, l. 16. *A quip.*—A sharp retort. 17. *Girders.*—Persons addicted to satirical reflections. Thus Falstaff declares "men of all sorts take a pride to *gird* at me " ("Henry IV.," Part 2, Act 1, Sc. 2); and in "Coriolanus" (Act 1, Sc. 1) it is declared of Caius Marcius—

"Being mov'd, he will not spare to *gird* the gods."

27. *Overthwarts.*—Sharp answers. 28. *A bitter bob.*—A satirical reply.

Page 118, l. 13. *O ys.—i. e. Oyez,* the old form of cry at the commencement of proclamations. 19. *Tush, say flie.*—It is evident, from this speech of Manes, that Psyllus had suddenly stopped repeating the proclamation when he came to the last word *fly.*

Page 119, l. 10. *So absolute a face.—i. e.* Complete, perfect. Thus in Shakespeare : "Thou would'st make an *absolute* courtier " ("Merry Wives of Windsor," Act 3, Sc. 3); "It is a most *absolute* and excellent horse" ("Henry V.," Act 3, Sc. 7).

Page 121, l. 22. *It is impossible.*—Dodsley alters this to "*not* impossible," which has been omitted in Blount, but occurs in the first edition, and appears to be the right reading. 24. *As treason in ours.*—Dodsley reads *from ours,* but all the old editions have the text as here adopted.

Page 124, l. 22. *God shield.—i. e.* God prevent or forbid. 29. *The haire of her head be yellow.*—An allusion to the fashionable custom of dying the hair yellow in the reign of Elizabeth, in compliment to the natural colour of that queen's. It was, however, a favourite tint during the Middle Ages, and considered the type of beauty. Thus in the romance of "King Alexander" we hear of a knight whose head is covered with curls, "and yellow the hair;" and in Chaucer's "Knight's Tale" we read of fair Emilie,

" Her yellow hair was broided in a tresse
Adown her backe, a yarde longe I guesse."

Bulwer, in his " Artificial Changeling," 1653, notes the fashion
as in use, and quotes from Schenckius an account of " a certaine noble gentlewoman, that would expose her bare head to
the fervent heat of the sun for some houres, that she might
purchase yellow and long haire." The ancients were equally
fond of the colour; but it went out of fashion in the early part
of the 17th century, as appears by a little book entitled " Ar-
tificiall Embellishments," printed at Oxford, 1665, where,
however, several recipes are given " to make the hair yellow."
The first is as follows :—" Take shavings of box, stechas,
cedar, liquorice roots scraped and bruised, coltsfoot roots,
maiden hair, of each two ounces, and a little saffron; set all
these over the fire till two parts of the water be consumed,
then strein it, and wash the hair therewith."

Page 125, l. 2. *New found.*—Erroneously printed " new-
sound" in Dodsley. 2. *Garden knots.*—The ornamental arrangement of the flower-beds so much in fashion in the days
of Elizabeth, which consisted of intricate "knotted" convo-
lutions, several excellent specimens may be seen in the wood-
cuts to Markham's " Newe Orchard and Garden," 1607. 4.
A more delicate consent.—See note to p. 108, l. 13. 10. *The
coale breakes.*—i. e. The charcoal used for the outline of the picture. 21. *Blotting of a boord.*—i. e. Painting a picture. The old
pictures were painted on wooden panels, and when they were
of small sizes had generally a raised and bevelled rim forming
the frame, and made in one piece. Of such pictures the Ger-
man galleries of ancient art possess many examples, and they
are generally termed "painted boards" in old inventories.
27. *Doth not this matter cotton as I would.*—i. e. Go right as I
wish it. In Beaumont and Fletcher's *Monsieur Thomas*, one of
the characters, speaking in a sanguine way of a plot, exclaims,
" This geer *will cotton.*" 31. *I will not contrarie your Majesty.*
—i. e. I will not contradict your Majesty. So in Gascoigne's
Works, 1587, p. 273. " The Lady Fraunces did not seeme to
contrary him." (Note in Dodsley.)

Page 126, l. 6. *A curst yeelding modesty.*—i. e. A modesty
tempered in yielding by a contrary emotion. To be *curst* was
to be crossgrained in temper—*shrewish.*

Page 127, l. 19. *Cloth of estate.*—The canopy placed over
royalty.

Page 128, l. 12. *Colices.*—Strengthening compounds used to invigorate the weak; from the French *coulis*, a strong broth or jelly. 25. *Song by Apelles.*—Omitted in all early editions before Blount's. It is printed in Percy's "Reliques of Ancient English Poetry," who terms it "an elegant little sonnet."

Page 129, l. 5. *Hee set her.*—*i. e.* Set as a stake in gambling.

Page 130, l. 6. *Hee is so light.*—This speech is wrongly given to Granichus in Dodsley. 16. *Yet tearme me.*—Erroneously read "yet terme me" in Dodsley.

Page 131, l. 1. *All conscience is sealed at Athens.*—Dodsley changes this to *seared*, but has no authority in any old edition, nor is the alteration requisite. The last edition of Dodsley, 1825, though retaining his reading, notes that "*sealed* is a term in falconry, signifying *blinded.*" 9. *The king's schoolmaster.*—Altered, without authority, by Dodsley to "the king of schoolmasters."

Page 132, l. 16. *Old huddles.*—A term of contempt for sordid age. Our author, in his *Euphues*, thus uses the phrase: "This old miser asking of Aristippus what he would take to teach and bring up his sonne, he answered a thousand groates; 'A thousand groates, God shield!' answered this *old huddle*, 'I can have two servants of that price.'"

Page 134, l. 3. *Not in love, but their love.*—This phrase, which is constructed in Lilly's occasionally obscure taste, seems to imply that Campaspe would have no dissembling in real love, but only in such simulated love as she despises. 22. For *tantara —sol, fa, la.*—*i. e.* Instead of the sound of the war-trumpet, he now enjoys the voice of the singer. 27. "*Bees to make their hives in souldiers' helmets.*"—This simile is evidently borrowed from Alciati's very popular "Emblems;" in which is an engraving, representing bees swarming into the face-guard of an helmet, this is reproduced by Geoffrey Whitney in his "Choice of Emblemes," Leyden, 1586, with the following verses beneath it:—

"The helmet stronge, that did the head defende,
   Beholde, for hyve, the bees in quiet serv'd:
And when that warres, with bloodie bloes, had ende,
   They, hony wroughte, where souldiour was preserv'd:
      Which doth declare, the blessed fruites of peace,
      How sweete shee is, when mortall wars doe cease."

28. *Foot-clothes of gold.*—Housings of horses, such as were worn

in times of peace, but not adapted to purposes of war. Lord Hastings, in "King Richard III.," observes that his *foot-cloth* horse did stumble. (Note in Dodsley.)

Page 135, l. 6. *Posies of love in their ringes.*—Examples of these rhyming posies engraved on rings abound in old authors. The following are selected from MSS. of the time of Charles I., published by the Percy Society :—

> "Constancy and heaven are round,
> And in this, the emblem's found."

> "Weare me out, Love shall not waste,
> Love beyond Time still is plac'd."

> "Weare this text, and when you looke
> Uppon your finger, sweare by th' booke."

15. *Gloves worne in velvet caps.*—Steevens notes this custom as used for three occasions, viz. as the favour of a mistress, the memorial of a friend, and as a mark to challenge an enemy. In the notes to Dodsley examples are given in illustration of this. Our author only alludes to the lover's use of the custom as mentioned in Dekker's *Satiromastrix*—"Thou shalt wear her glove in thy worshipful hat." (See also Lilly's play "The Woman in the Moone," Act 2, Sc. 1.)

Page 136, l. 27. *But content, &c.*—The whole of this paragraph is, by error, omitted in Dodsley.

Page 139, l. 9. *It is the next way.*—*i. e.* The readiest way. It was an ordinary phrase in our author's era, and is frequently used by Shakespeare. Thus in "Henry IV.," Part 1, Act 2, Sc. 1, the carrier, complaining of the Inn at Rochester, says, "Peas and beans are as dank here as a dog, and that is *the next way* to give poor jades the bots." 15. *Tryco singeth.*—This stage direction is given in the old quarto editions, but not the song, which first appears in Blount's.

Page 141, l. 8. *Thy carefull bed.*—*i. e.* Thy sorrowful bed. 13. *Unlesse it rubbe my heart out.*—I have adopted Dodsley's reading here, which is unquestionably correct, though the old editions, as well as Blount, read *thy* heart. 19. *For the nonce.* —*i. e.* Purpose, intent, design, occasion. (Halliwell's *Dictionary.*) "With a cord I have laid on the table *for the no[nce]* hand and foot.—Gascoigne's *Supposes*, 1587. howle *for the nonce.*"—Erasmus' *Praise of Fol[ly]*

Page 142, l. 1. *Pelting words.*—See note t[o] 4. *Curtall.*—*i. e.* Curtail. 10. *Pewter coat[s].*—[

cuirass of the soldier. 20. *Philosophy rates me from carrion.*
—Halliwell, in his Dictionary, cites the Kentish use of the
word *rate*, as meaning " to call away or off," which is a happy
explanation of this passage in our drama. 31. *First let us sing.*
—Here there evidently should be a song; but it does not occur
in any edition, nor even in Blount, who has usually given the
songs omitted in the old quartos.

Page 145, l. 18. *It skils not.*—i. e. It matters not. The first
edition reads, *it skilleth not,* which is adopted by Dodsley; the
third and Blount as in our text.

Page 146, l. 13. *Devising a platforme.*—i. e. Inventing a plan
or design; any sketch, either as the groundwork of a picture
or the plan of a building, was formerly termed *a platforme.*

Page 147, l. 7. *Loveth under hand.*—So in all the old editions,
but altered to *lov'd* by Dodsley. 11. *Campaspe, here is newes.*
—The entrance of Campaspe here is noted by Dodsley, but is
not so in the old editions, stage directions being generally
omitted. 21. *I ghesse unhappily.*—i. e. Unfavourably.

Page 148, l. 20. *Pricking in clouts.*—A somewhat contemp-
tuous term for female needlework. Thus Sir John Harring-
ton, in his *Treatise on Play,* declares in its favour that " men
cannot bee alwayes discoursing, nor women alwayes *pricking
in clowts.*" 30. *Be in a readinesse.*—The word *a* is omitted in
Dodsley, but is in all the old editions, and is good old English.

Page 149, l. 8. *Beare my hand.*—The word *bear* is omitted
in Dodsley, but is in all the previous editions, and is necessary
to the sense of the passage. 1. *On my word.*—I have adopted
Dodsley's reading, but I since think it erroneous; all the old
editions, including Blount, have " of my word," which is equivalent to the more modern " *on.*"

Page 150, l. 14. *Against the haire.*—Used as the modern term
against the grain. Thus in Middleton's *Mayor of Quinborough*
we read : " Books in women's hands are as *much against the hair*
methinks, as to see men wear stomachers."

Page 151, l. 10. *Though wee heare the neighing.*—The word
we is omitted in the old editions, but is necessary, and is intro-
duced from Dodsley. 22. *Like these torches of wax.*—An allusion to the torches which lit the hall at Greenwich when this
play was performing, and which are also mentioned at the
close of the Prologue. 24. *Ealder for a disgrace.*—It was popularly believed that Judas hung himself on an elder tree, in
remorse for betraying the Saviour; and hence the *disgrace*
which attaches to the tree.

Page 158, l. 17. *Bolts insteed of arrowes.*—Bolts were large and heavy, blunted at the end, used only to knock down, or stun; arrows were light and sharp for wounding. 30. *She hath her thoughts in a string.*—*i. e.* Under her own guidance; a simile borrowed from the leading-strings of a child.

Page 159, l. 1. *Yerke me.*—*i. e.* Kick me. Yerk, to kick like a horse.—Halliwell's *Dictionary.*

Page 163, l. 12. *Pantophles.*—Slippers; see note to page 23, line 16. 15. *Thy lerypoope.*—Loquacity. (Weber.) See note to "Mother Bombie." 20. *A mouse of beefe.*—That portion of the ox between the buttock and loin. It is still termed the mouse-buttock.

Page 164, l. 6. *Politian.*—Angelo Politian, one of the most learned men of his era, was born at Monte Pulciano, in Tuscany, in 1454. He was much patronized by the Medici family, who made him their teacher. His fame was very great, and he is commended as "rarum naturæ miraculum" by Erasmus. He is reported to have died of sorrow at the reverses which befel the Medici. 11. *Cogging at dice.*—*i. e.* Cheating at dice.

Page 165, l. 29. *Pranke yourself.*—*i. e.* Decorate yourself. So in "Winter's Tale," Act 4, Sc. 3, Perdita says:—

> "—— and me, poor lowly maid,
> Most goddess-like, prank'd up."

Page 166, l. 21. *Setting their ruffes.*—*i. e.* Putting them in order by arranging the pleats. "In print as puritans ruffs are set."—*Mynshul's Essays,* 1613.

Page 167, l. 19. *Passing fair.*—*i. e.* Surpassingly fair.

> "On a day—alack the day !
> Love, whose month is ever May,
> Spy'd a blossom *passing fair,*
> Playing in the wanton air."
>
> *Shakespeare's Passionate Pilgrim.*

Page 172, l. 7. *Unless thou perish, thou shalt perish.*—This passage is very corrupt, but it so occurs in all the editions, and can only be conjecturally rectified. It may have been "unless thou depart, thou shalt perish," for in the conclusion of the play he flies from Sicily at the confirmed advice of Sybilla. 17. *Put buglosse in their wine.*—Bugloss, or borage, was commonly mixed with wine in Lilly's era, and is still used to flavour mixed drinks and "college cup." It was also used by the ancients, and mentioned by Galen as healthful against rheum and melancholy. In Cogan's "Haven of Health," 1612, we are told: "Buglosse being drunke with wine, doth comfort the braine, and the heart, and increaseth memorie and wit, and engendreth good bloud, and putteth away melancholy and madnesse." 20. *Mandrage.*—Mandragora, a herb to which many magical virtues were formerly attached, and it was believed to be a remedy for most diseases; but its aphrodisaic virtues, and its power as a soporific, were especially dwelt upon.

Page 174, l. 17. *Browne bill.*—See note to page 55, line 22.

Page 175, l. 7. *A carbonado.*—A steak cut crossways for broiling.—Halliwell's *Dictionary.*

Page 176, l. 30. *Moe devils.*—The old form of the word *more.*

Page 177, l. 13. *Thou art a smith, therefore thou art a smith.*— There would seem to be an error here, did we not find equally miserable jests elsewhere in Lilly's plays. All the old editions concur in this reading.

Page 178, l. 17. *Unacquainted thoughts.*—*i. e.* Thoughts hitherto unknown.

Page 180, l. 4. *Quite.*—*i. e.* Requite.

Page 181, l. 17. *Grapes minde glasses.*—A word has been omitted here by Blount, which is also wanting in the second edition of this play; but the first edition has it thus : "grapes *are* minde glasses," meaning that the hidden desires of the mind are discovered as in a reflecting glass by those who drink wine. It is another mode of putting the old proverb *in vino veritas.*

Page 182, l. 8. *Strangers have greene rushes, when daily guests are not worth a rush.*—An allusion to the prevalent custom in our author's time of strewing chambers with rushes, and renewing them for a fresh guest. The favourite plant was the flowering rush (*Butomus umbellatus*), which emits a sweet smell when crushed. The term "not worth a rush" is still used by us as a word of contempt, long after its true meaning has been forgotten, but which is capitally given in our text. 13. *Filed tongue.*—*i. e.* Polished tongue. , 20. *Camockes.*—See note to page 32, line 24.

Page 185, l. 14. *Scamble in the court.*—To scramble; to shift. "Scamblingly, catch that catch can."—*Cotgrave.* 24. *Sachell.*—*i. e.* Satchel, or bag.

Page 186, l. 4. *Good wits will apply.*—*i. e.* Clever people can comprehend obscure sayings—an old jesting phrase, used as a sarcasm. 12. *Disgesteth.*—The old form of digest. See note to page 27, line 29.

Page 187, l. 24. *Song.*—Omitted in all the quartos.

Page 188, l. 1. *A drunken butter-box.*—A satirical term for a Dutchman, all of whom were popularly believed to be great drinkers, and inordinately fond of butter.

Page 193, l. 22. *Song.*—Omitted in all the quartos.

Page 195, l. 4. *Misconster.*—The old form of *misconstrue.*

Page 199, l. 17. *Like the stained turkis.*—It was formerly imagined that the turquoise had the power of foretelling danger to any who wore it, by changing to a paler tint. Swan, in his *Speculum Mundi*, says :—

"The sympathising turcois true doth tell,
    By turning pale, its owner is not well."

26. *The black oxe hath trod on her foot.*—An old popular saying to indicate advancing years.

Page 205, l. 22. *Song.*—Not printed in the early quartos.

Page 207, l. 5. *Deepe daine.*—*Disdaine*, in first and second editions. 16. *In the very loose.*—i. e. At the very moment of loosing the bowstring. 22. *No other white.*—No other mark, the white is the centre of the target.

Page 209, l. 25. *Fine knackes.*—i. e. Delicate devices.

Page 210, l. 22. *I marvaile, Cupid.*—Venus evidently enters at this speech.

Page 212, l. 1. *Cast your eyes on your feet.*—An allusion to the popular fable which states that the peacock was checked in its overweening pride by looking on its ugly feet. 7. *Nor feare me.*—An old archaism for *make me fear.*

Page 213, l. 15. *With my pen to write a fancie.*—Love sonnets were termed *fancies* in the days of our author. Falstaff's description of Justice Shallow is, that " he ever came in the rereward of the fashion," and " sang the tunes he heard the carmen whistle, and sware they were his *fancies*, or his *good-nights.*" ("Henry IV.," Part 2, Act 3, Sc. 2.)

Page 219, l. 21. *Pyble.*—i. e. Pebble.

Page 222, l. 1. *Thy fearefull father.*—i. e. Anxious father.

Page 226, l. 2. *Raughter.*—i. e. Rafter. 4. *Haled.*—i. e. Pulled, or dragged.

Page 227, l. 3. *A whole paire.*—An archaism for a *whole pack* of cards.

Page 228, l. 25. *It skils not.*—See note to page 33, line 2. 27. *Song.*—Omitted in the early quartos.

Page 229, l. 31. *Whist!—i. e.* Be silent. The word is still constantly used by the peasantry of Ireland in this sense.

Page 230, l. 13. *Make a curtesie instead of a leg.*—To *make a leg* was to bow with one leg considerably in advance of the other, shifting them, and drawing them back with a flourishing motion; a great distinction to the quiet, downward *curtesy* of a lady.　17. *No second thing.—i. e.* Not secondary.

Page 231, l. 2. *Blancht him.*—Frightened him from his course.　21. *Tuske these woodes.*—Beat the bushes to drive forth the deer.　25. *Hallow the deare.*—Halloo, or force the deer from cover by cries.

Page 233, l. 11. *Woodden lucke.*—Bad luck.　13. *Walking of hagges.*—Evil spirits who prowl by night.

Page 234, l. 25. *Angel.*—An angel was a coin of the value of 6*s.* 8*d.*, so called from a figure upon the obverse of the archangel Michael slaying the dragon.　26. *Tagge of a point.*— The *points* were the ribbons which fastened together various portions of the dress; the ends were cased in metal sheaths, or *tags*, to prevent unravelling, and which were sometimes ornamentally engraved.

Page 236, l. 17. *A pottle-pot.—i. e.* A two-quart measure.

Page 237, l. 20. *Grypes.—i. e.* Griffins.

Page 238, l. 9. *They say my father hath a golden thumb.*—An allusion to the old proverb, "Every miller has a golden thumb," because he judges the quality of the meal by rubbing it betwixt the thumb and forefinger.

Page 239, l. 1. *Play at quaites.—i. e.* Quoits.

Page 243, l. 26. *Swath-clowtes.—i. e.* The bandages in which babies were enswathed. In Cotman's "Monumental Brasses of Norfolk and Suffolk" are several examples of the manner in which unfortunate infants were confined in the 17th century. The body was entirely wrapped in linen cloths, and bandaged across, so that the arms and legs were perfectly immoveable, and the children looked like little mummies. The custom is still common in Bavaria, and the babies are sometimes hung up to the wall when the nurse is tired.

Page 245, l. 29. *My father had but one daughter, and therefore I could have no sister.*—Shakespeare has made use of this equivoque in "Twelfth Night," Act 2, Sc. 4, where Viola, to puzzle the Duke, says:—

> "I am all the daughters of my father's house,
> And all the brothers too."

Page 247, l. 22. *Concurre?* *condogge!*—This was a new-coined word, which seems to have excited the contempt of Raffe, who ridicules it by parodying the last syllable, and joking on the similarity between *cur* and *dog*.

Page 248, l. 18. *Hang them up at tavernes.*—An allusion to the constant occurrence of such signs for taverns as " the Sun," " the Seven Stars," &c. 22. *Signes which governe the body.*—The zodiacal signs were believed to have a mystic influence on the body, as noted by our author; and all almanacks were furnished with a woodcut of a naked man surrounded by these figures, each pointed toward the part of the body they governed. " Stuck with points like the man in the almanack." Persons regulated their diet, physic, &c., by the rules laid down for their guidance, as each sign was in the ascendant.

Page 250, l. 5. *Drib thine arrowes.*—To shoot at short paces. It is a technical term in archery.—Halliwell's *Dictionary.* 6. *Leys.*—*i. e.* Leas, open fields.

Page 251, l. 5. *Abateth.*—*i. e* Blunts. 27. *Pelting boyes.*— See note to page 27, line 3. So in Shakespeare :—

> " Every *pelting*, petty officer."
>> *Measure for Measure*, Act 2, Sc. 2.

Page 256, l. 14. *Enter singing.*—This entry is thus noted in the early quarto, but no song given, as usual. The burthen, " Let her come hither," bears a close resemblance to that in Amiens' song in " As You Like It," Act 2, Sc. 5. Lilly's is the oldest by some years.

Page 259, l. 7. *Lackie after Diana.*—*i. e.* Follow as a servant; from the old French *laquais*, a foot-boy. 11. *Arras.*— Hangings for chambers, so named from their having been manufactured at the town of Arras.

> " In clothes of Arras I have often seene
> Men's figur'd counterfeets so like have beene,
> That if the parties selfe had beene in place,
> Yet art would vie with nature for the grace."
>> *Taylor's Needles Excellencie*, 1640.

Page 261, l. 1. *There lie the mistrisse.*—A pun is here conveyed in the similarity of sound with " there lie the mysteries," which Gallathea wishes to conceal.

Page 262, l. 12. *He fell backward himself into a pond.*—This is an old classic jesting story against astrologers, who profess to tell others' fate without knowing their own. It was reproduced in the old books of Emblems, and by Whitney, who comments upon it as follows:—

" Th' astronomer, by night beheld the starres to shine :
And what should chaunce another yeare, began for to devine.
But while too longe in skyes, the curious foole did dwell,
As hee was marchinge through the shade, he slipt into a
    well.
Then crying out for helpe, had frendes at hand, by chaunce ;
And nowe his perill being past, they thus at him doe glaunce :
What foolish art is this ? (quoth they) thou hould'st so
    deare,
That doth forshowe the perilles farre : but not the daun-
    gers neare."   *A Choice of Emblemes,* 1586.

Page 264, l. 27. *Thou passest.*—*i. e.* Excellest. See note to page 25, line 10. 29. *Tagges of points.*—See note to page 234, line 26.

Page 270, l. 6. *It stretcheth not so far.*—*i. e.* It is powerless to do so much.

Page 272, l. 1. *It skilleth not.*—See note to page 33, line 2.

Page 274, l. 12. *Both fond.*—*i. e.* Foolish. So in Shakespeare's " Rape of Lucrece :—"

    " True grief is fond and testy as a child."

Page 275, l. 9. *Malepartly.*—*i. e.* Impertinently. 13. *We do not meane fortune-tellers, we meane fortune tellers.*—This is a similarly difficult passage to that noted on page 172, line 7, and is an instance of that love for small quibbles so prevalent in the authors of the days of Elizabeth and James I.; and from which Shakespeare is not free. The quibble seems to lie between fortune-tellers as professional revealers of destiny, and those who tell their own fortunes from their own experience. By bracing the two words together, in speaking, thus, *fortuneteller,* and dissevering them in the second instance, some better sense might be given by the actor to a passage which looks particularly senseless in all the old editions. 20. *Can you sing?*—All the answers to this question convey punning excuses on the words *base, mean,* and *treble,* or, as we should now term such voices, *bass, tenor,* and *treble.*

CHISWICK PRESS:—C. WHITTINGHAM, TOOKS COURT, CHANCERY LANE.